KATE RICE
PROSPECTOR

Other books by Helen Duncan

The Treehouse, Toronto: Simon & Pierre, 1975: Cloth; 1982: paper.

Helen Duncan

KATE RICE PROSPECTOR

Simon & Pierre
Toronto, Canada

We would like to express our gratitude to The Canada Council and the Ontario Arts Council for their support.

Marian M. Wilson, Publisher

ISBN 0-88924-210-0

1 2 3 4 5 • 2 1 0 9 8

Canadian Cataloguing in Publication Data

Duncan, Helen, 1909-
    Kate Rice, prospector

Bibliography: p.
ISBN 0-88924-210-0

1. Rice, Kate, 1883-1964. 2. Trappers - Manitoba -
Biography. 3. Prospectors - Manitoba - Biography.
4. Nickel mines and mining - Manitoba. I. Title.

FC3393.3.R53D86   971.27'03'0924   C83-098614-6
F1063.R53D86

General Editor: Marian M. Wilson
Editor: Lori Thicke
Copy Editor: Jean Paton
Typesetting & Design: Cundari Group Ltd.
Printer: Imprimerie Gagné Ltée
Printed and Bound in Canada

Order From

Simon & Pierre Publishing Company Limited
P.O. Box 280 Adelaide Street Postal Station
Toronto, Ontario, Canada M5C 2J4

For Will Duncan and Don and Jean.

ACKNOWLEDGEMENTS

 hanks must go first to Cathleen and Ian Morrison of Toronto for their kindness and ever ready help; to Hall and George Thompson, mining engineers at Cranberry Portage, Manitoba for their always reliable and excellent information; to their sisters, Edith and Rose for their hospitality and encouragement; to Charles Vance, former prospector and merchant in the Herb Lake area for his wonderful tapes.

To so many others I express my appreciation: the late George Bartlett, storekeeper at Herb Lake, for his letters and interview; Carl Beck, mining engineer, who ran the column, "One Man's Opinion" in the *Northern Miner*, for inserting an item asking his readers to help supply me with needed information and for his responses to my repeated telephone calls; Arthur Boissonneau of the Ontario Lands and Forests Ministry for his help; Lois Britten for her hospitality in The Pas, and her husband for his help with information; Winifred Courtney, Croton-on-Hudson, N.Y. author of *The Young Lamb* for her encouragement; Emily Crosby, Snow Lake, Manitoba artist, for her knowledge of birds and animals and her hospitality; Dorothy and John Eedy for opening up the resources of the St. Marys *Journal Argus*, and for their ready kindness and hospitality; Mrs. Babs Friesen, Winnipeg for allowing me to take notes on an unpublished manuscript by her father, the late Les Charles, former Chief Engineer, Western Division, Canadian Northern Railway; Joe Kerr, former trapper and prospector, partner of the famous Walter Johnson, Snow Lake; Larry Pfaff, librarian of the Art Gallery of Ontario, co-author of *Early St. Marys* for help far beyond the call of duty and information always reliable; the late Walter Reeves of Burlington, Ontario for reading the manuscript and giving his advice; the late Mrs. Lincoln Rice of St. Marys for lending the author three booklets; Vernon Wang, former librarian, Little Northern Museum, The Pas, for allowing me to read and take notes from an old diary by an unknown trapper; Mrs. Whitaker of The Pas for mentioning the article by Kathleen Rice about a canoe trip she took down the Sturgeon-weir River published in the *Toronto Star* Sept. 5, 1939; Mary and the Reverend Ted Williams for handing me the keys to their beautiful home in Brantford, Ontario for all my paraphernalia of papers, tapes, maps, reference books and typewriter; and finally, the people too numerous to list who wrote letters to me about Kate Rice and Dick Woosey for their consistent courtesy and information so willingly shared with a stranger.

Special mention must be given my editor Lori Thicke whose humour, unerring sense and good judgment saved many headaches.

Helen Duncan

TABLE OF CONTENTS

AUTHOR'S NOTE

athleen Rice was sixty years ahead of her time; her character, her conduct, the whole set and jib of her existence was stranger than fiction. She was great, she was different, she was beautiful, she was a feminist long before the expression was ever heard, she was admired, she was pitied; she was regarded with suspicion by the prospectors and trappers from Herb Lake, Snow, Chisel, Cook, and Elbow in northern Manitoba with their fuddled and simplistic ideas of the role of women, in particular women round mining camps: "It was strange her being educated and all that, and up here." Certainly Dick Woosey, her partner, admired and respected her.

Born in St. Marys, Ontario, Kathleen Rice graduated as a gold medallist in Mathematics from the University of Toronto in 1906. A few years later Kate was a trapper and prospector in the far north of Manitoba, discovering the nickel-rich Rice Island, in a lake named Wekusko by the Indians for the herbs growing along its shores and variously known as Wekusko or Herb on maps. She lived with Dick Woosey, another trapper and prospector, in a purely business relationship. Gradually, she became famous in the northern world: articles appeared in newspapers and periodicals in the United States and England, only one of which has been located.

I saw Kathleen Rice only once—I was a somewhat shy and mutinous nine year old. She made a tremendous impression on me; long afterwards I could recall every piece of clothing she wore, how she walked, her eyes, the cool, clipped voice, "Miss Brown!" I knew I'd be forced to write about her.

I set out on a voyage of discovery: what kind of person was she? The first source I turned to for help was St. Marys' *Journal Argus*. (Dorothy Eedy, the wife of the editor, met my train at the snow-crunched platform in a red and brown coonskin coat, very gay plummage, while I in ten year old wilted apricot felt drippy and dispirited—but then I always do feel dejected when I'm starting out on a new project.) I interviewed Mrs. Lincoln Rice, Kathleen's sister-in-law, in her home, and remembered being in that same parlour years before as a girl in dark green velvet dress

trimmed with rosy beaded guimpe for Sunday tea—canned salmon sandwiches and pale thin cocoa, piles of McCormick's cookies—given by an
anxious Sunday School teacher in the Methodist Church. (Everything
always happened on Sundays in St. Marys when I was young.)

Mrs. Rice loaned me three pamphlets, all good, but one which started
me writing letters: the *Centennial Edition of Snow Lake, Manitoba*. The
pamphlet from Snow Lake—a Hudson Bay Mining and Smelting town
(copper: HBMS won't touch nickel)—contained short biographies of all
the old prospectors and traders of the region. With a set will and greater
heartiness I wrote each one: "Please furnish me with any information
you can about Kathleen Rice and her partner, Richard Woosey (both
Kathleen and Woosey were given space in the Centennial pamphlet). I
plan to write a book about them and thank you very much for your help,
yours very sincerely." Then I sat back and waited, munching chocolate
bars and chewing apples with gusto and great optimism.

Dozens of chocolate bars and hundreds of apples later I was still
waiting for some replies—I dismissed the ones who never answered as
dead, dying or generally missing and unimportant. One wife wrote:
"What do you want this information for?" There were other replies in
that same vein. "You have your nerve sniffing around a person's private
life." Or, "She was a lady, what else can I say? Send me a copy of the
book if you finish."

Charles Vance, formerly a prospector and trader of Herb Lake, the
settlement on the shores of Wekusko Lake, and now living in Chilliwack,
British Columbia, answered cautiously through his wife, and once convinced I wasn't a voyeur, psychotic or simply nosy, answered fully. He
thought Kathleen had a screw loose somewhere but his knowledge of
the island where she and Woosey shared a cabin, of the mines round
the lakes, and of all the prospectors from that area was fascinating to me.
He sent tapes, many of them, interviewed ancient prospectors in out of
the way places, drawing out all he could from these age-silenced men,
all the facts necessary and helpful to a restless, sleuthing author, small
things like, "Their first Chisel Lake cabin was built of the biggest white
spruce logs I'd (ancient prospector) ever saw."

Vance didn't seem to be amused when I wrote back: "What is this
trenching you talk about? What are options? Drift? Overburden? Black
jack? Pegmatite occurrences? Hematite? Stringers? Ore shoots?" The list
was endless. I became his pupil, coached as for a hard exam; his patience astounded me and still does. He told me about the *Northern Miner*
where I got the name of Carl Beck who ran a column, "One Man's Opinion". Beck offered to insert a note in the column: "Anyone able to give
information on Kathleen Rice and her partner, Dick Woosey, once of Herb
Lake, Manitoba, please contact Helen Duncan" (giving my address).

Slowly, letters drifted in, many of the same pattern as the first batch.
"There was always the local gossip" (not outlining what the gossip was).
"We were well acquainted with Miss Rice and Richard Woosey but we

don't care to have anything to do with this project." But a mining engineer, Hall Thompson, a McGill University graduate, replied: he admired Miss Rice, liked Dick Woosey and would write later when he finished his income tax. He did and was invaluable.

Many letters had mentioned the name of Joe Kerr, an old prospector who had a camp on the next island to Rice and Woosey; he would know all there was to know. I'd already written Joe Kerr and given him up as dead or missing. I wrote again. Again, no reply. The library at The Pas had no information on Kathleen, the local newspaper and all its files had burned at some point in its career, the Canadian Archives had nothing, ditto the Manitoba Archives. Curiously, Manitoba Mines and Resources had some facts, all wrong: "Miss Rice was born in St. Catharines, Ontario. Her father was a clergyman, her brother an M.P." Ending on a somewhat sombre warning note: "Another person has tried to get information on Miss Rice and died."

I'd been disturbed by the contradictions and discrepancies between Charles Vance's and Hall Thompson's ideas of Kathleen. I was inclined to agree with Thompson—he'd known her better and longer, had a shrewd university-trained mind. From the very beginning the relationship between Kate Rice and Dick Woosey puzzled me.

All Thompson would say was, "There was definitely something between them; Woosey had this peculiar ability to find her when she was lost in the woods." But I also clearly understood he did not believe they shared the same bed, though many prospectors and mining engineers, now wealthy and established, did and openly said so. I let my subconscious mind mull over the problem while I went ahead to read government geological surveys, *Memoirs, Summary Reports,* the *Canadian Mining Journal,* books on Mineralogy, pamphlets from the Department of Mines and Resources, from the Department of the Interior, from the Canadian Mining Institute. Every day, including Saturday, for four months I presented myself at Toronto's Metropolitan Library, Science and Technology Division. When I finished, and without any seeming conscious effort on my part, I was certain she did not share her bed with Woosey and, just as important, that Woosey possessed a more special intuition towards her than she did to him. This was an important step.

Nevertheless, I quit suddenly, threw the whole thing up. Somehow, I'd lost Kathleen under the deep drift and sheer weight of my searching. Airily told my family, "It's all impossible!" They laughed at me, became insistent that I go to northern Manitoba and then finally produced an air ticket to The Pas.

I went. Joe Kerr was the first person I sought out in his summer camp at the south end of Herb Lake. But he disappointed me; he was too general, mixed his facts with a bit of bunco. "She was nice but suspicious everyone was trying to cheat her and Woosey, the two lived like hermits from hand to mouth—he was an old British Army man. In a way I liked him, he didn't yap too much, liked to joke but they were British jokes,

I didn't understand them." Asked about their relationship: "It was a bit odd their living together but I don't care who sleeps with who." While he talked he was drinking can after can of beer then trotting to his chemical toilet in a makeshift bathroom. I waited, staring down at a mouse testing the air from a hole in the sofa three inches away. Joe, who must have been close to ninety, was one of the few who made it; no one in Herb Lake or Snow knew the extent of his wealth. On a subsequent visit, the mix was as before, general facts, same bit of bunco. The hole in the sofa was still there but the mouse was gone.

On my way back to The Pas I changed buses at Cranberry Portage. It was a black September night with a gale wind blowing. I was greeted by a cheery voice, "This way, Mrs. Duncan."

"How did you know I'm Mrs. Duncan?"

"Oh, I know!" (Phoning Hall Thompson from a room in the Snow Lake Motel where men played crap, pool and drank beer, I'd been forced to scream my message. He had invited me to stop in at Cranberry Portage and meet his brother George, and sisters Edith and Rose.) The following morning, after their fabulous breakfast, I sat bemused while they reminisced about Kathleen and Dick Woosey.

At Snow Lake, walking along one of its three sidewalks I noted a woman sitting at the wheel of a half-ton truck; she got out, calling, "You're Helen Duncan, aren't you?"

"How did you know?"

"News travels faster up here than a forest fire." She invited me to her home (a cabin) thirty or so miles away in the woods—she had known Kathleen Rice slightly as a girl and knew I was up at Snow Lake searching for information. She was Emily Crosby, well-known Manitoba painter.

Returning to Toronto, I let all my new knowledge sink in, content for the time to be an ordinary housewife, dusting, scrubbing, trotting to the supermarket. But come January, I started back at the library studying transportation, railways in Manitoba and Saskatchewan between 1906 and 1917 (my own quite arbitrary dates, signifying not much of anything), the history of towns in Manitoba and Saskatchewan, the history of the prairie provinces, plant life, bird life, geography, social life, India in the nineteenth century, the history of various British cavalry units in India (Woosey had been a non-commissioned cavalry officer in India). Back in my home I sat with a plate of apples and studied maps: road maps, topographical maps, railway maps of northern Manitoba.

I'd solved, or thought I had, the riddles in Kathleen's character; still I had yet to deal with minor characters. The same contradictions dogged them—the Diamond Queen, the former London chorus girl, for instance: "She was the girlfriend of Sir Cecil Rhodes, he brought her to Africa...don't know how she got to Manitoba...she was a woman of easy virtue." Or, "She was a jolly, loyal person, very moral and kept a good house [inn]."

By June I'd quit again. Again, my family suggested I return to The

Pas. My former trip had yielded so much I knew they were right. From Snow Lake to the south end of Wekusko I went by taxi to Emily Crosby's cabin (my letter hadn't reached her, partly due to the infrequency of her trips to Snow Lake for supplies—it takes about three weeks for a letter from Toronto—and she had no phone). She took me by big aluminium canoe (loaned) up Wekusko Lake—something I had wanted to do since I'd first visited the lake. She was rather reluctant, carefully stowed food in the bow of the canoe. I found out why later. We never reached the full length of the lake, some twenty-five miles or so. The water became rough (I'd heard tales of its dangerous contrary winds), the waves high; we turned back, and on the return trip to the calm waters of the cove were badly shaken and frightened.

Back in Toronto I started to write. I knew I had to break out on my own, to give my own interpretation of the relationship I had established between Kathleen Rice and myself. I had to make my own diagnosis of the events of her life. It came easily then, or as easily as writing ever can, slipping around the inconsistencies.

After my exhaustive research, I worked and weaved my way among arguable facts, conflicting opinions and an almost total eclipse of dates until like a good judge I was forced to drop some so-called facts and "accept what the evidence obliged me to accept." And where even evidence failed, to stitch and sew, to make my own judgments, to use my own imagination, according to my conception of Kate and her partner Dick Woosey.

While I have had to add my own interpretations to historical events, in some cases certain facts have been left out. For example, Kate had a brother, G.D. Lincoln Rice, born 1892, but since his life, worthwhile though it was, was spent in St. Marys—except for the years in France during the First World War—far from the scenes of this story, he has not been included.

Little could be discovered about the early life of Kate's partner Woosey; he was born in Liverpool and served with the 18th Hussars, a prestigious cavalry regiment whose colonel-in-chief was first the Princess of Wales then later Queen Mary, and was known as Queen Mary's Own. It participated with distinction at Waterloo, Balaclava, Mons, India and South Africa. Woosey must have been soaked in tales of glory and this could account for his often arrogant behaviour towards the prospectors and trappers. He had been married to a woman who, when her eyes first lighted on the Citadel at Halifax, promptly left him, taking their son back to England. In 1917 his wife's address was York, England.

The name of the ship bringing Woosey and his family to Canada canot be discovered; the S.S. Tunisian Allen Line was plying between Liverpool and Halifax at the period of his probable crossing. In 1908 Woosey and Charles Krug were met by a government geologist, Robert C. Wallace and so were noted much later in the *Northern Manitoba Bulletin*, 1919, coming into Sturgeon Landing, Saskatchewan from a prospecting trip. That sighting could possibly place his arrival in Canada at least two years before, in 1906.

It is probable that Woosey reached The Pas by joining a railway road gang—this was the usual route for most of the early prospectors in northern Manitoba. Some of the work force would have been Indians and Metis, the latter being the fabled canoemen of the north. The railway camp details are from the unpublished manuscript of the Chief Engineer, Western Division, of the former Canadian Northern Railway, now part of the Canadian National Railway. Parts of a diary attributed to Dick Woosey are based on the daily records of an unknown trapper of his time.

Of the prospectors who knew Woosey, he was variously described as arrogant and strange, a kind of suspicious hermit, or as engaging, talkative, likeable and well-informed, a great British Army man. With one notable exception, a mining engineer whose perception and knowledge of Woosey was always reliable, most ignored an extraordinary trait where Kate was concerned: he could pinpoint with an uncanny precision whenever she was lost or in trouble, in forest, lake or lonely portage, and go to her assistance.

A gold prospector, Woosey was one of the old-timers working out of The Pas and knew well the five men who uncovered the copper on the west side of Flin Flon Lake in 1915. He discovered a gold mine on the east shore of Wekusko Lake and was responsible for the birth of a gold mining community. But Woosey lost everything. His Kiski gold mine was amalgamated with the Northern Mining and Development in 1916; in 1930 it was absorbed into Consolidated Mining and Smelting. Further stripping and sampling took place, but for whatever reason, all work stopped. The names of the promoter and lawyer possibly involved in the loss of the mine have been changed for legal reasons. Besides, there is only Woosey's word for what may have happened.

Woosey died penniless in September 1940 while having his hair cut and was buried in The Pas at Lakeside Cemetery. His military funeral may not be genuine—it cannot be authenticated.

The death of her partner affected Kathleen tragically; she did a number of strange things: she buried the forty-five thousand dollars earned by selling her nickel claims; she travelled to an asylum in Brandon and gave herself up saying, "I am insane." She was never pronounced mad, and died in a Minnedosa nursing home in 1963. Symbolically, I have shown the bushed Kate setting out in 1940 in her Duckling for her beloved Arctic. As for the money, as far as anyone knows it is still there, hidden on the island.

Both Kate Rice and Dick Woosey came to tragic ends. But since they carried out what they were compelled to do, their lives have acquired the lustre and grandeur of legends.

MANITOBA

MYSTERY LAKE

BURNTWOOD RIVER

OSPWAGAN LAKE

GRASS RIVER

SQUALL LAKE   PISEW FALLS

SNOW LAKE   SETTING LAKE

CHISEL LAKE   WEKUSKO LAKE (HERB LAKE)

FLIN FLON

CRANBERRY PORTAGE WOOSEY LAKE

WEKUSKO (MILE 82)

STURGEON-WEIR RIVER

ATIKAMEG LAKE   MOOSE LAKE

STURGEON R.

THE PAS

SASKATCHEWAN RIVER

PASQUIA HILLS

SASKATCHEWAN

YORKTON

REGINA

SELKIRK

WINNIPEG

PROLOGUE

he little girl came out of the front door of her house, a rare thing for her to do, the back door being the usual exit. Something about the February morning had summoned her with the red ball of sun rounding over the street of brick houses, their stern faces closed up.

From the neighbour's house, a door creaked open. She knew the sound of its whining hinges. The old gentleman who lived there with his old wife ran the St. Marys Milling Company; he was thought of, was spoken of, as a gentleman because he was learned, because he lectured on Genesis in the Methodist Church and could read, could actually speak, French and Latin. She knew the sound of his steps—the cleats of his galoshes made clinking, tapping sounds as he made his way over the ice and snow. What she heard now made her turn and stare.

The stranger was very tall, seemed to cave in at her waist (most of the women in the town caved out) and she was taking yard-long steps as though she wore seven league boots. In fact, she wore men's boots with thick soles and stub toes, the long black coat swished about the tops. On the stranger's head was a man's hat of black bearskin and great bearskin gauntlets reached beyond the elbows. The bearskin hat pivoted in the child's direction and a pair of blue-green eyes of piercing keenness nailed the little girl to the hoar-frosted February morning. She was beautiful, the most beautiful woman she had ever seen.

She stared, stared until the black bearskin hat had disappeared down the brow of the hill, stared after it had disappeared, long enough to feel the tremors shake her safe, tight little world: the short street with the humped bridge over the railway tracks; Form I; church three times on Sunday; Sunday dinner of roast beef, potatoes, gravy and apple pie. (No one living on this street would think, even dare to change this fare for their Sunday dinner let alone allow any other change.)

But the stranger carried something along with her; the little girl groped to puzzle out what it was. It was as if the woman travelled in a blinding light, the kind of light described in Genesis, the light sweeping the woman's life clean as she moved towards a wide and lost horizon.

15

While the child stared at the spot where the bearskin hat had disappeared, she was left, left alone on the familiar street, in her own safe world. But something had taken place; she felt strangely excited, with a burst of happiness, firecrackers, pinwheels and fountains of coloured lights setting off inside her brain as she ran along the icy street, over the humped bridge, along the fronts of the stern white brick houses, ran and ran and yet was not tired.

The old gentleman and his old wife had a daughter. She had discovered a mine far up in the north, so it was said in the town.

The little girl never saw her again.

PART I

o know the facts about Kathleen and why she acted the way she did, start with old George Carter, his granddaughter Lottie, Kathleen's mother, and Henry Lincoln Rice, her father. Of course Dick Woosey, a former soldier of the British Army, the 18th Hussars, a man who took part in great enterprises whose vastness he could but dimly comprehend with his intellect (it would need his sensitive nature to perceive the glory), played his role too.

Except for the Indians, the river and the creek slept in savage solitude until George Carter, having sold his army commission in County Tipperary, Ireland, made his final and successful move to St. Marys, a little town so bravely being born. (He'd gone from Tipperary first to a hundred acre plot in London township, before moving to St. Marys in what is now Southwestern Ontario). Other men were on the move too, restless men from the old world, from the new Republic to the south. The whole continent of North America was caught up in a mad push for land; everywhere they were tearing down the forests to plant. Or starve. They planted. George Carter saw his chance to set up a business. He'd buy wheat from the farmers round the little town and other little towns, and sell to the Maritime provinces and Great Britain, at a profit. Then, he bought the St. Marys Milling Co. and milled flour. He made more money. Such a man was Kate's great-grandfather.

George was tough, a type who could make it in these brutal trackless forests, now being ruthlessly hacked down. He built a white brick house with a long wing running out from the rear, and a double front door of solid oak, a replica of the church door in his native Tipperary—there was a connection in his mind between the house of God and his own dwelling. To the inhabitants of the town who lived in small log or white frame houses it was a mansion. His son George had an equal eye for business; during his regime as head of the business George had one son, James, and a daughter, Lottie.

Lottie had little ambition. She extended herself just enough to insure her privileges as the daughter of the town's richest citizen. She gave teas and receptions in the parlour among the tilting screens, the rose painted china and rose pictures, roses in baskets, roses hanging on a string. Even this entertaining was half-hearted. Perhaps her adrenalin was low; she had little enthusiasm for anything or anyone until her eyes lit on Henry Rice.

Henry was the son of the Reverend Dr. Samuel Dwight Rice; the elder Rice had been born in Maine in 1815, educated at Bowdin College, and been converted to Methodism, either at a respectable church service or by one of the roving revivalists, part minister, part showman, a camp preacher such as the hirsute Lorenzo Dow (Crazy Dow) who roamed the North American continent. Dr. Rice had revolutionary ideas, among them the education of women. He established the female college in Hamilton, preached at Victoria College in Cobourg, preached in St. Marys, preached in Winnipeg. He was everywhere and everything to all men. And all women. His son, Henry Lincoln, born in 1856, a graduate of Victoria College in Classics, had begun to teach at Dr. Tassie's School in Galt, the most noted secondary school in Ontario.

The town buzzed with rumours. The Rice family were cousins of Abraham Lincoln. Why was Henry's second name Lincoln? (Why indeed? They were descendants of Mayflower stock. The rumour was probably true.)

All this meant nothing to Lottie until one summer day when she was standing at the counter of Hutton's Grocery store beside a young man with a tall romantically-drooping body and golden satin hair; the blue-greeny eyes lifted indifferently to her. And Lottie, who had never wanted anything or cared very much for anybody, wanted this man.

In the end she won. Perhaps it was because Henry Lincoln regarded her as such an unlikely candidate for his heart he raised no guards to protect himself. While he remained obstinate against the wiles of an aroused woman, Lottie's mother had a talk with him. The words she used were brutal for someone accustomed to the cadences of that illustrious crew, Dr. Emerson, Henry Thoreau and Margaret Fuller. She talked about his intentions towards her angel, how the expectations of an innocent and beautiful young woman (by no leap of the imagination could Lottie be called beautiful) had been shattered, her virtue compromised. Henry could not understand how his honour entered into a relationship Lottie herself had begun and arcanely pursued. But in the end, the final end, he buckled under the attacks. He married Lottie in the cold month of December, 1880. Her wedding dress was a creation of silk tucks and lace with a train, false white lily of the valley in her hair, an ivory fan at the correct angle in her tight kid gloves of palest mauve, her face wore a rapt expression she would never achieve again.

Henry Lincoln Rice never did continue teaching Classics at Dr. Tassie's School in Galt but took up the duties of directing the Carter family fortunes; he became head of the Carter enterprises. Lottie's father had died and her brother James, finding the making of money too daring and mazey a path for him to follow—the business was beginning to lose a little money—committed suicide. Henry, the classicist, the scholar, the architect (he designed and built three fine houses in St. Marys), whose life had been fed and nurtured by the finest flowers of the human mind, now by his wife's demands, and of the female clan around her, was forced to study account books, ledgers, statistics, credits, debits, balance sheets, budgets—the whole business of a milling company and its various off-shoots teetering on the slippery slopes of insolvency. No man was more ill-prepared. No man tackled with more courage what heaven (with help from Lottie Carter) was pleased to call his lot in life. Such a man was Kate's father.

In 1882, a daughter was born out of Henry's marriage to Lottie and it was he who named her, Kathleen, Kate for short. As her middle name, the ubiquitous Lincoln. Kathleen was the joy of his life and during the everlasting days of childhood that nevertheless pass in a twinkling, they were inseparable. Lottie subsided into matrimony with ambivalence, outwardly active, enjoying her perquisites as the town's leading matron but privately sulky and suspicious. The more the mill lost money and dwindled in importance the more difficult and moody she became, until a lift of Henry's finely arched eyebrow, a word from his lips, even his silences sent her to bed for days—one of her headaches, she would claim to her friends.

Old Annie, the general servant would be forced to leave the preparation of meals and cleaning to care for her mistress. Kathleen was five when she knew what word, what lift of her father's eyebrow would send her mother to bed and for how long. Henry never learned, but then he would never understand Lottie.

2

"It must have been a Huron trail." In order to hear she was forced to run. "It would have been three to twelve inches deep, worn smooth and hard by moccasined feet and could be followed easily in the darkest night." Henry described the road he and his daughter were taking. The road was the main exit out of town into the south and west; it left Fish Creek in the town's center and after running parallel to the Thames for a few miles turned sharply at right angles and crossed it. They had reached the turn.

He sat down suddenly and she sat beside him, glad to rest. Instead of students scrabbling down notes as he lectured, Henry had the receptive ears of his daughter, and of all his listeners he preferred her. She believed. "The whole North American continent was seamed with trails that later became roads—that house behind us was once an inn, proof that this was an important route."

The blackened windows of the low white building stared wildly, its scarred black band running along the face where white letters had been painted and now only Blan House remained. Across the road, a log house, its roof fallen in, its logs porous to the shining air; behind the tumbledown building was untouched forest of oak, maple and elm, stretching to the river.

"Was all this part of the Northwest Frontier?"

He wasn't surprised at her question. "It was part of the long northwestern flank, one hook holding at Niagara, from there a line was flung out to Detroit, then the long angle to the Mississippi River—that was the Northwest Frontier."

She was seven and she knew where the Mississippi River could be located on her father's map, had known for years.

"But it kept changing, the Indiana and Illinois country then became the frontier." He began talking to her about Daniel Boone; something subliminal perhaps, some ancient nostalgia for his colonial American heritage was working in his subconscious. "Daniel Boone followed the Shawnee trail that broke through the Alleghenies." He stood up, started walking fast again. Kathleen ran after him. "Boone and that whole glorious gang turned their backs on the East and its civilization and became new types of men—no Indian could imitate the chatter of a squirrel, the calling of a crow, the gobbling of a wild turkey in signals to his fellows that the sharp ear of Daniel could not detect. If Indians crossed the country within ten miles he knew of their passing, how they were armed and what their purpose was. Except for a few vague tales seeping across the mountains he was unknown until the poet Byron devoted seven stanzas to him in his poem, *Don Juan*. Overnight, Daniel became a legend. When Audubon, the bird illustrator, first met him, he related that his stature seemed enormous though he was not a tall man."

"What made him die?"

Henry wasn't surprised at this question, either. "He lived to be an old man and knowing, as men do when they've spent a lifetime in the woods, that his time had come, he lay down under a tree and died."

"Was he just left?"

"His son Nathan gave him decent burial. Twenty-five years later Kentucky woke up to the fact he was a great man, a true Kentuckian. His bones were dug up and brought back to Frankfort, a monument erected." Henry was gazing down at his daughter, "I like to think you have eyes and ears as keen as Daniel Boone himself.

"His grandson, Christopher Carson, Kit for short, pushed the frontier beyond the Indiana and Illinois country into the Oregon Territory. Kit was the most feared white man amongst all the Cheyennes, the Apaches, Navajos, Comanches, Crows, Sioux. Even the fierce Blackfeet feared him. He was a little man with piercing blue green eyes and wore a fringed buckskin shirt and leggings. The shirt was ingeniously embroidered with quills of the porcupine and so were his moccasins. On his head, his hair was yellow as corn, he wore a coonskin cap but in his prosperous days it was otter. His rifle was always in his hand and under his arm he carried his powder horn and bullet pouch. A heavy knife for butchering as well as a whetstone to keep it sharp hung from his belt. The belt was of marvellous silver and gold ornamentation."

They reached the river, its water in full spring spate, browned by mud and silt with a glaze of blue reflecting the May morning sky. They stopped and then turned back toward the town.

"Kit used the horse to force the frontier, the same marvellous gold and silver workings ornamenting its saddle and bridle; his grandfather used the canoe and the axe. If you don't understand the axe Kate, you cannot understand North America. It's a wonderful thing, the axe, stern, simple, absolute, a truly North American instrument."

"But the rifle was good, too."

"And the rifle, always the rifle—it won the frontier."

"I want a rifle."

"A canoe first. You'll have one when you're ten and you will paddle round the mill pond."

"At first, then I'll have a rifle."

"Later in time came the horse and the frontier was held. Kit was true to the seed planted in him to push back the frontier and then discover new land, land full of mystery, land so great it could not be measured. And today Kate, the frontier has been pushed back and up and yet there is still another frontier, still there is land, land full of mystery, land so great it cannot be measured and—Kate, are you listening?"

"Yes, I'm listening."

"It is your land, not mine—I'm too old for such a young country. It's yours and it waits, a land of Boone's time when the canoe and the axe and the rifle were the implements of life and survival in the frontier . . . but I want you to remember that Boone did not regard himself as a trail blazer, the advance guard of a new civilization, but his grandson Kit did."

When they were back at the big double front door of the house an exhausted Kathleen was snuffing back sobs; if she was caught crying her father would catch it. Having run about seven miles, her arms and legs ached with tiredness. In bedroom slippers her mother answered the door, a crumb of chocolate cake clinging to the corner of her mouth; she gazed down at Kathleen, then the bitter accusing eyes lifted to Henry. "How could you take her on one of your crazy walks, fill her with your nonsense!"

Henry said nothing.

Lottie sniffed with victory (she always won in her combats with him). "I'm going to put you to bed, give you some supper and after . . ." her voice rose with plump self-satisfaction, "I'll read to you . . ." her tongue licked at a stray crumb of cake, brought it safely into her mouth, ". . . about the beautiful princess and the wicked witch."

Kathleen clutched the newel post on the stair. "I don't want to hear about a witch!"

Afterwards as Kathleen lay in bed, full of milk toast, Lottie brought her book of fairy stories. "I don't want to hear them!" A frown of rejection came to her forehead.

Lottie began, "In days of yore there lived a Princess, the fairest maiden in all the land . . ."

The frown eased out. Kathleen was hearing another voice, a siren voice. *Boone and that whole glorious gang turned their backs on the East and became new types of men . . . his grandson Kit was a little man . . . his hair was yellow as corn,he wore a coonskin cap and his rifle was always in his hand . . .*

"Many a youth hearing tales of the beauty of the Princess journeyed from afar to claim her hand . . ."

Kit Carson was true to the seed planted in him, to push back the frontier, discover new land, and yet there is still another frontier, still there is land. It is yours and it waits, a land of Boone's time when the canoe and the axe and the rifle . . .

"But none of the youths had come back to their own lands to tell their tale, for in the castle there lived a witch and this witch was filled with hate and with jealousy, a wicked witch . . ."

Kathleen was breathing evenly and peacefully, her thoughts a long way away.

Her mother stopped reading, gazed down with satisfaction at her daughter and stood up. Kathleen, roused by the stealthy movements, sat up in bed, asking "The canary? How is my canary?" The canary had been part of old Annie's possessions but Kathleen had adopted it after Annie died.

"The canary is dead. I threw it out."

Kathleen began to yell. Her mother stood in sullen apathy; without answering she went to the door. Kathleen yelled harder. Henry came, pushing aside his wife. "What's wrong, Kate?" He gathered her up in his arms, "Tell me . . ."

"She says the canary's dead! She's thrown it out!"

"I'll buy you one of your own—your own canary, Kate."

The door slammed behind them. Kathleen knew her mother would take to her bed and stay there five days.

3

She carried her rifle easily against her shoulder; she made no attempt to raise it, sight a squirrel or rabbit or other small animal and shoot. A kit fox peered from the underbrush of the deep woods to her left.

It was late October; the sky was a hazy pinkness along the horizon was the palest blue, with a few lazy clouds resting like dolphins tired of play. A crow watched from the telephone line. In deference to Emily, a classmate from Form V, she kept close to the fence rather than skirt the first layer of woods that stretched to the river. Emily had offered friendship from the first day of Form I in high school and it surprised Kathleen, then pleased her. When someone sought her out, she was always pleased, knowing, too well, how her mother and her mother's friends regarded her.

The boys in her high school classes admired her, chiefly because she was a beauty, entirely unconscious of her looks, a girl without airs or pretensions—but they were unprepared for her direct manner. Though they put her on top of their lists of girls, they never offered to take her home after corn roasts and picnics, skating and snowshoe parties. There was something inviolate and formidable about Kathleen that made them hesitate.

To Emily, walking over the fields with a rifle over one's shoulder was sort of crazy but not any more crazy than bringing along a canary in its cage. But then, Kathleen *was* different. Emily was glad she hadn't brought the canary along today because Kathleen always paid more attention to it than to her. The first time Emily had asked to come on one of the Saturday walks, Kathleen had said, "Are you sure you want to? I carry a rifle and sometimes my canary."

"You shoot things?"

"I don't shoot anything."

"Why do you carry a gun, then?"

"Because I want to . . . oh forget it . . . don't come unless you wish to." Kathleen could not explain the feeling of freedom, walking these fields with her rifle and her canary, escaping from the limitations of her mother and her mother's friends. She and her father had always escaped with a mutual secret joy to walk these fields and roads. Lately he spent more and more time in his office at the mill preparing his lecture on Genesis for the men's class at the Church.

The bigness of life filled her with happiness and sharpened her eagerness to set out on her own path; something else she was unable to explain, something that had been locked within her since childhood, was always drawing her on, as though some fortune or prize as marvellous as Kit Carson's damascene belt awaited her. How could she explain this to anyone, let alone to Emily?

Emily came.

Emily was small, dark and pretty and she lived in a world of high school, home, a little hot house and a fussy little mother. These circumscribed her life, her all. But she admired her friend, felt deep in her being there was something new and exciting about her and she reached out to draw her into her world, trying in a fumbling way to discover what it was that made Kathleen so apart from the others. When Emily did find out it was too late; her life had been crystallized and so had Kathleen's a thousand miles away.

In these days and on these walks she asked questions constantly and Kathleen didn't seem to mind though she could easily become impatient, and sometimes rough.

"What are you going to do when you leave school?"

Kathleen stopped walking and kicked at a brown daisy plant until it released fragments of dusty fiber. "I'll be expected to go to the University."

"You don't want to go?"

"Not wanting to doesn't enter into it. My father expects me to go—
he believes in the educated woman."

"Why don't you tell him you don't want to?"

"And what if I want to?"

A hundred things crowded Emily's mind, Kathleen in a big city
among alien people, eating strange food, studying more Math, more
English Lit. "I'm going to be a secretary—old Clarke will need one, his
is so old she'll be quitting . . . I'll keep his law office tidy . . ."

"Is that all you want?"

"What else is there?"

"Lots of things." Kathleen walked on again.

"Besides teaching, what?"

"There's law, a law firm of your own instead of serving Clarke."

"Are you crazy?"

"If I'm crazy you're foolish—or frightened or lazy or just too ignorant.
You don't know what you really want—this is the twentieth century now,
one year inside it!"

"Well, what do you know!"

The sky paling and wide above her, the crow caw-cawing, the woods
darkening, even menacing, Kathleen understood she wanted something
exciting for herself. She would know what to do when the time came.
And it was the twentieth century when everything would be new and
stimulating and she would embrace it all. She'd be another Kit Carson
or Margaret Fuller, she'd scale the heights of the wilderness, or open new
frontiers, something grand and heroic, bold and free. A new type of
woman. No little piggling life for her.

Emily was bound to unloose her soul. "I'll work for a few years and
then I'll get married."

"But you'll never know what you could've done."

"What do you mean?"

It was all so limiting—as though Emily had put a padlock on any
ideas that were original or exciting.

"It's all right for you to go to a big city and to college, your family
has pots of money."

"We have no money." She would be forced to pay her own way by
scholarships, and they were usually granted to men. The big lot at the
side of their house had been sold for an unheard of price and all the
cash had already been eaten up by the mill creditors.

A whistle made them both jump. On the road a boy was moving
leisurely along; he was Carl Bowers from their class, a big muscular boy
swinging his hips with arrogance. Handsome in a heavy, somewhat
graceless way, he was well aware of his carefully combed copper bright
hair. He was clever, Kathleen knew, came close to her in all his marks
except English Lit. She walked on with indifference, stopping only when
Emily called, "Wait!"

Leaning against the rail fence, he indolently surveyed the crow, whistling at it until the bird took off with imperious flapping wings. He didn't look at the girls. "Why don't you shoot it, Kate? What you got that rifle for?"

"Don't be superior, Carl."

He leaped over the fence and joined them. Kathleen and Emily walked ahead, Carl coming on behind. "Now what you two women think you're doing, huh?"

"Can't you see," Emily said, "we're taking a walk."

"Yeah, but why always the same walk?"

"How do you know?"

"Followed you two, three times."

"Run along, Carl," Kathleen said, "Find someone else to impress."

He strode up, a little in front of her; his eyes, which had wandered about the field, locked with hers now, brown eyes against blue green eyes. His were the first to drop. "Why always carry a gun when you don't shoot?"

"Why I carry a gun is none of your darn business."

He stepped back but kept on chaffing her.

Kathleen turned on him, "Three's a crowd, or don't you know, yet." He began to whistle.

She looked at her watch—it had belonged to her grandmother Rice and hung from a thin leather thong round her neck. It was time she was back home. "Come on, Emily, I must go."

When the three came to the outskirts of town, Carl suddenly disappeared down a side street. Emily left at the Fish Creek bridge. When Kathleen turned in at her own walk Carl appeared from behind the hedge, breathing as though he'd been racing. "What do you think you're doing, Carl?"

"Seeing you." He came up boldly close to her but he was nervous and swallowed, shifting onto one foot, resting his copper brown eyes flat on her.

"Take your fill." She stood tall, a full inch taller than he. She was nineteen and inviolable.

He swallowed again, flung his gaze about.

He was seeking her out, it was a little game. Most girls were associated with one boy by the time they reached Form V. She smiled.

Two women in dusty black with a jingling of jet passed them, bowing coldly to Kathleen, freezing Carl with their pudding eyes.

"Who are they?"

"Just friends of my mother."

He made a clicking sound with his tongue.

The women arrived before the double front door whispering among themselves. They would report Carl's presence to Kathleen's mother. But Kathleen was still smiling, wondering who would seek her out, want her, far in the future. It might even be Carl. She turned to him.

He was already gone.

The parlour, the whole house, was a mausoleum of every defunct and cranky craft known to ladies since the 1860s. It was crammed with paintings of flowers that never grew (those red roses hanging on a string) and sheep that never grazed; china covered with red roses filled cabinets and black satin screens crashed against Kathleen's shins every time she came within a foot of them.

She put away her rifle, fed her canary, washed her hands and slicked back her untidy golden hair. Possessing no pretty things, she did not change her clothes before she came into the parlour with a load of tea and cream and raisin tarts for the ladies. Her wild ways would already have provided most of the talk among the women. This young man, the son of the lumber yard's owner would only be another stick to add fuel to the latest evidence of the reckless and eccentric behaviour of Lottie's daughter. When Kathleen had served the last raisin tart to a fat woman with a mustache she disappeared. Privately, they had assured themselves Kathleen would come to a bad end, a disgrace to her mother's family and to the town. So they hoped. It would serve Lottie Rice right for her pretensions to superiority. Kathleen could follow the twists and coils of their minds up in her room while listening to the operatic trills of her little canary.

4

"I'm the new woman of the twentieth century." Margaret took the last two steps of the stairs and landed in the tiny foyer of the rooming house. It was 1906.

"Prove it," Kathleen said.

"I'm going to live an exciting life, none of your teacher-*cum*-wife-*cum*-mother for me.'"

"I won't stop you—I approve."

The rooming house had been Kathleen's home since the dean of residence at Victoria College had ordered that she get rid of her canary if she wanted to live in the residence. "Positively no animals!" she'd demanded.

"It isn't an animal, it's a helpless little bird!" She'd been forced to move to a large cold room in the attic of a shambling old boarding house. Her father made up the extra cost since her scholarship didn't cover rooming houses.

Margaret lived in residence. She had attached herself to Kathleen from the first year; perhaps a subliminal sense, a faint stirring of something new and different had suggested that Kathleen could help her reach some as-yet-undetermined goal. Kathleen regarded her as a kind of Emily, a different *kind* of Emily but essentially the same as her old high school friend, unless she was badly mistaken. There were differences of course. Margaret came from a wealthy family, was strong-minded and a blatantly handsome girl with dark brown hair and a small blunt nose; she'd always had her own way. For Kathleen the relationship was an easy, good-humoured one.

Throwing her tennis ball at the ceiling, Margaret caught it with her racket. "Then you won't have a game with me?"

"I told you I promised Ken and he'll be along, in fact he's overdue now."

"He's serious about you . . . hope you mean business with him. He means to get married."

"Who said anything about marriage?" Kate asked.

"Ministers sort of have to get married aside from the urge—it'll be the marriage of the twentieth century." She let herself out the door of the rooming house, stuck her head back in, "The tongues are wagging." She was gone, then her head appeared again, "Bet he asks you after Convocation."

Margaret's remarks disturbed her. She sat down on the chair below the wooden wall phone, rested her tennis racket against the newel post, and wondered just what her relationship was with Ken. It had grown under the big umbrella of her love affair with college life. She was free from her mother although she regretted the separation from her father, their nightly walks and his lectures on the stars; so important had these been to her she'd considered taking Astronomy. She admitted she'd gone along with Ken's attentions, not that he'd been very attentive until this, their last year, and then only after he was assured of being made assistant pastor at the biggest (and wealthiest) church in the city. College was a kind of melting pot and it had melted her down. What residue of her original self was left, she wasn't sure.

Now her college days were coming to an end. For the upcoming graduation exercises she had bought the prettiest clothes she'd ever worn and though she prided herself that clothes meant little to her she would be very happy to wear the high-necked lacy blouse, the black silk and wool skirt with its row of ruching an inch above the hem. And a long black woollen coat with the newest gathered sleeves to wear over everything. The skirt and coat reached her ankles.

She consulted the watch, hanging about her neck; it was long past the hour Ken had stated. He was always late and never excused himself.

He burst in on her then, out of breath—he'd been running or walking very fast—in white duck trousers, white shirt, a pale blue knot of silk at his neck exactly matching the blue of his eyes. The effect was a studied note of harmony. (She'd always thought every move he made was done after careful and cautious balancing of facts.)

"Hello there!" He bent forward as though he'd decided beforehand to kiss her and then at the last moment something about her eyes, her whole stance made him change his mind and he straightened.

"What kept you?" She did not rise.

"Kathleen, I had duties."

"They kept me waiting."

"I think you're impatient, Kathleen."

"That's certainly no secret."

"Are you in a hurry to get married too?"

"What! Who mentioned marriage?"

"I did."

The placid face gazing so straightly at her with the pale blue serious eyes, the pig-coloured white skin sent a jolt of alarm along her spine—his colour wasn't right, he was driving himself into exhaustion. "I think you ought to rest before Convocation."

"Kathleen, I asked you a question."

"I'm not quite sure what you're driving at but if you must have an answer right at this moment . . . it's no."

He frowned as though her answer was unacceptable to him. "There's something equivocal . . . almost a double meaning . . . you've always been so clear."

Ken was a difficult person to say no to. "What gives no a double meaning?" In some ways he was like an obstinate little boy who, deprived of what he reached out for and desired, lay down on the floor and kicked. She stood up. "Seriously, I think you should rest."

He frowned as if trying to switch his mind from one set of facts to another. He had no sense of humour.

"Let's stop this. If you insist on playing, let's play—but I'm against it. Besides I've got to get back and dress."

They went out into the splendid June day in silence. He didn't know her at all and yet he'd asked in his queer, angular way to marry her. She had a glimmer of how he would be as a husband, always late, always conscientious about his duties, always expecting too much of her her and perhaps always ailing (that peculiar pig-white skin). And quite without any humour. She swirled the tennis racket round her long white skirt; it made small slashing sounds. She ceased when he looked down, scowling at the racket, "Stop that, Kathleen."

They reached the grass court behind the women's residence. "What a lovely day," she said. "I wish I'd brought along my canary, the air would have done it good."

"Kathleen, you're being too silly!" Now he was very annoyed with her.

They were in the middle of the game when she shot back the ball and he ran, lifting his racket, appeared to stumble and then fell. She waited. "Hurt yourself?" When he didn't get up, didn't answer, she went to the net. He lay still, his eyes closed as though rejecting all further action. "Ken, what is it?" He seemed suddenly to be so small. She was running around the net bending down, touching the face raised to the sky. She lifted herself up shakily, her whole being vibrating with shock. He was dead.

She didn't attend the graduation exercises to receive her first class honours in Mathematics, her Gold Medal, but busied herself informing the college authorities, Ken's parents, his friends, her father, her friends. She wanted her father; he had decided not to come because of the expense but after her telephone call, promised to be with her. She received condolences from Margaret, from everyone as though she was Ken's fiancée. His sudden death was a terrible ending to the happy years of her college life.

The funeral was conducted in the college chapel; Ken's father, assisting with the service, asked her to sit with his wife in the front pew. She was a slender woman, almost frail, hiding the grief in her washed-out eyes behind a black veil. To Kathleen she was the perfect Methodist minister's wife, her personality obliterated by duties to her husband, her church, her only son. Even to her own self she was merely a symbol of service, never venturing to claim her own beliefs, her own unique desires. The complete servant.

Occasionally, a black gloved hand squeezed Kathleen's in sympathy and mutual mourning.

Kathleen sat with her shoulder drawn up, her eyes set above the open coffin onto the three rounded windows, arched in varnished oak. She was appalled by the lifeless body so close. Would it have been better, would it have made a difference to Ken's fate—she couldn't yet make herself say the word death—if she had said she'd marry him, acted an eagerness she hadn't felt and cancelled out her own life, handed it over to his custody as he wanted, expected her to do? She knew she could never have done it; she'd have always been fighting for her freedom.

She drifted into irrelevancies; the three windows, a symbol of God, the Son, the Holy Spirit—the Trinity. Their roundness was the result of Charles Wesley's theories on church architecture. She was unaware that Ken's father had announced the hymn until she felt the sympathetic squeeze.

The owner of that hand regarded her as her beloved son's fiancée and believed her to be strangled with mourning.

She was sitting down but had no awareness of doing so. Her mind was screaming denials, NO, no, I could never have done it, never married him. Never. She was furious with herself for drifting into a relationship for which she had neither preparation nor talent; furious with Ken for pressuring her to be his wife with his terrible sense of duty towards the church, towards her, towards his unborn children.

Her emotion drained her of any ability to reason, even to think with clarity. The hand that held hers was fever hot.

There were two sermons and they were interminable. What did it matter now that Ken was dead? Dead. She could use that word now.

Her mind drifted. Far back she heard other words, another voice, a siren voice. *He was a little man with piercing blue green eyes . . . Kit Carson was true to the seed planted in him to push back the frontier, discover new land, land so great it could not be measured and yet there is still another frontier, still land . . . It is your land and it waits, a land of Daniel Boone's time, when the canoe and the axe and the rifle were the implements of life and survival.*

The hand squeezed hers. They were standing up, singing.

Afterwards, she stood beside Ken's mother at the coffin. Why had it taken a tragedy to bring her a glimpse of her future? Choking back her sobs, the older woman said, "You must come to us soon, dear . . ."

Ken's father came down from the platform and stood beside the two women. Gazing deep into Kathleen's shining eyes, "May God help you."

Kathleen spent the next year teaching in St. Catharines, Ontario, a small town. She liked the pupils and the teaching of Mathematics, but not the succession of boarding houses, icy bedrooms, stiflingly hot dining rooms, wretched meals, the roast of beef that lasted in one way or another all the week, the other teachers, their pettiness—as if her very differences constituted a threat—their gossiping. She led a secret life, ordering mining manuals from the government, biographies of explorers Samuel Hearne and La Vérendrye.

Margaret had retreated to her wealthy parents' home and no longer talked of the new woman, the thrilling life she was about to lead. She bombarded Kathleen with letters, occasionally spending a weekend with her. "I thought you were going to set the world on fire but here you are—a schoolmarm in a small town." Kathleen was glad when Margaret left.

One Saturday near the end of Kathleen's first year of teaching, an ad appeared in *The Globe*. Wanted: Male teacher, mathematics, Salary $1,400, New high school, Yorkton, Sask. Apply Secretary.

Kate consulted her atlas; Yorkton was close to the Manitoba border and adjacent to a kind of parkland, a belt of trees, tall grass, small lakes and streams. It was a frontier town, halfway between civilization and the Arctic, a good place to listen to sounds from the north. She applied for the job and within the month had been hired. The Secretary informed her a male teacher would have been preferred but none had applied with her qualifications. Her salary would be $1,200—all they would allow for a female teacher. She did not protest.

When Margaret heard the news she wrote the Secretary to inquire if there were any positions still vacant. There was one teaching English Composition, Algebra and Art to Form I. She applied and was accepted. Kathleen could help her with the Algebra. Once more she returned to her old theme: she was the new woman of the twentieth century leading a thrilling life of her own. Her parents were satisfied with their daughter's job, so far away; Kathleen Rice would be there also, and Kathleen, in their opinion, would temper any inclination to wildness, she was such a solid, sensible young women.

Kathleen left for Yorkton in mid-August, stopping over in Winnipeg to outfit herself, with a man's heavy high-necked grey sweater, man's overalls, cap, mackinaw, lengths of canvas, canvas sacks and a twice handed-down sleeping bag, said to have been in Admiral Peary's expedition to the Arctic.

With her canary in its cage she rode from the station at Yorkton on the top of a hay-wagon drawn by a team of oxen along the main street, passing a hardware store, a funeral parlour with a verandah where an old man snoozed in a rocker, a blacksmith, a general store; a lumber yard, a hotel, a hospital in a private house, the Queen Victoria, and a pool room splattered with tins advertising Sweet Caporals, King Albert plug tobacco. Quite a lot of civilization, but the main street ended abruptly, breaking up into branched winding trails that led to a skyline of trees, the park belt of the atlas.

She found the secretary at the Yorkton Grain Exchange, leaning against a bale of hay, sucking a straw. "Young lady," he said, "you might as well go home, we have boys and girls older than you and they'll eat you alive."

Kathleen was staying. "Let them try."

Her boarding house was frame with a verandah and a peaked roof (not unlike the houses on certain streets in Toronto). Her landlady, very satisfied she lived in the best place in Yorkton, fluttered about her first boarder, eager to impress with refinements brought from her old home in Nova Scotia. Kathleen had expected a landlady of Slavic origin— perhaps with an ikon as a relic of her homeland—not this talky, excited little woman and her fussy talky, excited little woman and her fussy parlour filled with nicknacks, last year's frilly valentine, an upright piano and two unframed photos of her late lamented husband leaning against a plaster cast of Minnehaha painted in imitation bronze. In the exact center of the little parlour was a square table on high legs, its embroidered scarf holding a stereoscope and slides and a family album; on the lower shelf was Eaton's catalogue and a Bible.

Yorkton had the most modern high school Kathleen had ever seen, with large airy rooms, many windows letting in light over the pupil's left shoulders, and modern desks, built according to the latest standards of 1906 for educational purposes. But the town had no post office: mail was distributed once a week, vaguely around four o'clock of a Saturday afternoon, from the newspaper office, *The Enterprise*. At night, lying in the high-backed varnished oak bed, Kathleen heard coyotes howling and the lonely wail of a locomotive echoing across the empty prairie south of the town.

Margaret arrived two days before school opened with a trunk full of fine clothes, enough to delight the heart of the homesick Ada Ames, the landlady. The first day of school Kathleen formed a baseball team and organized walking trips into the park belt; it was seven miles from the high school. The boys and girls were eager, playing baseball after school on the fine autumn days and joining in the walking trips, pointing out Yorkton Creek and some of its contributory streams, an old trapper's cabin. At first Margaret came along on these Saturday jaunts but it was so much easier than walking for miles along Yorkton Creek and a lot more comfortable to stay in the boarding house, chit-chatting with Ada Ames (they were early on first name basis), eat her baking powder discuits, her drop cakes, and view the slides on the stereoscope of the Eiffel Tower, the Roman Forum, the Houses of Parliament in London. The stereoscope and its slides had a strange and compulsive effect on Margaret. Little by little she began to wonder if the new woman was not more attuned to the Elysian fields of Europe than the boundless and chilling frontiers of the Canadian north.

5

May 10 1906

I am not a hero but I have taken part in heroic exercises. This is my diary of life in this new land.

Steady, boys! I have made a beginning but I may never finish this opus since I have no idea what Destiny has in store for me. I'm headed for a land called District of Keewatin in the Northwest Territories. The northwest seems to make a pattern in my life since I was stationed on the northwest frontier of India.

I ride now in a colonist car one day out of Montreal. It jogs along its tracks like a stately matron never pausing, never increasing its pace, like majesty on parade. I leave the train at a place called Winnipeg. I leave it because my money will be gone; more of that later. Winnipeg is an odd name but no more so to an Englishman who has served in the Indian Army than Nowshera, Malakand and Secunderbad.

The train follows a course through deep and gloomy forests, some of the great trees rising out of swamp water still covered with patches of snow. The little Russian woman with the flowered kerchief on her head stops at my lower bunk and nods and becks and continues on down the aisle; she's probably not a great deal older than I and I am 25 but she looks old, too old to be starting out in a new raw country. Last night she brought me a slab of hot sausage on black bread. Tasted mighty good after my diet of biscuits and cheese and tea. I have the strangest feeling my bones will be buried somewhere in this cold land. I had the same strong feeling (and it proved only too true) when I was embarking on the troop ship for India that my mum standing on the dock shading her eyes would be dead when I got back to England. And such proved to be the case. That same feeling overcame me when I looked from the dock at Halifax to the third class deck of the S.S. Tunisian trying to find my wife May and my son, knowing only too well they would have gone below after we parted.

When May saw the Citadel of Halifax she turned into a whirlwind of fury. I don't care what the name of the place is or the name of that hill or the name of this country, I hate it and I hate this country too and if you insist on staying here I never want to see your face again! Strong words! The man she had married had not proved to be the gentleman she wanted. May believed because my pater lived in a forty room house

32

free of rent from some relative that we were County and therefore gentry. I suppose we were but without money, my pater being the younger son of a younger son though he always had enough to buy nailing good hunters and be out all day at point-to-points and race meets. Never did a day's work in his life. I knew May was building up to some big scene in which she was the offended one, the martyr, during the 13 days it took the S.S. Tunisian to reach Halifax from Liverpool, but never thought she'd leave me on the dock with just enough Canadian money to get me a ticket to Winnipeg and buy a few supplies, mighty few. April always lovely in England but it is no time to be on the North Atlantic Ocean which kicks up some big equinoctial storms. Our cabin below water line, bunks on three sides, fourth was door to passageway. Third side occupied by man and wife, complete strangers. May seasick before ship began to roll and because his mother was sick my boy sick too.

I had to decide in one minute what I was going to do. At one moment we were together the next we had parted company. May said she was returning to England on the S.S. Tunisian back to Liverpool. I to go ahead with my plans to find gold. Didn't have to worry too much about May and the boy they'd make a straight line for pater's house she to be mistress there. The boy would be sitting astride a small grey cob and sent cubbing. It's a good arrangement: my pater has the boy to train into a good horseman and May is doing what she wants to do though she will never be accepted as County, her father being in the hierarchy of the servant world fairly high up an assistant of an estate manager to an Earl. But she will make out in the drafty cold mansion, dusty too since pater had no more than 3 servants after my mater's death, 2 of them in the stables.

A bad trip, ship crowded, must have had 2000 passengers most in class 3. Dining salon below water line steamy with great caldrons of pork and you helped yourself. Most passengers single fellows in peaked caps wearing their best, all eager to make fortunes. It's said fortunes made every day in this part of the Empire. I was in old Army trews, jacket unbuttoned, tan galluses, with trusty Lee Enfield in the cabin. When I began Army career we were issued the magazine-fired Lee Metford. Before setting out bought myself a good Christy in London, wide brimmed good black felt. Was wearing it and carrying rifle when May sounded off. My best West Country tweed packed in trunk in hold and it'll go back with May.

Setting sail from Liverpool was happy doing what I wanted to do having seen an item in paper about men discovering gold in a place called Klondike in Canada. On map encountered lands as big as whole continents with names like Keewatin, Yukon, Athabaska. Took months to persuade May but the sound of gold and the very good possibility of my finding it did it.

Like a good letter well written is what a diary should be and Mum used to say a letter well written was the mark of a lady or gentleman.

I never had any schooling except what she and the Hussars taught me but I'm doing well enough. Mum was a real lady being eldest daughter of Squire Hutchinson. Her family have been Squires since Saxon times. When she sat side saddle on a horse she looked what she was.

May 11 1906

In the afternoon. We are proceeding along the shore of a big lake. Sun sparkles on its waters and there are islands with stands of timber. Glad to leave the gloomy forests; have just made myself a cup of tea and feel jolly good. Have one small Army duffel bag to my name and a couple of Canadian dollars left but I am free for the first time in a very long period and freedom is the thing. I must keep my wits about me and my powder dry when I disembark in Winnipeg.

Colonist cars comfortable with cookstoves and heater each end as well as washrooms where I can shave, clean my teeth and wash up. There are upper and lower berths, uppers let down by brass chains during day, and a lot of fellows lie there; some play Scottish airs on mouth organs or unknown tunes of far away places such as Russia or Poland or Italy or Bulgaria on their harmonicas and accordions. What will happen to a nation of such diverse peoples? Good thing it is part'of British Empire to give it steadiness! Some of the fellows just lie there in upper bunk staring at people passing up and down aisle in constant procession. My favourite is the little Russian woman. She passes now nodding and smiling and patting my shoulder. There are no questions in her eyes as there are in the eyes of the fellows lying up there in their bunks. She'll make it.

Her husband wears a wide brimmed black felt hat though not as good quality as mine not being of British manufacture. They have a son about 13, very shy but no doubt full of dreams of making a pile of money in this new raw land. Last night his mother by a series of gestures invited me to join her family for a meal. We had boiled potatoes, boiled cabbage, sausage, black bread, pretty good fare for passengers coursing through a black forest and along the shores of a great lake. The father speaks a little English. I gather they are disembarking at Winnipeg and going at once to some kind of Immigrant Office. Invited me to come with them. Declined nicely as I could don't consider myself an Immigrant. This is the Empire on which the sun never sets and I am old Imperial Army man.

Conductor a friendly bloke comes through coach with big smile, a joke or two, told us we would be in Winnipeg tomorrow morning or very early in afternoon. Will never forget another conductor calling out the strange words All Aboard in Halifax. Never heard them before. The train rolls on in its measured course and I roll too.

Aug 8 1906

I have been working here since May 16. We are camped beside a lovely lake; it's a late summer paradise, the bluffs about us covered with heavy timber bogs and sloughs, they are breeding grounds for ducks and geese. And mosquitoes. Thank heaven their number has moderated; we've all suffered from their ferociousness. They cover everything, men, food, especially cakes, and have caused a lot of sickness. Some of the men have died from fever. I am employed as cookee to a railroad construction gang. There are 3 cooks plus Chief Cook cookee and bull cook. I spent one night in the attic of Bell Hotel in Winnipeg, heard in the bar of a new railroad line being constructed and applied at the home of location engineer. Only place left was the second cook. Hired on the spot at $30 a month and board. I admired the location engineer's team of horses in front of his house, noted the new type (new to me) of harness and was told it was the western way of hitching a team. The chief cook is an old Imperial Army man, ramrod straight and over 80 so the men say, but doesn't look a day more than 65. He lost an eye at the Siege of Ladysmith and carries round in his pocket glass eyes of different colours, red green yellow blue, changes them frequently and scares the Indians in the gang, they say he's bad medicine. When moving camp to a new location he has a trick of placing a red or green glass eye on a stump and saying, "Now you so and so's you get to work, I've got my eye on you."

So far it's solid comfort but the nights are becoming much colder tho' early in August. I do not wish to think of winter in this country in this camp. We are somewhere north of Selkirk laying track which will eventually I'm told end up on the shores of Hudson Bay. Our camp composed of 5 pyramid type tents of various sizes, the bunk tent being 14 x 14, the cook tent and dining tent joined together each 10 x 10, the office tent the same size. There are 18 men including the chief location engineer, topographer, the draftsman, rod man, axe men, line men, and the cooks. Everything well organized.

We eat breakfast at 5 in the morning; line men leave camp at 7 and work till 8 in the evening. The 3 cooks sleep in the cook tent, rise at 4, go to bed at 11, work almost all day. Food is excellent, breakfast of oatmeal, hot cakes, bacon, with maple syrup and coffee. I miss my tea. Cooks take a few hours off in the afternoon after taking sandwiches down the line to the men and then feeding themselves. Rather than taking to my bunk I go for a tramp to become better acquainted with country and so discover habitats of wild animals and game birds. Noted partridges, curlews, Wilson snipes, usual ducks and geese. Freedom in the life at camp means a lot to me.

The stove is made of sheet metal and can be taken apart when we break camp and move to another site on up the line. Table tops are made from canvas nailed to laths which can be rolled up for easy moving, table legs and benches are cut from the bush at each camp. Tent sites must be cleared, poles cut for tents, firewood for cook stove, brush for bunks, wood to mark the proposed railroad line each time we move on. Very efficient. When the line is projected across the numerous small lakes and bogs the Chief and the rodman wade straight ahead, often to the armpits in water, sometimes forced to swim. Emerging they remove boots and pour out the water and continue on their way. The principal instruments are the steam shovel and dinky locomotive fired with wood, the small cars being used for excavated materials. Sundays the Chief, the transitman, draftsman, and topographer spend day reviewing work so far done and planning ahead. Other men like myself wash clothes by lake or stream.

Sanitation is a pole set over a hole in the ground. Toilet paper unheard of, you use leaves or moss, anything handy.

Aug 10 1906

So far I'm fairly content but this life has nothing to do with finding gold. An axe man Billy Todd tells me months and months of this life will change a man. He tells me I'll lose my good humour. He comes from the United States and has been working as axe man 2 years and is ready to quit. Has a half finished cabin in wilds about hundred miles or so north and east of a mining town called The Pas; sometimes he calls it Le Pas. I wonder once in a while about May and our son but my memories become dimmer with each passing day. I also wonder about the little Russian woman and her family. Shook hands with great solemnity at the foot of the steps of our coach. I wish them well. All those fellows on the S.S. Tunisian seemed to vanish in the thin air of Canada. Never saw any of them again. I wonder if it is any use keeping this diary or if I'll ever read it again.

6

Winter fell suddenly that year in Yorkton. At the end of October a blizzard struck, fine dry snow drifting and sifting and whirled by gale force winds; at night the temperature fell to fifty degrees below Fahrenheit. It was to prove the toughest winter since the young town had its inception. Kathleen's activities, the hockey on the frozen Yorkton Creek, had to be curtailed but the social life broke out, an epidemic of suppers, a raging of festivities, a deluge of hard time dances.

A team of horses or oxen hitched to a wagon on sleigh runners or to a red cutter waited every Saturday afternoon before the boarding house door; often she would ride postillion behind a student's father. Kathleen was popular with the students. Most of the suppers had a strange familiarity, rabbit of one kind or another—the farms were overrun with rabbits, rabbits sitting round frozen haystacks, darting into houses— roasted rabbit, stewed rabbit, fried, ground for hamburger. The ways of serving rabbit were endless. Occasionally, and it was a sign of honour, she was given boiled or roasted beef. The true glory of the suppers and entertainments were the cakes of many layers with cream, jelly, custard or fudgy mixes between the layers and covering the whole of the great concoction. If the farmer or homesteader was Scandinavian she would be handed innumerable cups of coffee, floating with cream so thick it was spooned into the cup.

The hard time dances were held in barns; she learned to square dance. Whole families would come by sleigh, babies and young children made comfortable and snug along a wall close to the huge stove glowing red with heat. Nearby stood the fiddler and the caller, the caller's voice ringing out over the dancers and up into the barn's rafters. "Take yer partner, swing her round, over and under, away yer go!" All the favourite songs were sung or hummed while the fiddler thrummed until he ran with sweat and the caller shouted until his voice was hoarse: *By the Banks of the Saskatchewan, The Moon Shines Bright on Red Wing Sighing*, over and over and over again.

She discovered she had an excellent digestion but Margaret was forced to take great doses of baking soda for days afterwards when she accompanied Kathleen.

On one of the Saturday morning walks or snowshoe jaunts into the parkland Kathleen met an old trapper; at first he was shy with a woman who was interested in trapping, but when she shared the food she had brought, he told her where she could place traps to catch mink and marten. When he knew her better, he told about setting muskrat traps in spring.

"I'd come along on raft and water not gainin' and jes make little hollows on bank big enough to hold trap, set it in 'bout inch of water and put any kin' of veg. on li'l stick and put it into hole, rats smell it. Works good."

From the lips of this old man she first heard of The Pas. It was the gateway to the north. A place of dreams. "What kind of dreams?"

"Eh, why dreams of gold. Trappin' prospectin' exploring gold. If I was a young nipper I'd sure go . . . gold . . . nothin' like gold."

She asked her landlady about The Pas. Ada Ames shuddered. "A shanty town filled with rough men and loose women—no fit place for a lady teacher."

But new rails were being laid from western Saskatchewan through Yorkton and across the border, a hundred miles north into The Pas. According to her trusty atlas, The Pas was on the North Saskatchewan River. A few passengers could ride the open gas car, one of them steering, legs dangling a few feet above the uneven rails. One Saturday morning she examined the road bed; it was rough, steering would be tricky, the car could easily jump the rails and throw the passengers onto the rocks along the side. They would be forced to stop in order to shoot a prairie chicken, or rabbit, boil it on a fire and camp the night. In good weather the progress would be slow, in winter almost impossible, but it was a way of getting to The Pas.

Towards the end of her second year she announced to Margaret she planned to finish her teaching career forever at the end of term, and take the gas car to The Pas.

Margaret was lifted brutally out of the pleasing monotony of her life in Yorkton where she was the apple of Ada Ames' homesick and genteel eye and quite aware of it.

"Remember I'm not asking you or even recommending you come— if you do you're on your own just as I am."

For the first time in her life Margaret was forced to make a tough decision. On one side Kathleen meant business: it would be a hard life. On the other side, the coddled life in Yorkton and later, the Eiffel tower, the Roman Forum, the Houses of Parliament in London. Perhaps she could persuade Ada to come along. The choice unnerved her. She seesawed back and forth for weeks, then finally said she'd go along; it was the line of least resistence when she couldn't make up her own mind. Ada Ames cried bitterly.

It was 1909.

And so, into The Pas, the end of the rail and the gas car. They walked the tracks, crossed the ditch by a two-foot plank, wound through muskeg, found a path full of puddles blocked by a manure heap, and passed through a tangle of bushes to stand in the mud of the main street of The Pas. Kate's pack sack hiked on her back, sleeping bag rolled on top, a fry pan and tea pail hanging from the bottom; her belt hung with pick and axe, she held her rifle in one hand, her canary in its cage in the other. Margaret carried the smaller load. Men stopped on the dirt street and stared. Women prospectors! They stayed at the De Pas Hotel, a two-storey structure with a wooden front and tar paper sides.

The Pas—a French word meaning a narrow passage on a river or lake—was used for centuries before the coming of the prospector as a crossing place, a resting site, a camping ground by Indians of the western plains and the eastern tribes round Hudson Bay. And where the Indian was, the French trader was sure to follow with his fine red French wool cloth, his red blankets, beads and trinkets from Paris in exchange for beaver skins. The explorers and voyageurs knew The Pas, too. The two sons of La Vérendrye built a stone fort at the confluence of the Pasquia Creek and the low-banked Saskatchewan River, called it Fort Pascayac; that was in 1741. Later, in 1750, Pierre, the one nicknamed "the Chevalier", rebuilt the fort and named it Fort Paskaiao, sometimes called Basquia; by 1759 it had been abandoned. The Pas went through many more name changes: Opasquai, W'passkwayaw, Au Pas, Le Pas de la Rivière, Le Pas and finally The Pas.

The Saskatchewan River racing beside The Pas had been called Ki-sis-kah-chewan by the Indians meaning the river that runs swift.

Now, excitement breaking over the tar paper roofs, The Pas was a habitation of rumours, jumping off place for the riches of the north. Trappers, prospectors, girls: Suicide Sally, the Moose Jaw Kid, Cut-Throat Rosie with the scar running round the base of her throat, girls with gold

in their eyes. Husky dogs roaming the streets, new railway bridge beginning to span the wide Saskatchewan, Gateway Drug Store, shacks, furs
furs furs, every store trading in furs. Buy a pail of water, twenty-five cents
a pail out of the river from a stone scow drawn by buffalo. It was the place
of Kate's dreams. Shanty town, gateway into the heart of her new life.
Striding through the gateway, not seeing manure piles, mud puddles,
wild dogs, her gaze cosmic; she was in the thrust of seekers for new
freedom, new frontiers, new faiths. No comfortable, no ordinary life would
do for her.

But Margaret hated everything, the mad dogs, the mud puddles, the
Moose Jaw Kid who lived in the next cubby hole at the De Pas, worst
of all, hated herself for being weak-minded and merely a follower of
Kathleen. The change of name to Kate was an offense to her ears. She
hated it; this wasn't what she wanted. Ada Ames and her cosiness, her
drop cakes and pretensions to refinement would do for a while but she
longed in her secret self for broad avenues dazzling with light that led
to the Tour Eiffel and elegant shops full of beautiful clothes. That was
her frontier.

There were rushes the first winter to Island Lake up near the three
Cranberry lakes. Gold had been found years before but the prospector
hadn't staked his claims; Kate joined the rush, marching behind the
cortege—six horses with a snow plow, two horses dragging a tent, the
rear sleigh with four horses carrying a caboose-like structure where the
men and Kate ate and slept. Once a night she would threaten to use her
rifle, "No dammit, I'll shoot!"

They never found the gold but it was a journey of discovery for Kate:
now she was a real prospector, now she'd seen the lake country. She would
return. Margaret stayed at the hotel, storming out when the noise of the
men visiting the Moose Jaw Kid next door became too raucous, to walk
the muddy streets, her cheeks grainy and salty with unwiped tears.

With an unexpectedness that delighted Kate, she was offered a
teaching position in the town, a ragout of subjects—Arithemetic, Algebra,
English History, English Literature—a good place to assess rumours from
the north although at Yorkton she believed she'd given up teaching for
good, she accepted; she arranged for a small cabin to be built in the Indian reservation north and east of the town, located in the forest beyond
the new railway bridge over the Saskatchewan River, intended for the Hudson Bay Railway when its tracks reached The Pas.

Margaret resisted with force. She would return to Yorkton, board with
her old landlady, teach school again for a year, perhaps two, until she
went home again, and then perhaps to Europe and its domes of pleasant-
ness. Enough was enough. She would leave at once. Kate suggested caution; she should write Mrs. Ames before making a move which could
prove useless. She wrote Ada Ames all her plans and waited for a reply
in the new cabin darkened and dampened by forest shades, tortured by

ague, the disease of streaming eyes, shivering fits and enlarged spleen that crippled so many pioneers. She waited two months.

Ada Ames answered in a long letter bayoneted by exclamation marks, though the words were a kind of sober rebuke for such frivolity from a former favourite of hers. "You gave up against my most considered advice, may I say it, and an honourable position in the town, leaving my home and fine board, if I do say so, for a wild, unmaidenly venture! And now you want to return! You can hardly expect me to hold a room for you, knowing as you well do I have only three bedrooms in my house! They are at the time of writing and I hope for a long time to come, occupied by a most respectable young man who teaches Mathematics and a young lady from Winnipeg who has your old position and a very good teacher and friend she has proved to be! I can only wish you the best in all your future plans!"

Margaret knew the proper young lady would have won over her landlady with a gluttony of clothes and been rewarded with drop cakes and hot baking powder biscuits. She gulped down her pride at the defection of Ada Ames and mourned to Kate, "I thought she liked me."

Several months later she was looking after the accounts of the new drug store, the Gateway, run by Dr. William Sinclair.

The Pas was sweetening with new bustle, new growing: a theatre, the Dreamland, a newspaper, the *Hudson Bay Herald*, wooden sidewalks. Margaret met the excitement with indifference, Kate with eagerness. A new rumour, the biggest, juiciest of all, gold on Beaver Lake, gold in the cracks and seams of rocks, gold found by two men, well-known to the town, Dan Mosher and Tom Creighton. It was the middle of June, 1911 and Kate left the cabin and her teaching.

Her enthusiasm carried Margaret along like a bit of flotsam (she had become almost inert, caring little about anything) into the stern wheeler *The Saskatchewan*, to Sturgeon Landing with its white Hudson's Bay post, into Kate's canoe, the Duckling, into Sturgeon-weir Lake. They reached the evil Sturgeon-weir River with its hairpin bends, its rocks sharp as needles, and finally its terrible rapids; they portaged past the Snake and the Bent, and the unnamed others to a low point of land at the south end of Beaver Lake. They had arrived.

7

The mid-day sun glaring down on rock, land without form, water cold as though of primordial substance. The canary resting on the shelf outside the cabin door, silent.

She'd come in here for gold. Veins of gold in the quartz rocks had been found north and west on the shores of the lake. Once, it had been called *Lac aux Castors*, Beaver Lake now; the native's name for Beaver Lake was Amisk Lake but it was never used by the trappers and prospectors. Kate wasn't sure why Margaret had come and didn't believe Margaret herself knew either.

This place at the south end, the source of the Sturgeon-weir River tumbling over its rocks, haunting her; voices of men who'd voyaged to this point, had crossed here, the lost sound of their paddles hissing in the water, floating back to her out of the long years since those voyageurs and explorers had ploughed their canoes through the waters out of Montreal along the mother of rivers, the St. Lawrence. And this very summer, men clearing drift and sludge, panning gold a day's journey from the lake's inlet; most of them too had gone, now. Others, though in smaller numbers, were coming to take their place, tadpole prospectors off the farms of Manitoba and the prairies of Saskatchewan; they also would leave. And she would be left alone. She told herself she had no fear of being alone in this harsh man's world, treacherous; she'd been warned about the Sturgeon-weir River, a killer right on her doorstep. A tadpole prospector herself, she'd been in here since July. But she would stay, one winter, two, she was contemptuous of time, then she would go east into the lake country.

Gold dolomite cliffs with a stand of pine to her right, sloping into muskeg and floating bogs whose tough matted surface moved if she stepped on it, the slightest pressure submerging her feet into the blackish water. Behind the cabin, burned-off trees suggesting to Kate that every three or four years there had been a forest fire—those voyageurs and explorers must have been careless. Winds whimpering round the corner of the makeshift cabin she and Margaret had taken over. The Crees in their wigwams down the river told tales of the wind in here. To her left, the evil Sturgeon-weir raging against its banks. The Maligne, the early voyageurs had called it and that was its name for her.

This place Margaret loathed.

They were standing on the low point of land between the dolomite cliffs and the Maligne, waiting for Dan Mosher the prospector who had his base camp somewhere halfway up the east side of the lake to come with his big canoe and take Margaret out.

"The whole country in here is malignant and you're cruel Kathleen . . . I always guessed it . . . you persuaded me to come."

"I never even asked you to come."

"You did all that talking when the landlady wan't around . . . you believed what that old trapper in Yorkton told you . . . you pored over those old maps . . . I should have known."

"I studied David Thompson's map, an old trapper's with lumps for lakes and curvy lines for creeks and rivers, not much else."

"You don't tell the truth. There was Samuel Hearne and a man with a French name and all those manuals on how to prospect. And you kept it all secret from Ada Ames."

"I repeat, I did not ask you to come."

Margaret was bushed. The crystal clear lake reflected the cold, non-colour of the October sun. Before them hundreds of small islands sprouted magnificent stands of white spruce—the fires hadn't reached out across the water to destroy them—all those islands staked stolidly, and most of the staking without regard to mineral showings. A sense of her own power stiffened Kate's will. She was here. She wanted to be here.

She wore the clothes purchased long ago: the pair of a man's overalls over a thick man's grey sweater, heavy grey socks pulled over the legs of the overalls and thrust into high miner's boots; on her head where her hair had been cut short, a kind of fireman's cap, its peak jauntily turned back to show her piercing blue green eyes. The outfit intensified her beauty, but she was oblivious. She was lean, lean in her body and without ornament or trappings; she had even changed her name to plain Kate as her father had called her—it was more fitting as future trapper and prospector. But her spirit, oh her spirit sailed and streamed and swept over muskeg, burned spruce, Sturgeon-weir and polished lake.

"Are you listening to me Kathleen? You never listen to me."

"I'm listening." Unwillingly.

"I'd go crazy if I stayed here a week longer."

"Can you stand it another hour, maybe only a few minutes more?"

"Don't be so hatefully logical."

"Well you won't have to go crazy."

Margaret, the new woman, the twentieth century woman as had been her boast in college, in Yorkton, was showing signs of hysteria, or the malady of the bush; the long daylight, the loneliness, the timelessness.

Kate didn't bother to remind her that they'd only been in the bush three months. The last few weeks Margaret had refused to go prospecting, had hung about the cabin alone all day and complained bitterly when Kate returned about the isolation, the terrible scariness of the isolation, the lack of proper food (the landlady's drop cakes, she meant).

"You could fish," Kate said.

"I've never fished in my life!"

"Time to learn, then."

It was impossible. Margaret had to go. Then Kate would be alone, free to steer her own life as she steered her own canoe, the little Duckling.

Ever since Ken's funeral when she knew what she was going to do with her life, a flame had consumed her, drawing Margaret along in its vortex despite all the brave talk about the new age. "I'm going to startle this old world, you'll see, Kathleen Rice!"

"I wish you would."

And now she stood before Kate defeated. "Supposing this Mosher doesn't come?"

"I think Mosher's reliable."

"You don't know anything of the sort! He has no use for you or for any woman . . . the way he treated you . . . us."

Mosher had been in the woods a long time, since 1906 she'd heard, though no one was sure of dates in here. He'd grown so unaccustomed to women, the very sight of one meant trouble to him.

"And what will you do when I'm gone?"

"What I planned to do from the beginning. You want me to say I'll be lonely, that I'll suffer. But I'll be prospecting until the snow gets deep, then I'll lay traps. And there'll be the aurora borealis at night. And I'll explore."

"You'll be all alone." Her words had a bitter sound.

"I'll make out."

Margaret had become her main problem. Four nights ago Kate had been brought out of a well of sleep by Margaret's misery. She was in her sleeping bag, head flat down, mouth open from exhaustion when, floating up into awareness, she felt heat and sensed the acrid smell of an over-heated stove. The other side of the bunk, which was nothing more than a crib with branches of pine covered with moss, was unoccupied. Kate slipped out of her sleeping bag, bare feet curling away from the cold clay floor. The room was dark except for the dull red light round the lids of the little drum cookstove. A shape bent over beside the stove, a concealed sob moving like a convulsion up the bowed back. Margaret was weeping hysterically. Why were people weak when it didn't take much more courage or will power to be strong? Kate wondered. With the tips of her fingers she touched Margaret's shoulder. The convulsions ceased. Margaret was waiting to hear what she'd say, what she'd do. Behold the new woman! "Stop crying!"

Margaret waited. There was the problem of ways and means but Kate's attention had shifted. It was too quiet in the cabin. At the slightest stir in the morning the canary would start its singing. She threw off the old sweater covering its cage, knowing that bright eyes were regarding her though she could not see them. "Can't you sing, sweetie?" The bird raised itself over the tiny claws, and was silent. "If anything happens to you..." She fussed, trying for its attention but the eyes had closed now. She took out the little glass dishes, filled one with water from the pail, the other with bird seed.

"Aren't you going to help me?"

It was a cry from the heart. Kate moved away, shivering from the cold pressing up from the icy clay floor. She must seek out Dan Mosher. "I'll be off for a few hours; you'll be responsible for my canary."

She paddled along the east shore through a scattering of poplar leaves crisped by frost and floating on the water, through the purplish shadows cast by the cliffs. Above their rock face, a paleness, over the water a fuzz of grey, over all a terrible stillness. She wished she'd brought along her canary for company. Where was Mosher's camp? Where was Mosher? The big brutal man with the dull eyes that never rested on her. Mosher wouldn't want to have anything to do with her, let alone give his help.

Down the east side of the lake her cabin made a small rectangle of darkness in the greater darkness. No one had any idea who had built it or how long it had been there. An old-timer in The Pas had said,

"There's a cabin on the low point of land at the south end of Beaver." And now it was her base camp. But contemplating the cabin she felt no satisfaction, no happiness; there was something wrong with that.

She had no idea where Mosher's home base was, or whether she would find it, or even whether he'd be there or in his temporary quarters up the lake which would mean three or four more hours of paddling. She was cold and hungry as though she had not tasted food in days but strong and full of her own powers, her body responding easily to the rhythm of her paddling, dip and twist and lift, dip and twist and lift, dip and...

She'd been paddling two hours, perhaps three, her brain half mesmerized by the smooth passing of the Duckling through the still water. Dawn had come to this universe of original substance. In an anguish of loneliness she shouted, "Is anyone alive?" "Live live live", the stillness took up her cry, ringing along the cliffs far ahead, far behind.

By an inch she missed the crib of rock. Small birch saplings, a creek, a path beaten hard by feet. Mosher's? Along the path, tin pails, jelly pails, lard pails, butter pails, a fish net, tar paper, a gold pan, traps, all leading to a cabin of newish logs. A thick smog of smoke, white against grey sky, waved bravely from the stove pipe. Whoever he was, he was home, cooking his breakfast. Running the canoe along the crib, she jumped out, legs aching like a toothache. They didn't obey her and she stumbled. An old black felt hat had been tossed on a log. It was Mosher's.

She faced into the cabin, remembering her first encounter with Mosher, early in July. She'd run the canoe up the mud on the northwest channel of the lake. Getting out, rifle in hand, she approached the group of men—there'd been five—bent over stripping outcrop. They'd straightened sharply. A woman! Except the man she'd come to know as Dan Mosher. He'd come up slowly, lips barely mouthing, "Hear there's a coupla of y' down there."

"I'd like some information if you please." Her words had sounded proper as she formed them but here in front of that man, they took on a mincing foolishness.

His eyes had deepened as if he was searching back to some memory, something unpleasant. His eyes were dull mud.

One of the five, younger than the others, wearing a navy handkerchief tied about his face to keep off the black flies, stepped over. "My name is Charlie Krug," his voice eager, nervous.

"What d'y' want?" Mosher asked, his dull eyes pouring down at the bared rock.

She hadn't been prepared for the sullenness of this scraggly man. She was prepared now. That was the way he was going to be; she would accept it.

Behind the cabin a couple of huskies howled, were joined in a fury by others, one howl answered within the cabin. The young birch trees quivered and a shower of golden leaves descended onto the path.

A man opened the door, "Shut up!" It was Mosher without his ubiquitous hat, his long greyish brown hair swirled round his pate like silk threads. With awful fixity he gazed at some rocks along the path.

"I'd like to speak with you."

A young husky appeared beside him, baring its teeth. He gave it a kick. "Wall, c'mon, you're here."

Inside she patted the dog; it stood by her side wagging its great furry tail. The cabin permeated by the cheerful messiness of men with things on their minds other than cosiness and sociability: tins of food, snowshoes, paddles, axes, picks, mackinaws, caps, the smell of old burned fat, new burned fat, of hot food, fish, dog, and a kind of male smell, of men in confined quarters, sleeping bags still warm from their bodies. Krug stood by the cook stove. Without the navy handkerchief about his face he was very young with dry khaki coloured hair and blue eyes.

"All right," Mosher snapped, "stash up the grub."

Kate took a chair though no one asked her to sit.

"What d'y' want?" Mosher's response to her was the same as it had been in July.

She was going to give him trouble. She told him about Margaret, how it was important that she get out.

A grunt as if he'd found a tree that'd have to be removed from the outcrop. He was standing, eyes boring into the clay floor.

Charlie Krug brought her a tin plate of fried bannock and whitefish. There was no fork; she seized a piece of fish and swallowed. While she gulped down the food, drank the scalding tea, she was aware of another man, his eyes glued to her in an insolent lustful stare. She'd seen him before in The Pas: a huge man in a bearskin coat who'd stopped her, "Who ya cookin' for?" Her hand had tightened on her rifle, then. Neither the two brothers she'd come to know as the Dion boys nor the prospector Creighton were in the cabin.

Mosher said he was going out to register claims at the Recorder Office in The Pas, take gold to be assayed. Krug would be going, maybe another of the boys; Creighton was over Lake Athapapuskow way, had made himself a makeshift camp on Phantom Lake. Creighton was interested in copper and nickel, not gold.

Creighton must be someone to reckon with. She knew she'd heard something important.

He wasn't sure what day they'd be going out.

It was been enough. She got back to camp and waited with Margaret. Four days had already passed. Surely today Mosher would arrive. Kate was anxious to be rid of her; she had great plans for the time left before freeze-up.

Then it was there, a big freight canoe veering round the tree-decked island so silently it seemed a mirage, bearing down on the two of them. Mosher at the bow, beaver-tailing, two others. The husky on the pack sacks, wagging its tail.

Margaret turned to Kate. "Don't forget me, will you?"

"You'll forget me before you've reached Snake Rapid."

The canoe ran up the soft black earth. Mosher jumped out. "Let's go!"

Kate gave Margaret the record of their gold claims for the Recorder Office in The Pas, wondering if Margaret actually would go to the office (in the end, it turned out, she did not). Picking up Margaret's pack sack, she handed it to Mosher who passed it over the dog and the third man to Krug. To Mosher, more impatient at each second of time passing, she produced the canvas bag of gold flakes to be assayed and a list of supplies to be paid for by the gold after Margaret had taken her share (she didn't stop long enough to take it). Charlie Krug climbing over the third man, smile eager, dry khaki hair spiky, hands nervous on Margaret's pack. Mosher irritable now—it was like a photo being posed; his body tensed with impeded action, his mouth opened to blat out, "Get on wi' it!" Krug holding out a hand as Margaret readied herself for the jump, the big man with the insolent stare directed at the camera's lens, Kate herself. "We're off!" Mosher breaking past the lens pushing the big canoe out into the water, leaping in before his female passenger was properly stowed like another canvas sack at the feet of Charlie Krug. Margaret was shouting, her face above the gunwale, white and scared. "Write..." her voice small and thin, "I'll..." blurred already as the canoe rode into the tossing white water of the Sturgeon-weir River.

Kate turned toward the cabin. She was alone. Her life was her own. She looked over to the canary in its cage on the shelf by the door. It was lying on its back, thin legs held stiffly to the sky. "Oh no, no..." She put her hand through the cage door; the small body was ice cold, "The things we were going to do together, you and I."

She buried it in the muskeg, parting the tough mat of vegetation, pressing the body down into the brackish water. The sun, having gone behind a wall of soft grey cloud, wouldn't return today. She went into the cabin, shut the door. Was she the only living being left on the lake?

Every movement she made, the clatter of the fry pan, the sound of water boiling for tea, her footsteps on the clay floor, made lonely echoes. She swallowed a few mouthfuls of cold bannock, drank the tea, and instead of cleaning up (she had constantly hectored Margaret about the necessity of a clean camp) went outside. In the northern sky a beam of broad light glittered, was cut off sharply as if a giant switch had been turned, came on again, illuminating the whole of the sky. She raised her glasses, a pair of small opera glasses of gold wash and mother of pearl that had belonged to her mother. She watched until the aurora left the sky and the earth was plunged into darkness, went back into the cabin, took her black notebook, a scholar's cheap little scribbler and began the first of a series of observations on the aurora borealis that would eventually fill many books.

The habit of life in the bush is not nocturnal; but at the same time the idiosyncracies of the Aurora itself present special difficulties to the discovery of laws which govern it. The hours of the occurrences, from early evening on all through the night, till the sunrise appears in the east; the ever-changing position of the lights above the earth, sometimes apparently so low overhead that one's scalp seems to tingle at their touch, on up through every stratum of the atmosphere into the highest airs; their fantastic colours and motions; all these combine to produce effects as infinite, in variety as fancy itself—and correspondingly difficult to reduce to a set of law-abiding facts.

8

Margaret had gone. She was alone on the lake. It brought a sense of emptiness but Dan Mosher would be back in a week or so and it wouldn't be so hard then. In the meantime she had much work to do before freeze-up.

Every evening the light faded more quickly on its relentless march towards winter. Above the cabin roof, hundreds of wavies headed south; a large flock of pelicans wheeled in great circles, suddenly formed into an arrowheaded figure and struck out, straight south. The lake was still clear of ice.

Keeping close to the small river, she searched for the ruins which Charlie Krug had suggested as a wintering place; early builders would have chosen a site near water. She found herself among low mounds of stone. The floor was of clay two feet thick out of which grew a clump of white birch. At the north end was an enormous fireplace of stones; the wreck of a building was not a place that could be made habitable at this late season and by her alone, now that Margaret had gone. It was curious how often she reminded herself of the fact that she was now alone.

She lingered, wondering if La Vérendrye had built it—the old French forts always had huge stone fireplaces. He could easily have been here this time of year; it would have been getting late and he would have noted the pelicans, the same today and all the yesterdays, forming their arrowheads, and watched the beavers working busily to complete their winter sleeping quarters. He might have hurried to build a cabin before winter came raging in. It was only a theory, but a rather nice one, too.

The wind changed quarter, a cold blast out of the northwest, a warning. She continued to stand, listening. It was too still, too lonely and haunted. Actually, the bush was noisy with wind, with small limbs twitching and thrashing, golden leaves hissing to the ground. She went to her canoe and followed the little river back to shore and along the coast of the mainland.

Everywhere around her were staked claims, hundreds of them on birch and poplar posts, their bits of paper recording claims, names, dates of staking, often hours of staking, location; they were more rain-washed, weather-worn, unreadable than when she'd first encountered the men last July and had dared to complain to Mosher: "It's hard to find a place where no claims have been staked."

"Those fellows gone fer good, jus' hoped for a boom, didn' plan to stay, do any hard work, be a year 'fore all this free ground." He'd given her a warning. "Any man come too close or jump my claims, I shoot to hurt, best I shoot to kill." It was a warning to be off.

Now, she beached the canoe, worked her way along the creek bed, through thin strands of poplar and birch, raising her face to the weakening sun. The trees ended in a sharp demarcation: here was the cleared space, each of her claims a thousand five hundred feet as was prescribed, quite a little clearing it was, hers and Margaret's, the boundary lines north and south, east and west, as near as they'd been able to judge, their posts at each corner. The No. 1 post at the northeast corner, the others known as No. 2, No. 3, No. 4 in clockwise order. Her No. 1 post stating Kate Rice, July 30, 1911, 3 p.m., was about ten feet from a square boulder in the creek bed, the claim neatly written in indelible pencil. Margaret's No. 1 claim post (she had borrowed the pencil) had her facts scribbled in an illegible jumble.

In those early days of July, Mosher had been free enough with his advice (normally, he spurned conversations or any unnecessary talk) telling her to forget her books, that there were no hard and fast rules of prospecting, and showing her how to scrape and pit after tracing fragments of gold. Pointing out how few veins were exposed enough to allow appraisal of their width, length or possible extent without removal of overburden, dirt, moss, roots, stones, shallow tangled underbrush and even small trees, he'd gone out of his way to make it sound very hard because she was a woman.

But even Mosher, that tough old hulk of a man without an ounce of chivalry or of kindness, had once said, "Prospectin's kinda romance, 't'sn't science, you look't rocks and dirt an' it's adventure, I tell y'."

She'd learned the names of the old-timers who'd been in here since 1906: Dan Mulligan, Koller, Hugh Vickers (the first man to prospect north of The Pas), two Frenchmen, the Dion brothers, Tom Creighton and Dick Woosey.

"Woosey wintered with us back '07 ways, he's Cockney and Cockneys allys arrogant, why he didn' spot gold, him allys searchin' gold gold, allys gold, workin' alone now that Mike Hackett has gone off, doin' trenchin' east of the Cranberries, not good workin' alone, come here wantin' this boy here," indicating with his thumb, Charlie Krug, "work wid him." She'd learned there were metals other than gold and they were important and that there was a man called Dick Woosey and Mosher was of two opinions about him.

Scraping at the rocks, she could even now find traces of gold. She'd always thought of it in nuggets but it came out of these rocks in small flakes and grains. Panning had been the worst job of all and she loathed it. The pan always filled up with small particles of pulverized rock and earth and she'd been forced to stir the mix with her fingers. Following the illustrations in her manual, A. B. C. D., she hadn't dared to ask Mosher or even Charlie Krug for advice. The backbreaking part had been rotating the pan under the stream's water until all the upper material, as the manual called it, was washed away. And she did it not once but three times, panning her own gold and then either helping Margaret or doing it for her.

She made her way back from the claims through the birch and poplar to the Duckling. The north channel was protected from the wind by the high rocky ground and was calm and surprisingly green. She paddled furiously down the lake, leaving the protection of the bifurcated shore and letting the winter lay claim to her gold deposits. Battled by gusts of wind pushing the little canoe out towards the open water, she felt no attachment to her own cabin. There were too many disadvantages—it was too close to the Sturgeon-weir, the Maligne, too exposed, and there were few animals which would mean a lack of meat. Its shortcomings oppress-ed her. In truth she was beginning to hate the place.

Her only hope for the winter just ahead was the return of Mosher and Charlie Krug.

She sat on her bunk making notes in her little black book. Outside, footsteps on the hard ground. She grabbed her rifle and waited. The door was pushed open, a young man stood there, gazing transfixed at her.

"Excuse me, ma'am...didn't expect a woman."

"What did you expect?"

"Thought it'd be some old prospectors."

"And mayn't I be a prospector?"

"Sure, ma'am."

He was little more than a schoolboy. She put down her rifle.

"Glad you put that down."

"What do you want?"

He gazed about the cabin. "Where's your man?"

"Isn't any man here."

"You alone?"

"And if I am?"

He smiled, showing good strong teeth. He was younger than she'd first thought, his shirt, his boots were new. She figured him to be one of the fledgling prospectors, wooed off some good farm in southern Manitoba or Saskatchewan. "Sit down and have something to eat."

"Mind if I stay the night?...got caught...don't know my way round here."

"Don't suppose you do. You can stay, that'll be your section of the cabin..." indicating the side towards the river, opposite her bunk. "Understand this side is mine."

"Sure m'am...whatever you say ma'am...you a school ma'am?"

"Do I sound like a school ma'am?"

"Kind of."

"Where do you come from?"

"A farm near Dauphin."

"Bring in your pack—you can use my cookstove."

He went as she ordered, brought in a sleeping bag and a sack of food, took out sausages, potatoes, honey, scones already buttered and full of raisins. He laid the sausages in an orderly line in his new frying pan; her appetite became almost ungovernable at the smell of the frying sausages. He was talky, telling her he and his married brother farmed a half section of land but if there was any free gold, as he'd been hearing, he was going to make a try for it. Optimistic about his chances, he'd hired himself a guide in The Pas, got charged too much to bring him in but he'd make it up later when he made his find. She warned him and hated to do it that everything was well staked. He ought to go down river, inland a bit; she planned to go down herself tomorrow.

He invited her to sit with him and eat, and only too willingly she became his guest. He had pale blue eyes with whitish eyelashes and he seemed to get younger by the minute. As he ate he regarded her shyly; he'd been led to expect all kinds in a gold rush but not this, not a tall beautiful woman and a schoolma'am to boot. Then, he was holding back words, so many things sitting on the tip of his tongue, things he couldn't bear to say. He was awfully homesick. She too, had words hard to hold back: he should never have left the farm. She demolished the scones, hard as rocks, and the sausages offered her.

"I won't trouble you any more, ma'am." He began to tidy up. How handy he'd be about a farmhouse kitchen.

She went outside with her rifle, her little golden opera glasses, to look for an aurora. There was nothing alive in the sky, blackness had fallen on the world of crude forms, the shape of her visitor's canoe barely outlined against the cabin wall, too big for one man unless he'd been paddling for years. She came back inside, lit a candle, made a few notes in her notebook.

He was already in his sleeping bag; she stood over him with the lighted candle. "What's your name?"

He stared up at her, eyes foreshortened and drawn back into his head. "Hardie Jones is my name, at your service, ma'am."

She turned her face away to hide the smile. It was the kind of name found in any school roster.

Closing his eyes, his mouth fell open. She blew out the candle, undressed and got into her sleeping bag, her rifle beside her.

She was up early, went outside, Hardie Jones appearing with a tin pail, new and shiny, for water. He shared the last of his sausages and scones with her; the butter on the scones had gone rancid but she ate everything offered, wondering what he would do for his next meal. Again, she warned him about the claims to the northwest, stressing how much better it would be if he would try inland from the river.

He was stubborn, but cocky and cheerful, talking about the farm, how it looked in the spring with the first new shoots of wheat, so beautiful it gave him goose pimples, about the animals they had, his favourite horse, one he called Pinky because it was so young and kind of pretty like a girl. Definitely, Hardie Jones was not created to be a prospector for gold. She wondered if she'd sounded so credulous last summer when she'd pestered Dan Mosher with her questions. Probably so, and preposterous besides.

It was time for him to go. "Be seeing you," he called and jumped into his canoe. He handled it well. As he disappeared round a big island she wished she'd asked about his equipment, his camping gear—his cheery gumption had silenced her questioning as it did her pity.

Turning away from the lake, she took the trail along the Sturgeon-weir. The portage was like a village road, hard from the tramp of many feet and lightly covered with crisped birch and poplar leaves. With her pick and axe dangling from her belt she went about five miles and was close to the infamous Bent Rapids where the river swerved on one of its hairpin twists and the trail swerved beside it. Over to the east was muskeg with a forest of small ugly lobsticks. The banks of the river became high, the poplar and birch gave way to pines and among them were scattered Indian graves, their crosses painted in glossy black with a coating of light, rather mauvish pigment. Beyond the graves were tepees, one of which had smoke pouring from its smoke-hole. A small trail led to a partially deserted Indian village; she found Indian houses, abandoned, their doors hanging or gone. A few Indians dissolved into the trees as she appeared. In front of the largest tepee the skin of a young bear was drying, its hair long, black and silky.

The shadow of her passing brought out an old Cree woman. "*Nokum?*" she used the only Cree word she knew. The old woman gave a toothless grin. Kate struck her chest, "I am Kate Rice, a prospector."

The Indian seemed to understand her gestures if not her actual words. "Mss Custer." Was she part Sioux, her ancestors having fought against General Custer?

She was beckoned inside to the fire. It was an old tepee, smoke-darkened, with several bunks in its gloomy interior and someone hovering among its shadows. In the center was the brightly flaming fire with its whispering tongues leaping through the pile of carefully crossed sticks to the fire hole above. No wonder the Indians loved to tell tales with darkness outside and a storm fighting the wigwam, the heat, the relatives, the safety inside. The old woman gestured—Kate was to sit; she was brought a tin mug of tea. She removed her cap. The old Indian leaned over her, patted the short blond hair, smiling and nodding and speaking her Cree language. She approved; she was a progressive Indian and she said something quickly to the shadow figure. It must have been an invitation to come and see a white woman with her short hair but the figure remained in his shadows, said something sharp and fast. The old ideas were for him.

She was cheered; she'd found a friend in the old Cree woman, a human being who was near her on the river. She left, cut through to the river bank where there were long exposed flanks of quartz now, flecked with yellow moss and traces of gold. She scraped here and there, pulling away moss and dried grass. A snowflake fell, melted instantly, she went on working; there was gold here, how much she couldn't yet tell. The air was a queer grey black with a vast stillness held in it as if all its movement among the trees had been withdrawn and she was standing in a vacuum. The next moment there was a soughing noise and the snow came, furious, out of the north. She was forced to quit. All life flowed with the weather in this country. She returned to her base camp.

During the night she was wakened, sat up, rifle in hand. The wind was coming in short angry gusts with intervals of absolute silence. Whoever, whatever had wakened her, had passed on.

In the morning, the sun was shining, snow covered the lake which had frozen over in a few hours. But the air was gentle now, moving almost playfully about her face. A stake had been set into one of the bays to the west of the Sturgeon-weir's source and a claim paper fluttered on a post. Only the most inexperienced man, accustomed to snow on the prairie, would plant his stake on ice covered with snow. Hardie Jones had passed through last night.

After breakfast she left to set up her own claim posts and to visit her new friend, Mss Custer, the old Cree squaw. But the tepee in the Indian village was cold, the cheery fire was out, only the gloomy interior remained: the old woman and her husband had gone early this morning to their traplines, the husband having hurried his woman away from the influence of the white woman and her modern ways. She stood outside the tepee, the wind mourning in the pines. She was alone, completely alone in all this country.

She headed back to the cabin. Surely, surely the time had come for Dan Mosher's return.

He appeared that afternoon, coming out of the river, the husky riding on the pile of canvas sacks. She didn't notice the absence of Charlie Krug so happy was she to have this solid, brutal prospector back on the lake. He threw down her sack of supplies. "No money left."

She noticed then he was alone. "Where's Krug?"

"Dead."

"Dead?"

He turned to her, his face blurred with shock as though for one minute he had let himself go, given up to mourning his partner. He looked away abruptly, explaining in a voice gone hard and matter-of-fact how at Snake Rapids Charlie saw a nice fat jack rabbit and decided he'd get a move on and get it for their meal. They spent the next two days along that river poking among rocks, diving into the water, thinking that he must have slipped and fallen into the rapids. "Not the first one to drown in them waters, feller name of Billy Todd, one-time partner to Dick Woosey drowned a while back. The woman with us had a kind of fit." He spit out the last sentence as if he blamed the death of Krug on the bad luck of having a woman passenger.

"Come in..." As soon as she'd made the offer she knew it was a mistake.

"Nope. Got to find Creighton tell him 'bout Charlie, see how he gettin' on, mebbe found somethin', never know wit' Creighton, gone all winter, mebbe back in spring mebbe no." Without bothering to say good-bye he dipped his paddle and was gone into the newly unfrozen water.

She was stunned. She carried the sack of supplies into the cabin, an unbearable pall of loneliness shrouding the small interior. She became obsessed with the need for another human being; even Dan Mosher, that tough old brute of a man felt the need and had gone off to find his other partner, Tom Creighton. She sat on the bunk, the sack of supplies still unpacked. Why must she always test the last remnants of her strength?

She was here because she wanted something bigger than herself, had wanted it since her father told her the wonderful stories of Boone and Kit Carson. She'd wanted a big new frontier but this bigness was too much: Boone had a wife and children, he had relations and friends; Kit had a child wife, later a Mexican wife who stuck with him, keeping a base camp for him to return to. This frontier was too immense, the loneliness too great for her to bear alone. Dan Mosher knew it. Pulling herself finally off the bunk, she went with her glasses and her rifle to survey the northern horizon.

There was a beautiful aurora, its ribbons of green fluttering out of the north and the whole well of the sky but she turned away, her mind too busy warning her to get out before it was too late. She was unready for winter and its white solitude; she was quite unprepared to be alone on the lake.

9

Jan 19 1907

Still banging out porridge and bacon and hot cakes in the cook tent. Everything frozen in the night no fires allowed in the tents, occupants take turns to cut dry kindling before going to bed and in morning jump out of their bunks in bare feet and shirt tails to ignite fires and in few minutes there's a roaring one. It is impractical to use coal oil for lighting as it taints the flour, use candles and they are in very short supply usually forced to use melted tallow with a wick in a tin saucer. There are no holes for the toilets in winter you sit on frozen logs; after a year or two of winters men suffer greatly from hemorrhoids. These are just a few notes of life in a railroad camp in winter. But there is warmth in the cook tent and plenty of grub.

There are always accidents and yesterday was a bad day the steam shovel was buried in the snow and the dinky ran over the end of the trestle and fell into the gully. One man hurt. But at the end of a bad day men are angry and take out their vexations on the cooks. The bull cook is apt to pull out his knife and get ready to fight indeed think he'd kill. Dining room in a great melee but the Chief Cook the old Sergeant of the Imperial Army bawls out 'Silence' in a voice that makes tin dishes quake and order is established. He tells me he is seventh son of a seventh son and they always die on May 12, he has prophesied his death to me as 12th of May this year. I don't believe him. If he has a wife and children he never says.

Billy Todd joins me now each Sunday when we go snowshoeing an hour or so away from camp. I borrow mine from location engineer. Todd wants me to leave next June. I tell him I'm honour bound to the location engineer to stay another year. Todd says are you crazy? He suffers from hemorrhoids and says if I stay longer I'll suffer too. He knows quite a few blokes who worked on the railway and who walked off and made it in gold in copper too. You must have 2 fellers at least in this kind of enterprise Todd says.

There is so much monotony about this life and it galls me. Work is hard and constant in the cook tent and you go on day after day without let-up or change. I believe I have learned everything I can in this place. My plan to find gold seems lost. I go from day to day of bitter cold with neither the time nor the inclination to try something new as Todd wants me to try. I can't even remember my old life with the 18th Hussars. I have no plan for the future except listen to Billy Todd. I exist only. I do not know whether I will continue this diary, it does not seem to serve any good purpose.

May 12 1907
I have news. Went as usual down the line with coffee and sandwiches for the mid meal of the line men. Walk pleasant because was full of bird song. Felt free of winter at last with faint stirrings of hope and expectations in my breast. On return found camp in an uproar. The Chief Cook had died on the 12th of May just as he'd prophesied. The location engineer had already chosen the bull cook as Chief thus passing me over. Can't understand, thought he liked me. I was chosen among 3 others on work detail to dig grave for the old soldier. I was plunged into sadness as we laid him out in the shallowest of graves. I wanted to dig a good deep pit but the others would not expend their strength or give up their time. I was shocked, went on digging round the body to deepen the old sodier's grave but then bull cook sent word I was to return to cook house to fill out my stint. Any animal can sniff him out. Then and there resolved to

give ear to Todd and leave as soon as possible. We'll be bound for the Unknown and gold.

Sept 15 1911
     Note my last entry was in May 1907 and this is 4 years later. Consider Destiny to have been kinder to me than to Todd. He must have drowned in the Sturgeon-weir River there's no other explanation. Never saw him again after he left me near the cabin we'd built. Consider the Sturgeon-weir the wickedest piece of water ever met up with.
     After Todd and I slipped away during the night of June 1 from railway outfit we made for The Pas a miner's town on Saskatchewan River. When first my eyes lit on it it went beyond my imagination. Forget law forget order forget anything you ever met up with before. Met prospectors Todd knew. You speak Cockney? You Cockney? That was my name then, Cockney. These prospectors tough men, they know only one thing. Gold. They all had partners I noted or if not were in P. looking round for one or two. There was a bloke called Dan Mosher, another called Creighton, two French Canadians the Dion brothers, and a young feller Charlie Krug. I liked Krug he had a little refinement, that doesn't mean he was a gentleman but wasn't as rough as Mosher and the others. Din and smoke and heat and pool rooms and women in bars (one was called Saratoga). Funny thing I noted when a couple of prospectors took off and were so to speak lost in wilderness they were in some queer way connected with one another though miles of bush lake and burned-over country separated them. Think it's called moccasin telegraph.
     I was forced to buy complete equipment at inflated prices. Canoe, down sleeping bag, traps, gold pan, fish net, lengths of canvas, pack sacks. When we left for Todd's camp at Chisel Lake we were accompanied by Charlie Krug which pleased me mightily. Took a week of hard going to reach camp through what was known as lake country but only about 130 miles as crow flies, reason for slow progress and slogging was each carrying about 200 pounds. We had cement and glass, tar paper for roof as well as usual grub and my extra equipment. My money almost all gone and I'm worried. Todd thought it funny to worry about money in here. Camp turned out to be a 1 roomed cabin made of biggest logs I'd ever seen and quite roofless. Logs came from white spruce forests down the lake. Afterwards had what I thought to be twinges of rheumatism, Krug thought they were muscle strain in right arm from carrying heavy load over portages.
     After 2 days of rest the 3 of us set to on roof and windows. Krug got restless after few days of work and set off to do some prospecting on his own and came back same day with news there was a whole wall of black jack right on our doorstep; didn't know then black jack was copper nickel and silver. Todd and I looking for gold so the black jack meant nothing. After Krug with us a month he went back to The Pas. Maybe Todd and I too quiet for him.

Todd also became restless, find this common among miners in this country and he left me to finish cabin which I did willingly while he took off to lake called Squall. He came back with gold scrapings which whetted my appetite for that metal. What the heck he said, they're only scrapings. We took off again for The Pas to replenish our supplies for the long winter just ahead. Filled with rumours as usual. Creighton there his partner Dan Mosher just gone. The two men had built a camp at north end of lake called Beaver over in Saskatchewan and prospecting for gold though Creighton said he would prophesy copper and nickel would be as valuable as gold. He planned to look around Flin Flon about 100 miles north of The Pas.

To my surprise Todd wanted to go to Beaver Lake with the 2 men. I could either come along or go back to Chisel and hole up. I opted for Beaver good way to see the country before settling down. Terrible journey along Sturgeon-weir River, too late in season for one thing. Were forced to build temporary shelter on low point in black mud already half frozen at south end of Beaver. Bad choice but didn't know then. Day after we finished Todd restless went prospecting for gold into country west of the river. He must have tried to cross rapids rather than going up along west coast of Beaver. I kept going up and down that river both sides but never found him. Ran into Dan Mosher on one of my searches and seeing me pretty low because of Todd's disappearance and probable death asked me to join up with him and Creighton. He said that cabin we'd built no good to spend a winter round in here. I went to his base camp. Spent freeze-up that year yarning about gold and trapping and hunting for meat. Meat's scarce in there. Mosher still staking gold claims, Creighton too but he also said he was going to Flin Flon L. to look for copper and nickel. After break-up made up my mind to return to Chisel L. and prospect all through there.

Been at Chisel since I left boys in 1908 making trenches through the muskeg, good chance of finding gold in low places. Learned this from Mosher. Discovered beautiful lake don't believe it's seen the print of a white man before, named it Woosey Lake. Make regular visits to P. for supplies. Understand why it's so necessary to have a partner or partners. Started to look for a new partner in P. thought maybe I'd run into Krug but he'd gone in the rush last spring to Mosher's camp. Returned to Chisel but plan to go to Beaver L. before freeze-up and that's at once. Will ask Krug to join me. As for continuing my journey to the Klondike I understand it is half a continent away and that is too far. I am quite content with my life in this bush country. I am free and I'll make it in gold for sure.

.

10

Any hour, any day, she expected winter to blow in and still she stayed on. It was the first time in her life she was paralyzed by indecision.

She was standing on the low point of land with her rifle on the ground beside her, her little golden opera glasses raised to her eyes when silently out of Sturgeon-weir a canoe rode out, its occupant riding up the partly frozen mud at her feet and jumping out before she was aware she had a visitor. In surprise, she dropped the glasses. Picking them up, he put them to his eyes, "One lens is cracked," and handed them back to her, grinning; he was shorter than she—five-seven to her six feet— and of stocky build with mild brown eyes, black, coarse sideburns just visible under the wide brim of his black felt hat. He took off his hat and she noted a big scar cut across the left side of his face and into his hair. He had no prospector's beard.

"Who are you?"

"Is it important for you to know?" He was still grinning.

"Certainly."

"You using this cabin?"

"What's that to you?"

"Alone?"

"What is it to you?"

"Nothing, a ruddy nothing."

"But who are you?"

"I built that cabin with Billy Todd back in '07."

"'07? Who are you, anyway?"

"Woosey's my name."

"You're Dick Woosey?"

"The same, ma'am."

So this was Dick Woosey, another old-timer, the man Dan Mosher had two minds about. He wasn't so old in years, couldn't be more than a couple of years older than herself, certainly years younger than Dan Mosher.

"You've been talking to Mosher?"

"He's a neighbour up the lake."

He was on his way now, he told her, wanted Charlie Krug to come back with him, work in the lake country, thought he was on to something good having done a lot of trenching and found more than traces of gold.

His accent was cultivated, or cultivated in comparison to Dan Mosher's kind of talk. Charlie Krug, she explained, was dead, lost in the river.

The grin left his face. "Dead? Charlie Krug dead?" His brown eyes swept the river. "It's a cruddy one, that water, Billy Todd lost his life . . . but Charlie was young and no fool . . ."

"I hate it."

"Get away, then."

"I've been thinking of it . . ." She didn't want to admit she'd be running away, that she couldn't handle something she'd attempted.

His eyes quizzical, curious for a moment ran over her, "It's a good idea . . . for you . . ."

"What do you know about me?"

"Nothing, ruddy well nothing." He was gazing up towards Mosher's cabin as if he were about to push on. "So Krug got caught . . ."

She told him then that Mosher had gone to Tom Creighton's somewhere up near Flin Flon Lake where he was looking for copper. She knew very well she was trying to keep this man who had appeared so suddenly at this time of decision in her life. She suggested he come inside and she would boil a pail of tea and open a can of apricots Mosher had brought in from The Pas.

"Thank you, no—I'm pushing on."

"You won't find Krug." She was trying to hold him back.

"No, but I'll find Mosher." He pushed back his hat, showing the tough black hair growing in a peak over his forehead, and surveyed the sky. "No time to waste . . . snow today . . . tomorrow, any day now . . . freeze-up is here." He moved to his canoe.

"You won't find Mosher either, he's left his camp."

"I'll catch up with him, somewhere on those portages to Athapapuskow." He was stepping in, picking up his paddle. It was a change from Mosher's solid indifference.

She wanted to call out, "Stay, stay . . ." She said nothing.

The canoe was slipping away. He turned, "You're a fool to stay here."

Panic in the lengthening blackness of water increasing between them gripped her whole being; her voice made small ineffectual sounds. "Wait . . . I want to go . . ." He disappeared round an island. It was too late.

The lake country was two hundred miles to the east and north, over lakes and muskeg, rivers and creeks, along trails and portages, through tangled black spruce forests, across a jungle of burned-over land with its ugly ubiquitous lobsticks. The man known as Dick Woosey belonged to it all, had proved himself, just as Dan Mosher had proved himself. She was still living on the surface, a kind of traveller who didn't belong. This was the new frontier, this was what she'd chosen but she had yet to earn her way by strength, by will power, by whatever it took. She needed a partner, too. Margaret who had refused to touch the surface of the life in here had failed.

Most of the night she was packing supplies, leaving behind most of those she and Margaret had brought in with such pains—the little cookstove for instance—and all the supplies Mosher brought except four cans of beans, some bacon, flour, lard, jam, sugar and tea. Just once she stopped, sat down on the bunk, overcome by a sudden recall: Dick Woosey was clean-shaven, when he'd grinned he'd shown teeth that were white and sound. He was a cultivated man, not some old unkempt prospector with shaggy beard and rotting teeth. That seemed important, somehow. She stood up and went back to her packing. She was taking no more than the foundation of a load, about seventy-five pounds—a good man could carry one hundred and fifty. And all to take to The Pas.

11

When dawn's first light touched the Sturgeon-weir, she closed the door of the cabin wondering what difficulties she'd run into if she had the nerve to take the river below Bent Rapids. There was no sound at all except the feral voice of the Sturgeon-weir. But if she didn't try she would never respect herself: this was her chance to prove her fitness for the life she'd chosen. For this one moment she allowed herself to be scared, her mind, her whole self telling her there were thirty miles of continuous rapids, the channels of safe water were erratic, there were shoals and rocks and the wild fury of water rushing out of the Arctic and roaring headlong towards the Saskatchewan River.

"*Deo volente.*" She was going to try.

She got down on her knees, struggled into the shoulder straps of the pack sack. Leaning forward to work the weight onto her back, her feet planted under her, she could not budge the pack. Then it came in a rush, sliding too far forward and coming to rest too high on her shoulders, throwing her head to the earth; her nose hit the hard ground and she waited, expecting a rush of blood. All this five minutes after she closed the door of the cabin. Blindly she grabbed a sapling, toppled her load sideways but her knees had locked; she could neither move them nor get her head off the ground. Panicky, she jerked the pick and axe from her belt, pried herself off her knees. She rolled over; what would Mosher say if he came upon her rolling on the ground, unable even to get into her pack? She tried again. This time the pack stayed in the right place on her back. One thing was clear—she could not carry her fourteen foot canoe on top of her pack as any good man could do; she'd be forced to leave it against the cabin and come back for it. She started down the portage at a fast clip, her moccasined feet scattering the crisped fallen leaves.

About five miles below the Indian settlement, below Bent Rapids, there was an old trap cabin where she and Margaret had spent the night on their way in. Here she rested, putting her pack inside before going back for the Duckling. By the time she returned it would be afternoon and she'd be forced to camp the night in the cabin: she must have seven hours of daylight to tackle every imaginable variety of water. The sun had a greenish sour haze over it—the good weather would surely end by tomorrow.

She was back with her canoe in time to build a small fire in the windowless cabin and make a meal. She hung her tea pail on the iron hook that swung from a rusted iron rod built into the hard clay fireplace. There was a smell in the cabin she didn't like, something to do with the little room's darkness; she ate outside and afterwards went down to the river, trying to read it like a good old-timer could read a river to find its safe channels. It was a straight shoot of flat deep current, margined by boulders that broke the fury in a series of precipices, the ferocious voice crashing in her ears. She remembered a story Charlie Krug had told. He'd been working hard up against the terrible current when something on the shore attracted his attention. He turned to look—it was only a second but the canoe drifted sharply sideways onto a rock and in a flash he was thrown out, his canoe smashed, his supplies lost. Tomorrow would be a test of her strength against the river's power.

She didn't sleep, the sound of the Sturegon-weir was too loud, too insistent, it had drowned too many men; its depths must be littered with the bleached bones of their bodies. During the few hours of rest she allowed herself it seemed to be daring her to come, to pit herself against it. She hadn't been able to read the river, hadn't been able to sense its safe channels. Before the light came she was up, a few points of sleet pricking her face. She built a fire, fried some bacon and beans, made tea and coming out of the cabin again to test the weather, another point of sleet pricked her face. To add to her difficulties she would have sleet or snow. Of all the old-timers, Mosher and Tom Creighton, the Dion brothers, Charlie Krug was the only one who had dared take on the river and Charlie had been drowned. Her canoe waited, loaded and set between rock outcroppings in a quiet backwater. She must get into the current, never take her eyes off that current, not for an instant, not even the flicker of an instant, not for seven hours. Grains of sleet were swirling in the air; it was as though she'd been living all her twenty-nine years for this moment.

"*Deo volente.*" She stepped into the canoe and paddled out.

It shuddered as the current caught it. The violence took away her breath and she fought for air but her eyes held to the rolling sheet of water; she was being driven down a channel at terrific speed and all she could do was steer; steer and never take her eyes off the water just ahead, and forget the danger of hitting a submerged rock. The north wind was at her back, pellets of sleet attacked and stuck to her mackinaw. Gradually she became accustomed to the speed and to the pain in her chest muscles from fighting for breath, from fear and finally from excitement. The swiftness of the little Duckling was like fire in her veins. Breathing almost normally now, she was beginning to enter into the spirit of the river and its violence, becoming exhilarated by its frenzy; she was not its conqueror, she had become one with it, a part of it. The river had accepted her. For five hours she shot down the slide of water without once lifting her eyes, not for a second, not for the flicker of a second. The river demanded complete and total fealty.

The current was growing visibly more calm. Skirting the outskirts of a whirlpool at furious speed she entered a deep pool of tranquil water. But the ride was not over. Ahead, just above Sturgeon Lake, were the worst rapids of all. Even Krug had refused to tackle these rapids, their voice hoarse above the pool and the water behind. She intended to rest a minute before making up her mind to risk them and was guiding the canoe towards the bank on the western side when the river decided for her:

some freakish current thrust her out into the mainstream, all the force of the pushing headlong water that reached far into the Arctic tearing her forward. Twice she was turned at right angles to the river and swept along, down, down without will of her own—the river's will was supreme and it would do what it wanted with her. She was only vaguely aware of the tortured sheaf of rocks on both sides.

It lasted two hours. Then it was over. Suddenly she was in choppy waters at the mouth of the open Sturgeon-weir Lake; towards the center the water smoothed out, a sheet of grey glass. The sleeting had stopped, the wind had died down. She paddled straight across the lake, exhilaration gradually flickering out into tiredness, finally into exhaustion. Past the Landing, past the little settlement with its white Hudson's Bay post and on towards the Narrows. She'd reached the end of her day. It was just dark. She made a landing, unloaded the canoe with slow, stiff movements, dragged her pack up into the old trap cabin there, too tired to feel any elation over its dryness. She built a fire in its clay fireplace, made herself a cup of warmish tea—she couldn't wait until the water boiled—drank it as a toast to the river first and then to herself, and worked into her sleeping bag. She was out at once. During the night she was wakened by the whispering of snow on the cabin's roof, and fell asleep again. Tomorrow came and with it another decision. The cabin was bitterly cold, the fireplace was poor; either she would lie all day in her sleeping bag in a freezing shack or take the snow, the strong head winds in the Narrows.

She launched the Duckling.

Out on the water the cold was unbearable and before she was halfway through the Narrows the falling sleet had stuck on her mackinaw and melted from the little heat in her body, soaking her. Desperately, she searched for a landing place but the banks were high and smooth. She was shivering badly and frightened when she noted the rocks gave way to a small sandy inlet. She ran the canoe up the inlet and jumped out. Her pack was wet, her matches wet and her teeth knocking together; if she didn't dry her clothes, she'd have pneumonia. It was life or death, now and at once. She must have a fire.

She'd never been able to do the trick of lighting a fire by shavings. Now, it was a matter of making one or freezing to death, it was as final as that. With shaking fingers she took hold of some deadwood, trying to open her big green jacknife; it was too stiff, her fingers almost too weak and shaky to pull out the blade but it finally gave and then she was splitting out the heart of the wood and shaving it. Managing to start the fire in a sheltered crevice of rock, she ripped off her mackinaw, her heavy sweater, her overalls and hung them on branches close to the fire.

The flames burned greedily. She set her tea pail in the center, tossed tea into the boiling water and drank, eating a piece of hard tack, standing up. The weather was changing, snow was beginning to fall, softly, persistently, and there was no wind. When her clothes dried she started out, paddling hard to make it to the Cree settlement at Budd's Point. It was hard to tell if it was noon or early afternoon; a white pall covered land, the banks and the Narrows. The snow slowly tapered off but each moment the cold increased.

She was tired and shivering again when she drew up at the wharf. It was deserted. When she had come through with Margaret in July there were Indians standing around seeming strangely displaced. The wharf was high and she climbed the piles hand over hand to the top. The log cabin in which the schoolmaster lived sat on top of the hill in a stand of thick timber. She went along the plank covered with half-frozen snowy earth, hesitating before the door. She had a resurgence of strength and despite her weariness, a rock core of triumph rang in her veins. She would have to be careful to avoid the temptations of food, a warm soft bed, to resist telling the story of her descent down the Sturgeon-weir River, the Maligne. She knocked and smelled food.

There was a soft pad of moccasined feet and the door opened. The schoolteacher in a blue plaid shirt confronted her. "Why hello there..."

"Hello." When she'd stayed with him on the way in she'd thought he had some Cree blood in him although his name, George Martin, was English enough.

"I've been thinking of you the last day or two, wondering how..."

"How was I managing?"

"That's it." He was holding the door open for her to enter.

She stood there. The white oilcloth-covered table was set with a large bowl of stew, steam rising richly above its rim in graceful garlands. Beside the steaming bowl sat a blue and white cup with a spiral of vapour from the scalding tea, a brown teapot with a pattern of turquoise dots. Her eyes followed the convolutions of the dots.

"Come in, come in. And how have you managed?"

"I'd like a couple of guides to take me through the Tearing River today."

"You don't mean today—it's almost evening."

"Now—I want to push through to the Saskatchewan..."

"Woman, are you out of your mind?" He had the beautiful hazel eyes often resulting from white blood mixing with Cree.

"I've set a goal."

"Forget your goal. The weather's poor, it'll go down to zero tonight. I don't think an Indian will..."

An open book was propped against the round sugar bowl. What was he reading while he was eating?

"Come on, forget it, join me..."

She moved a step onto a bear rug, its hair long and silky, squelched under her damp moccasined toes. He closed the door behind her. The warmth soaked into her cold bones; the steam spiralled so gracefully out of the stew and the cup of tea, the cabin was so cheerful with its one red geranium in bloom. She moved onto the second bear rug. She could savour the meat between her teeth, taste its succulence, the potatoes redolent with fat, the cabbage hard and gristly, and after she'd eaten he would ask her to stay the night, she would have a whole room to herself with a real bed covered with a white hare blanket. Her body began to cave in, her backbone became putty as though she were a ball, rolling across the floor to the table. Then, she straightened up to assure herself that her backbone was there, upholding her body and her will.

"I remember last summer thinking you were a woman who would live too dangerously. You positively seek out danger."

"I haven't even started yet."

"I'll wager you rode the whole of that thirty miles of rapids down the Sturgeon-weir alone."

"Most of them."

"Two days ago, the body of a young man was found at the Landing— he'd tried to do what you've done but he wasn't as lucky as you. It was luck you know, not know-how."

"Was the young man's name Hardie Jones?"

"Nobody knows his name."

"Where is the body?"

"Already buried back at the Landing."

"Will you get me the guides?"

"It's crazy, you know..." He waited as if she'd change her mind. "If they do go, which I doubt, you'll have to take three of them, one for your canoe, two for theirs—and you'll have to give them something extra." He waited. Then he turned and went outside.

His moccasins thudded softly on the plank. Stepping onto the third bearskin at the table, she sat down. She began to eat from the bowl, the hand raising the spoon to her mouth in such rapid succession it seemed not to belong to her. She finished the stew, stooped over the open book, *The Warden* by Anthony Trollope; George Martin had reached page 126. It was as though someone was reading aloud to her while her body rested, wrapped in warmth and comfort, as though she was lying on the sofa behind the cookstove, the warmest place in the room. Draining the cup of tea, she went to the stove with the bowl, lifted the iron lid of the kettle and spooned out the rich mixture. She sat down again to eat, pouring tea from the brown teapot with its turquoise dots into the blue and white cup, spilling out plenty of sugar. One hand reached for the book: *"Well, well, well!" exclaimed the Archdeacon impatiently. "Oh, it's as long as my arm," said the other; "it can't be told in a word, but you can read it;" and he handed him a copy...*

She got up for another bowl of stew.

The door opened, George Martin had returned. "I've eaten your supper." She was stupid with gluttony.

"I hoped you would."

She replaced the bowl on the table and stood in the center of the room, part of her mind miles away. He regarded her with curiosity.

"I've got your guides."

"Yes, thank you. I must go."

"Why can't you act what you are—a woman?"

His words jerked her out of her trance. She stiffened her shoulders, her eyes flew to him.

"If you don't act like a woman, you're going to get into trouble."

What he meant she was to know a long time later. He had a lot of Cree in him, she decided and let the remark pass. "I have some unfinished business back at the Landing, the guides will take me..."

"I don't know if they'll go back, I was at some pains to say you'd go through to the Tearing River rapids tonight."

She went to the door. "Would you give me some bacon and two nails?"

"I'll give you bacon, but nails? Why, may I ask, will you need nails?"

When she didn't reply he went to a shelf, pulling down a can and taking out the nails, then to another cupboard for the bacon. Regarding her sadly he put the two separate items into her outstretched hands.

Outside, the air was heavy, her breath spinning out before her and falling. George Martin padded softly behind her. Down on the dock the three guides were ready, one in the Duckling, the two others in a big canoe; they sat patiently waiting. There was something about an Indian's patient waiting that had a kind of force about it. Silently, the two steadied the canoe while she jumped from the dock. "Back to the Landing now," she said, attempting authority, and expecting them to refuse but the big canoe swung out into the water, turning back towards the Landing, and the Duckling followed. She lifted her face to the quiet man on the dock. "Thank you for the grub," she called. He did not reply.

The canoe ploughed through the rough waters as the cloudy, wintry landscape swirled above and around them. Someday she'd buy the Trollope book and find out what it was that was as long as his arm in *The Warden*.

The canoes were swept along between high concave banks with willows growing on their tops. At the Landing she would put up a claim post over Hardie Jones' grave. In a few years his name would almost be forgotten by his brother who shared the running of the farm, and his sister-in-law; his nephews would look over the land, the beautiful ploughed land that had given Hardie goose pimples and they would not connect him with it; his name would be lost forever. She would write his brother at Dauphin. Instead of a claim to a gold deposit she would do his obituary notice. "Here lies Hardie Jones, a gold prospector from Dauphin, Manitoba. *Ave atque vale.* Oct. 14, 1911, written with an indelible pencil on a page torn from her little black scholar's notebook.

But at the Landing she had trouble finding the grave, indeed was not sure she was standing over the site—the ground up here, high above the lake where the wind whistled was covered with snow. At the Hudson's Bay post the manager was absent and the clerk, an Indian, was deliberately vague—there'd be some Indian theory about it. Her guides would have no part in it. She went alone, cut down a small cedar, sliced off its branches with her axe and nailed the page torn from her notebook using the priceless nails for the corners. She lowered her head, "Our Father which art in Heaven..." a gust of wind tore the words from her mouth, "Hallow'd be Thy Name..." another gust of wind, "Thy Kingdom..." The bitter wind forced her to quit. She jumped into the waiting canoe, ordering "To the Saskatchewan," wondering if they'd obey.

When they reached Budd's Point again the canoe headed for the wharf. "No no...on on..." she directed and waited for them to murmur it was too late, too cold, and they were going home to their families. The men were talking among themselves but they kept on paddling. She relaxed against her pack sack, "Thy will be done..."

The channel made a short turn into the swift current of the Tearing River; they were on the uplifted edge of the limestone plain of illimitable distances. In the dying day's greyness was the bluey haze of the high Pasquia hills far to the east. The canoe sang in the too eager current, twisted between limestone banks and sailed into the crinkled brown flood of the Saskatchewan. There was no place to land.

As the last light hovered over the rim of the universe, the river divided round a large island. The Indians took the south channel and as the island ended in a long tongue of frozen sand jutting downstream, there was a landing place with a solitary wind- and water-tattered willow bowing to the river. Above the strip of sand the banks were high with willows on their tops.

"Camp here," one of the Indians, the natural leader, said. And the day ended.

They camped a little distance back from the shore, a grove of big trees giving protection from the weather and providing fuel. They made a great fire. She cooked the schoolmaster's bacon and opened a can of beans, raspberry jam, hard tack and tea. The Indians stayed on the far side of the fire, tending the flames, lying in their one blanket and talking in low voices among themselves, probably, she surmised, about their families and the crazy white woman who insisted on travelling at night and in bad weather. She didn't sleep but lay in her sleeping bag, quite content, one hand on her rifle. During the night some heavy animal poking round the frozen sand at the river's edge got the Indians up. It was almost too late for a bear and it couldn't be a moose for there was no sound of twigs or branches being torn off the willow. She sat up in her sleeping bag and waited. There were two rifle shots and an Indian came up the bank, "Bear," he said, and went back down again. She worked back into her sleeping bag, the rustling sound of water and the soft Cree voices blending together.

At the first sign of light she got up and went down to the river. It was a young brown bear, the frozen sand matted with its blood. She turned away. The Indians kept their eyes carefully away from her—she'd brought them good luck in the form of fresh meat to be carried back to their families. The river running with slush and ice was more than a bad omen for her Duckling: it was a catastrophe. She clapped her hands to hurry the Indians and pointing to the cakes of ice went back to camp and waited. It was no use to hurry Indians, especially Indians who'd shot a bear. To her surprise they came up, bringing a steak for breakfast. At the sight of their bloody hands, the bloody piece of bear carcass, her appetite fled and she could only drink innumerable cups of strong sweetened tea. After they'd eaten, she paid them off, went down to the frozen sand, carefully avoiding the slaughter, and launched the canoe. She worked it out among the ice cakes convinced that her chances of reaching the Point today or any day, for that matter, were nil. The alternative she refused to consider. But the ice cakes she feared dissolved under the bow of the Duckling although the Arctic wind cut her to pieces. She reached the Point in two hours. The hard-looking ice at the river's edge gave way when she stepped onto it and she sank deep in mud.

She climbed up to the schoolmaster's cabin. The towheaded young man who taught here was from Minnesota. There'd be no bear rugs, no geranium, no books and little comfort as in the other schoolmaster's cabin, just friendly chit-chat, at which she was never very good. She and Margaret had slept here on their way in. If he should invite her to stay the night, she would accept. But there was no answer to her knocking; as she opened the door a whiff of icy dead air swept her face. She'd been hoping for a good meal at least, the tea at breakfast having long since worn off, leaving her ravenous. She went inside, opened cupboards; no flour, no sugar, no fat—in fact the cupboards were bare. She got out. She launched the canoe again and started down the Saskatchewan. The condition of the river was worsening, it was almost solid now with floating ice. Her Duckling would be cut into ribbons; she was too hungry, too tired to care. She began looking for a good camping place but the banks above the swirling water were low, then rose steeply to a great height. Landing on a flat strip of frozen mud and sand she scaled the banks, the trees on top indicating a good enough place for a camp. She built a fire, opened the last can of beans, fried the end of the bacon and made tea. Afterwards she got into her sleeping bag; it must have been afternoon. Before falling off she wondered what the condition of the river would be in the morning.

It was light when she wakened the next day and not bothering to build a fire she went down to the river and launched the Duckling out amongst the ice. To her surprise she could ride the ice cakes; their momentum being enough to offset the strong headwinds, she had little paddling to do.

Two or three times during the day ice jams brought the canoe almost to a standstill but always she was able to find a ribbon of moving ice in the stationary fields. Sometimes, a line of ice would move much faster and she'd manoeuver the Duckling into this current. By the middle of the afternoon she was exhausted again and decided to camp if she could find a landing place. It would be her last night on the river. If it wasn't, she couldn't think of the consequences.

The banks were still very high with their strip of sand along the river's edge. Almost any place would do and she ran the canoe up the frozen sand. She scaled the heights to find large trees growing close to the cliff, well spaced—a fine place for the last night. She built a great fire, ate the leftover beans and bacon and the hard tack covered with raspberry jam. The river was an awesome sight: an unceasing procession of ice forms, pinkened by her camp fire and soundless except for the eerie rustling of their bloodless shapes, jostling one another, crowding along the line of current as though their whiteness shrank from the drab ugliness of the silted yellow river. She sat on the edge of the cliff, her back resting against a tree trunk, drinking her tea, the fire crackling and red-hot behind her. The day began to darken, the ghostly white cakes of ice forever moving downstream. Life in the bush allowed a few moments of beauty.

It was a mild night but the snow melting on the ground dampened her sleeping bag. She slept poorly, rose three times to build up the fire. The change in temperature made it certain she'd reach The Pas tomorrow, a most cheerful prospect. Just before daylight she fell asleep to the rustling of ice cakes jostling their way down the great river.

12

Nov 1 1913

I was mighty glad to get out of The Pas though advised not to start out at this time of year. Epidemic of measles especially among Indians, many of their children dying. A big fire in Northland Hotel. Weather very stormy. Intend to keep diary to help fend off loneliness until I get a partner, if I do. Don't know this part of country well, always go other way from base camp on Chisel L. through the Cranberries to reach The Pas and vice versa. Had an old blighter in P. draw me a map. He did it like old time explorers in North, squiggly lines for rivers creeks, circles for Cormorant and Moose Lakes. I'm more or less between two in here. There's some muskeg other side of river and beyond that country burned-over long ago with now smallish trees coming on fairly big white spruce my side of river, with this cabin under biggest, a huge old fellow. Spotted it from river before I saw cabin. Cabin empty, made myself at home. Fairly roomy of its kind and built by some Indian trapper by the looks of it where my river and a creek meet—a good place. Indians always have a sense of the fitness of things in the bush.

Old sod who made the map told me there's a homesteader east side of Cormorant called Cowan who named the Cowan River, flowing at right angles on top of Cormorant into Reed Lake. Cowan raises potatoes. Not likely to meet up with him at this season.

Coming in had to portage almost continuous rapids; they'd frozen in peaks almost instantly in the cold and were mighty pretty. Saw 2 otters but not in range. Pride myself on landing in comfortable places (if I don't I get out) with good meat handy and promising trapping. Caught 4 partridges, gave 3 to dogs, having spent money on 3 huskies and toboggan—brought them along part way in canoe.

Am sitting on my bunk, there being no table or chairs. I'll probably spend winter here trapping so should make me a table and a couple of chairs. Am enjoying a roaring fire after being out all day, lord of all. Feel on top of the world. These Indian cabins of the ancient type perfect of their kind. Built of square timbers close fitting along the walls and interlocking at the corners, over the outside of chinked walls and under inside of roof a plaster of well-worked clay which also is used to cover inside walls, and floor window frames and door made of hand-hewn boards held in place by wooden pegs. Best feature of all is the clay fireplace with built-in iron rods on which hang stout iron hooks to carry cooking kettles.

I'm just returned from P. after travelling to Phantom L. Tried to persuade Mike Hackett to join me as partner now Charlie Krug drowned. No luck. Later, H. said he might join me do some prospecting round Wekusko Lake. Stayed with Creighton and pals. Talking about rocks all the time and how they were bound to make a killing in sulphides. It used to be gold they talked about. I didn't turn a hair with their talk of making it. So will I by George, so will I. On gold.

Mosher's at Phantom, though still has the Beaver L. camp. He and I went hunting for moose to keep us all in meat but Tom was off to Flin Flon to have a look see. Noted Tom was cautious because I was there, nobody trusts anybody in this business. Dan and Tom can't lift their eyes off the rocks for fear of missing something and they miss plenty—the earth the sky the berries all those raspberries blueberries snowberries bearberries. As an old Regular Army man I like to take in the terrain, even a little soft wind means something to me. They got tired of me eating and taking up air. Hey Cockney, hear that Cockney? I'm no Cockney but no use telling those pukkah wallahs. In P. I stayed at Bacon's a one bit flop house. Meant to ask boys about that woman on Surgeon-weir R. at Beaver L. but with my ears ringing from rock talk I forgot. Seems a nice enough woman, very good looking, a bit on the vinegar side. Strange her being there alone. With the fire blazing must be 90 degrees in here. It's the life but wish I had a partner.

Nov 2 1913

Not as much ambition for writing now trapping in full swing, out every day. Today snow on the ground. Laid traps behind cabin. Circled from creek back through bush to south branch of river setting 5 marten traps. Also it's good rat country but their houses frozen. Saw moose tracks and came back to my river got lynx. About 5 miles from cabin shot 4 bulls and skinned all 4 at once packing some meat making a new meat cache and so back to camp about 5. Snow falling. Tired but content.

Nov 3 1913
   All day drying moose, made trip to 2nd moose cache put poison bait round it. Went up river saw 7 moose shot 6 made 3rd meat cache also shot some partridges. Then went touring lower down. Somewhere towards evening looked through my load for more shells having bought 9 boxes of 303 shells for my Lee Enfield at P. Missing. Damped my spirits I can tell you. Stayed about camp doing chores, cutting wood, making supply of bannock.

Nov 4 1913
   Much rejoicing. Found boxes of 303 shells in morning going over load. Found I'd packed them with traps. Took canoe and toboggan and dogs went up 4 rapids in quick succession, the water at the head frozen with ice. Proceeded, ice became thin, proceeded, ice became very thick, got out toboggan hitched dogs and went on 12 miles up river. Then went to 2nd meat cache then set some fisher and marten traps. Continued on down river. Ice treacherous, went through got wet feet. Got a marten and some squirrels. Made 1st meat cache and on down river. Dark and very cold because of wet feet went back to cabin.

Nov 5 1913
   Returned to 2nd meat cache for moose meat, circled all through bush and set 6 traps for marten here. Snowing. On way back found 1 ermine in trap 1 mink and 1 fisher. Heavy snow set in. Returned to camp. Wearing heavy rubbers over woollen socks a mistake, feet badly blistered.

Nov 6 1913
   Pretty sight this morning snow heavy on trees and still falling softly. Went to 1st meat cache with dogs and circled about snow, deep and hard going. Shot 2 grey squirrels. Set traps. Found a beaver dam set some marten and beaver traps. Came back close to camp found 2 marten 1 mink the mink's eyes eaten by whisky jack while in trap. Cooked up a big feed. Had roaring fire.

Nov 7 1913
   Took day off. Snowing heavily. Fixed up shack, started to build table. Too much snow to examine rocks on Moose L. for gold as I planned to do.

Nov 8 1913
   Got lost today. Went up river on snowshoes then crossed the ice and cut straight through to rough muskeg, set some traps it's good rat country. Snowing a little still. Saw tracks of moose. I must have gone 12 miles found a shack about 4' x 8' a curtained burlap bag for door. Must be someone's trap shack, nothing inside except poor fireplace and musty smell.

Kept on going then seeing it was getting dark started back couldn't find that shack then night came on fast. I hit straight across muskeg thinking I'd make it to river, couldn't find river. The fresh snowfall wiped out my tracks of this morning and when I'd almost given up and decided to make a make-shift camp recognized a clump of willows and knew I was near river. Then heard dogs howling to right about 3 miles down and found my cabin. It was almost midnight when I'd fed dogs, got fire roaring and cooked some grub. Odd thing someone had been inside cabin. Certain I had more moose meat also the flour was much lower than I thought. Nothing else disturbed as far as I could find. Tired.

Nov 9 1913

Went up river at daylight laying 7 traps on way, then into bush locating big lake not on old blighter's map, made tea on its shore. Wolves howled during night. Went out and shot 2 missed other 2. Went back to bed.

Nov 10 1913

Skinned wolves then went to 3rd meat cache. Wolves got almost all moose meat. Put poison bait round remainder. Went to lower end of trapline below 1st meat cache. No luck. Then up to beaver dam got ermine in beaver trap. When I got back to camp found 3 dead wolves. Skinned all 3.

Nov 11 1913

Went over trapline set from north of 2nd moose cache some luck. Got 2 marten 1 fisher and on up to beaver dam got 1 marten, 1 ermine. Visited poison bait found 3 dead wolves many dead ravens. Hauled the 3 wolves back to cabin, too frozen to skin.

Nov 16 1913

This is Sunday slacked off and read a novel called *Love Made Manifest* that some old bloke in P. had given me. Bum book as Mosher used to say. Wonder what the boys are doing now and wonder about the copper find. When I make my killing in gold will buy real estate in P. Build a house raise Indian ponies. Too bad May and boy couldn't stand it in Canada. Wish I had a partner though.

Nov 17 1913

Didn't set out till about noon to lower beaver dam with dogs and toboggan. Got 1 marten on creek. Returned at night. Heard wolves howling direction of 1st moose cache went out again, heard 1 very close, set poison traps, couldn't locate trail back, hit straight through and made it 1/2 mi. north of cabin.

Nov 18 1913
Went back to 1st meat cache. Wolves cleaned up everything. No meat left there. Visited traps at 2nd beaver dam and got 1 fisher 1 mink.

Nov 19 1913
Went round trap lines getting 2 marten. Returned to cabin and in afternoon went over lines to east. Got 1 ermine. Tracked a bear, late for him to be out, didn't get him. I'm low in butter, jam lard have no tobacco, smoked tea and willow berries. Rum.

Nov 20 1913
Took day off. Small pain in right arm think I did damage to muscles or tendons carrying in that heavy load the first journey I made with Billy Todd to Chisel L. Hope it goes away soon. Laying on bunk resting with roaring fire. Keep thinking what I'll do when I make it in gold. After buying a good lot right on Saskatchewan R. near old French fort will build a good English type red brick house, have to import the bricks but cost no object. Will always keep my hand in prospecting in summer but no more grubstaking in winter. Will certainly raise Indian ponies always liked horses since my stint in the 18th Hussars. It's a great life. Wish I had a partner.

Nov 21 1913
Still have a little flour tea and sugar left. First thing today I saw a bull moose, shot it. He was blind. Made a complete circle through bush from river to creek to lake through muskeg. Took dogs, they needed exercise. Noted harness needed repairs must be repaired before trip out with furs to P. Got 1 mink 1 beaver at 2nd beaver dam. Saw snowshoe tracks probably some Indian.

Nov 23 1913
It's Sunday again. Chopped wood cooked up some of blind moose, those 3 dogs eat everything in sight. Will be glad to get out to P. Need company. Wonder how Mosher and Creighton are doing. It's getting colder by the minute. When I went out today saw the sleeping place of 5 caribou past creek at head of river. Followed trail on snowshoes and found the bull broke his leg with my first shot. It was about 4 p.m. Partly skinned him and then and there brought some meat to cabin for supper, making a cache of rest.

Nov 26 1913
Bloody tough living in this cold. Pulled up traps behind cabin, travelled up creek then to north branch of river at mouth of creek, got 1 mink. Saw snowshoe tracks a few days old presumably the Indian. Then went to 1st beaver dam and found house broken into by some previous visitor. Wondered if it was that Indian again.

Nov 29 1913

Went over traplines got 1 ermine. Took dogs, circled to river through bush setting 3 marten traps and 1 mink. Went to moose cache for meat. Came back to cabin baked bannock. It's rum smoking tea and willow berries.

Dec 1 1913

Went to upper dam on river found 3 rats all frozen to ground. Going over other traplines found 1 ermine. Returned to cabin did chores and fixed up for trip out. Left foot very sore, slightly frozen day before yesterday.

Dec 6 1913

Tomorrow or day after I'm off to P. Went down to head of river and brought back rest of caribou then back to camp, cooked bannock and caribou meat for trip out, chopped wood, mended harness. A little pain in right arm and then lay around. Roaring fire.

Dec 7 1913

Took dogs and crossed river heading straight north looking for my rat traps and found 3. Tried to find that 4' x 8' camp but couldn't. Wonder if it was a mirage that I'd first seen but then I was inside and remember the musky smell. Kept on going came to small unnamed lake then a river with rapids frozen solid. Country badly burned over, rum kind of land. Found a small creek with willows decided to camp out it being late in day. A cruddy rum decision, dogs howled all night, wood green and smoking. At daybreak broke camp and headed back gloomy dark all day. Stopped once more where I thought 4' x 8' camp located but it was not to be seen. Saw fresh snowshoe tracks though. Got back about 3 p.m. Decided I'd go out tomorrow.

Dec 8 1913

Changed my mind about going out. Too lazy. But I did go over traplines for last time to see what I could find. At beaver house found 2 ermine 1 beaver 1 marten. Set 7 more traps will leave them till after trip out. Went to creek found someone had cleaned up every trap. That Indian. Pulled them up. Went to 2nd beaver house got 1 beaver. Got dark, very mild out, tough going. Thought of roaring fire caribou meat and tea.

Dec 9 1913

Stayed in camp all day skinning animals. Piled on logs and had roaring fire. Feel much better. A good fire makes me feel as though I owned the world. Keep adding details to house I'll build when I find gold. 3 bedrooms and each with a big brass bed. Tomorrow definitely I'm out to P. with my fur catch. Start at dawn.

Dec 14 1913
    Writing this from Bacon's. Left cabin on December 10 with heavy load dogs went slow. Turned very cold. Travelled over portage. Reached Halcrow's place at about 3 p.m. camping that first night with Indian family. Reached Frog River at lake at 3 p.m. and left about 4 and reached Atikameg Lake where I camped with a bloke called Stanley. Asked about Mosher and Creighton. Stanley said he hadn't heard anything since they went to Flin Flon. Made the Big Bend the next afternoon and camped with a man called Alex Ballantyne. Reached The Pas and the flop house Bacon's yesterday and today sold furs for $876.50. Not bad.

Dec 15 1913
    Still at Bacon's. So noisy here I can't think. There's a woman here her real name is Miss Sophia O'Ryan she belonged to a song and dance team in old London town called "Troubadors" been dancing since 15 but she's known at Bacon's as the Diamond Queen. Seems she went with troupe to South Africa and the miners threw diamonds at her. That is what is being told here can't guarantee the truth of it, said to have been a friend of a wallah called Sir Cecil Rhodes. She's small very good looking wears men's clothes. Her man here used to be a blacksmith in Prince Albert, he ran away from his wife to be with her leaving 9 children. His name is Gilbert LaCroix. They are living common law. Big stir at Bacon's last evening when she chased a man with horsewhip down the stairs and out along the wooden streets.

Dec 16 1913
    Still at Bacon's. Forgot to say Diamond Queen is supposed to have crossed ocean with a bloke called King of the North, real name Ernie Montimer. Also in flop houses is a woman called Cut-Throat Rosie, she has a scar at base of her throat which some feller is supposed to have cut. She's not my type. I kind of like Diamond Queen maybe because she's English and so do a lot of other blokes. She's choosy though.

Dec 17 1913
    Still here but clearing out tomorrow getting supplies to start back to camp. Have been looking round for Mike Hackett but he's off to Crowduck Bay he's got a lake named after him east of Wekusko. Think of buying a big piece of real estate everything booming here. Picked out a good spot at bend of Saskatchewan across trail from Christ Church and not far from old French fort. Poked about. Those Frenchies built great fireplaces plan to use the old stones and copy the one in the cabin. Intended to go to Christ Church, the evening service is for whites. One of these days I'll be attending regular service taking up the collection and be a regular pukka sahib. Couldn't get chance to get cleaned up at this flea joint.

Dec 24 1913

Was back on trail December 18 as planned reaching Big Bend that very afternoon and camping in Ballantyne's cabin again. Persuaded him to come with me but he said he'd meet me, had some business to attend to didn't promise to stay. I noticed he had a cough. I left Big Bend and reached Atikameg Lake at night. Very mild. Left Atikameg in the morning and arrived Frog River at noon. There was a dance that night. One white woman, rest squaws. Squaws don't attract me we have too much trouble communicating. Left at 10 and reached Halcrow's place at 5. Left early making the portage halfway. It was still very mild. Camped and waited at muskeg mouth of small river beyond portage till Ballantyne showed up. An Indian came to my camp all in and out of grub. He'd eaten a trapped marten the previous day that's all in 4 days. I fed him bacon potatoes canned fruit and tea and sent him on his way. B. showed up at dusk. We noted lots of tracks of moose but no luck.

We made big river but B.'s cough was much worse so we didn't push on to my cabin but camped here for night. There was very heavy snow and high winds during night, by late morning it had cleared and we set out reached cabin about 7 p.m. Heavy going. B.'s cough bad he's pretty sick. Somebody had been using cabin while I was away. Flour all gone great haunch of moose meat I left on my table gone too. Wonder who it was. B. says it's an Indian. Settled in after roaring fire and big meal of bacon potatoes beans apricots raspberry jam and tea. B. not very hungry.

Dec 25 1913

Decided to slack off this being Christmas Day, built a roaring fire. B. on bunk, think he's pretty sick. Had another good feed but B. didn't eat he's now sleeping heavily. Kind of ruddy rum Christmas Day.

Dec 26 1913

Tried to go over my 8 traplines but snow waist deep. Shot a bull moose and chopped enough meat for 2 days and returned to cabin. B. up but cough still bad. Built up fire and cooked big meal. B. hardly ate.

Dec 27 1913

Took dogs and went back to moose carcass and chopped him up. B. didn't come says he'll rest up and go back to Big Bend. Tried to persuade him to be my partner told him I'll be discovering a big lode of gold but he says he's too old and wants to be closer to The Pas. What happens to old trappers? I'll have a place of my own before I think of that question.

Dec 28 1913

Went to lower beaver house and set 3 traps. Very mild out and thawing. Most of meat I brought back is for dogs. After round a big fire told B. about property I'm going to buy in The Pas and house I'll build. B. impressed. They'll never forget your name in The Pas he told me. At bend in the big Saskatchewan right in front of the property I want I noted you could step from ground right into brown flood.

Dec 29 1913
Turned much colder. Went to lower beaver house and found traps set yesterday frozen to ground will have to wait till break-up now. B.'s cough much better says he's off tomorrow. Said I'd go as far as portage with him if he'll leave at daybreak.

Dec 30 1913
Left at daybreak. Beautiful out. Left B. at portage came back and went straight up river. Night when I got back to empty cold cabin. Made a big fire and cooked grub. It's ruddy lonely. Think loneliness stems from fear.

Dec 31 1913
Set marten traps though saw no tracks. Saw tracks of a hare and set a snare. Tramped about came back and there was my hare. Took it back to cabin made a big fire and cooked a stew. Plenty to eat. This is good trapping country but I want to get back to my base camp at Chisel L. Lonely I guess after B. gone.

Feb 1 1914
It's 1914! Time rolls on! Heavy snow during night. Went moose hunting in afternoon. No luck. Missed whole month in my diary. Too weary to write.

March 10 1914
Big gaps in my diary now. No ambition. Did go to Moose L. sometime back but not able to examine rocks for gold snow too heavy. Very cold with high wind stayed indoors all day and slept on bunk, still no ambition. One of these days I'm going out to The Pas. Getting tired of this lonely life.

March 22 1914
Today I got a three legged bird in one of my traps!

March 27 1914
Got 5 rats today at beaver house and shot moose in evening. This good because getting low in meat. Days definitely longer.

April 2 1914
Saw first goose flying north over me this a.m.

April 20 1914

Definite signs of spring, a wind that's actually warm and snow is loose sun is more yellow. Starting to go over traplines preparing to leave Merry Widower camp.

April 25 1914

Travelled with dogs to little lake getting 5 marten 8 rats set more traps. Ice beginning to leave, river was running out all night. It was almost dark when getting home noted snowshoe tracks leading to cabin door. The snowshoes were left against the wall of cabin. Opened the door with some caution. A woman was sitting on my bunk drinking tea a roaring fire in fireplace pot boiling on hook with moose meat stew in it. She was the woman I'd met at Sturgeon-weir on Beaver Lake 2 years ago, would recognize her anywhere.

Hello I said.

Hello she said. Close the door will you, you're letting in cold air.

Mighty cool. I've been seeing all the snowshoe tracks for some time, I said. They yours?

They could very well be mine, she said.

Did you help yourself to my flour and moose meat?

I was hungry.

Twice someone robbed my trapline.

I made stew.

The 4 x 8 shack disappeared.

I needed the boards.

Cool cool.

Last time I saw you you were at Beaver Lake—how did you get here?

I rode down the Sturgeon-weir rapids and then on down to The Pas. Went back and spent two winters alone in the schoolmaster's empty cabin at the Point. Why the cross examination?

No one ever attempts to ride the rapids on the Sturgeon-weir.

I rode them.

What are you trying to do? Kill yourself?

I'm trying to get to the lake country and I haven't too far to go now.

You spent the winter close by robbing me.

I've been in a trapper's cabin behind George Cowan's homestead. Soon as break-up I'll be off and out of your hair.

Not out of my hair—you're into my food supply.

And so?

And so we're both headed the same way. One thing though, I have a camp in the lake country and you have not.

I'll travel along with you until I see a lake or creek I like then I'll stop.

Cool cool.

I've been wanting a partner, how about it?

I'll think about it.

She was mighty cool. I like her.

PART II

1

ou've got to do the thing properly if you're going to do it at all."

"My word as a gentleman and former NCO in the 18th Hussars is as good as any bond."

"Fiddle dee dee! Don't dangle your Army in front of me, the point is you don't own a bond, any more than I do."

"I don't need any signed paper is what I'm trying to say."

"I insist that a document be drawn up between you and me in a proper manner. We're two consenting parties. It is a business arrangement—this is not a man and woman thing at all, do you understand?"

"All right, all right."

To Whom It May Concern:
That the said party Kate Rice and the said party, Richard Woosey have agreed—
That their work relationship shall be that of a partnership.
To share any mineral claims or mineral properties they shall have prospected singly or together.
That these claims or properties, houses they shall inhabit, or lands laid claim to, shall be held in joint tenancy.
That each party shall have unlimited liability in the general partnership agreement.
That the acts of one partner in the course of the management of all mining properties shall be binding upon the other partner.
That the partnership of the said two parties, Kate Rice and Richard Woosey shall be dissolved only upon the death or withdrawal of one of the said parties and the acceptance of a new partner.
Signed and sealed this day, May the fifteenth, 1914.

"So help me God, what does it all mean?" He signed after her name.
"We're going to make it, so what does it matter?"

2

At the end of May, they went to Woosey's cabin on Chisel Lake, travelling in two stages. They kept well out in the centre of Cormorant Lake to avoid the George Cowan homestead on the northeast side.

"What's wrong with George Cowan?" Woosey wanted to know. "He's only a potato farmer—he wouldn't hurt a fly."

"I'm not a fly."

He understood. "George never sees a woman except the occasional squaw."

"That's no excuse."

Kate had stayed at the Cowan cabin a week last fall, been compelled to move out by the sexual advances of the homesteader, and had occupied a cabin ten miles back on a small river until she'd been forced out by the severe winter storms.

Paddling round the big stone bluff that looked from its profile like a man yawning hugely, they entered the Cowan River, coming into Cormorant Lake from the west. Cormorant was surrounded by stands of exceptionally fine white spruce with their tall clear trunks, and then, wiggling, twisting its way through marshy ground, it expanded higher up towards Reed Lake into two small round lakes. The land on the east was burned-over.

Woosey stopped when they reached the reddish sandy soil of the portage running between low hills into Reed Lake. It was well-wooded here with small poplars, banksian pines beneath which grew the red mealy bearberries, blueberries and cranberries. "How about camping here, no ruddy use killing ourselves."

She pulled up in her Duckling, the sun slanting down gold with a sheen of green in its rays. "But there'll be two more hours of this, and then there'll be twilight; I want to push on."

Good-naturedly, he got back into his canoe; it was big, almost the size of a small freighter. He paddled ahead across Reed Lake, a sturdy, rather square figure in a wide-brimmed black hat and wide tan galluses over a black shirt.

Reed Lake fascinated her. It was the first lake in this lake country, a body of exquisitely clear and shining water, so clear that the blocks of white quartz on its bottom showed up as though mirrored. Ahead Woosey pushed his way into a creek, almost unnoticeable with its tangle of last year's hay crop through which its new growth was just bursting out. He went in a few yards, jumped out on a small sandy beach, turned his face with its ingratiating grin to her, "Steady, boys!" pushed back his hat showing the coarse bushy black hair, the swarthy complexion, almost too dark for an Englishman. "This is it, our first camp, it's Woosey Creek." She was now willing to stop.

The trees were bush willows, not much taller than she was and shivering slightly in their new green from a night breeze. They made a trackless tangle of overgrowth, with an awful solemnity, a terrible loneliness full of whisperings. It was a camping place of no horizons and she loved far distances. She was glad Dick Woosey was there, cheerily unloading his canoe, and glad she had a partner. A white-throated sparrow sang its mysterious little song from some hidden place as she jumped out of the Duckling. Where was its partner? Or was it too early and the sparrow travelling alone within a flock of small birds? She took out her gold opera glasses, the left lens still cracked, feeling that the one call added to the loneliness and mystery of the place. Standing on the sand in her moccasins, trying to sight the bird, she towered above Woosey.

But she liked him; he was a compulsive talker, always cheerful and sometimes arrogant. She felt herself superior to him and in this place with the twilight fading so slowly to blueness to greyness she wondered if in order to like someone she must feel superior to him. With a flutter of wings the bird darted from its secret covey and dipped into the twilight.

"I think I'm difficult at times," she said. He turned and stared at her.

Methodically, Woosey had set about to build a big fire and fix a makeshift camp, then began to cook the meal: potatoes brought from The Pas, bacon, bannock, hard tack, jam and tea. She had wanted to come to the lake country and here she was; she had wanted a partner and she had a partner, his busyness, his cheerfulness making a dent in this closed-in, eerie place.

Was it strength and dependability, know-how, someone wise in the ways of this country she had really wanted? In the back of her mind she'd thought of someone like Dan Mosher; he was a man who knew exactly what he wanted: to find minerals—gold or copper. Dick Woosey wanted a partner as a sounding board for his rotarian sociability, his barrack-room camaraderie; neither she nor Woosey got exactly what they had wanted though she believed he got the better of the bargain. Yet as bargains went, it was a good one and she was content. The smile she bestowed on him in this twilight, solitary land was dazzling. It was one o'clock in the morning.

When they were sipping their tea, he started the story of his life. This would go on at intervals for a long time. He began abruptly, "I was a soldier of the line, one of the Old Mob, a Hussar in my fine blue and silver uniform, my chin strap gleaming, my horse shining, its long tail combed. You should have seen us! We'd come out of the barracks at 'Shot, when the Sarnt barked "Ey-ees Ri!" in a voice like the Bull of Bashan. I can remember it all—jingling down a country lane, the music of the creaking saddles, swords and rifles, the hedges gleaming with frost, the morning sweet on our cheeks, a rabbit scuttling by, and oh the lovely odour of sweating horses." He was silent, aware of his partner's indifference. "You don't think a soldier can be a poet or an artist? I tell you he can see and feel things over the rim and know of sensations where there seems to be nothing."

All his life he'd been around polo ponies and could ride like a centaur; he was coach to his officers, teaching them the art of tent-pegging, mallet-handling and lance-wielding. The regiment's sport came to an end when it was ordered to India, to go by train to Nowshera. There had been an uprising by Pathan tribesmen, aided by the fanatical preaching of some mad mullah. "At Nowshera we were directed to move by forced marches through the terrible summer heat to Chitral, with men collapsing from sunstroke, enteric fever and malaria. Chitral was a roadless state far to the north of the main road into Afghanistan, one hundred and twenty miles of Himalayas between it and nowhere."

She listened sleepily and without much interest to this tale that happened long ago and on other continents but gradually it took on the assonance of a saga, an immense world away from the flames of their little campfire lifting into the interminable twilight of a May night near the Arctic. In the end, the end of their relationship, she listened willingly and with wonder, both at herself and at him.

His voice stopped. He yawned and stood up. "Time to kip in." They slept on opposite sides of the fire, her hand always outside her sleeping bag, clutching her rifle.

After two hours of sleep, he rose, went a short distance from their camp, hung a small circle of polished steel on a tree and shaved himself. After a cup of tea and a piece of hard tack they set off into the sun, yellow as butter. They followed the zigzag course of Woosey Creek to its source, a lake with a narrow waist and two arms, each pointing in opposite directions; it had many indentations with wide sandy beaches where a cabin might be built. In its wide parts were wooded islands; it was beautiful. "It's Woosey Lake," he shouted back to her. In his search for gold he had trenched this entire area to the east. The trenches were wide enough for their canoes to pass through and he pointed to the intrusions of pink and grey coloured granite which she had already observed. "There's gold all through here." He was proud of his knowledge of the country.

They were canoeing now north and east. The country around them was hummocky and swampy. Flocks of small birds flew over their heads, warblers, nuthatches, tits, sparrows; she wondered if the white-throated sparrow was among them. On the shores of a lake they stopped to build a fire, warm up some potatoes and make a pail of tea.

"This is Cook Lake and my cabin on Chisel is right over there..." and with his paddle pointed into the pink and saffron tinted eastern sky. Afterwards they headed in the direction indicated by his paddle, entering a creek. The ground had changed again, becoming almost park-like with very large trees, snowberries and bearberries growing beneath them. He waited for her. "I've trenched through here too, we'll come to it, soon— connects with Chisel Lake."

The park-like country was the last good camping place before they reached his cabin. "If we stop here, we can take the trench early in the morning." The day had been an easy paddle and she who was always in a hurry to push on, who never had time for details, explanations or small pleasures was happy to stop, build a big fire and cook grub.

During tea round the fire, he took up his tale, telling Kate about marrying May and her return to England with their son. His frankness pleased her. It all came out: the story of gold finds in the Klondike, setting out with his family on the S.S. Tunisian, May and the boy leaving at Halifax, his stint with a railroad outfit and the Chisel Lake cabin begun by Billy Todd. She listened, setting up no barriers in her mind, suspended between this camping place, this story and the unknown cabin which would be her home.

Before settling into his sleeping bag on the opposite side of the fire from her, he went to a small creek and cleaned his teeth.

He did not ask about her life.

The next morning with the first shafts of sun they took the trench he had built. It was filled with black water cut through underbrush and it opened into Chisel Lake. Chisel was different from the other lakes they had crossed; it was lined with high walls of rock, covered with lichen and coloured incrustations which at first glance could be mineral stains, rusty outcroppings here and there ranging from yellow to chocolate brown. They were gossans and sometimes gossans meant gold or secondary minerals, sometimes were unimportant. At a levelling in the rocks Woosey ran his canoe up beside a wharf whose end had slipped into the water. She brought the Duckling in behind and jumped out, following Woosey up the path to his cabin. Its logs huge and weathered, it sat low under the boughs of a great jack pine. Inside it was large as cabins go, one room now musty from having been closed half a year, dead flies on the window sills, fireplace draped in cobwebs, two black bear rugs on the floor (perhaps a little too cosy for a grubstaker and prospector), a cooking stove, two windows with real glass in them. Dick Woosey stood, legs astride, in the center of the room, his pride of ownership exuding a welcome to her. "If anyone's stayed here while I've been away, he's left no signs."

The blue green eyes blazed about his cabin. "I'm going to put a rope down the center—one side will be yours, the other mine."

"Are you bushed or crazy?"

"We'll both need a certain amount of privacy. Now, where is that wall of black jack?"

"Don't you want to settle in first before looking for metals?"

"I'm going now."

"I'm starting tomorrow, looking for gold on Squall and maybe File, the black jack's on the way."

"You're looking for gold, I'm looking for copper and nickel."

"You've been too influenced by Mosher and Tom Creighton."

"You've told me that before, change your tune, or can't you?"

That first afternoon she began her search for the mineral occurrences, leaving him standing on the slanting wharf staring after her. She paddled along the high rock banks which continued to climb for two miles until they became a wall. On the northeast side the sulphide body was exposed to wide sections of quartz gabbro carrying what she judged to be a large percentage of copper, silver and zinc, exactly as he had said.

Where a small creek, a mere thread of water tumbled down, she beached the Duckling but did not ascend the rocky uneven course of the stream, and instead made her way along a shelf of rock about two feet wide, examining the gabbro, getting out her knife, making scrapings every few feet. He was right, it was a rich lode of copper and silver. The trouble was, it was already staked, something he had not told her. Every 1500 feet there was a claim post. A second stream came sliding down the rocks and she climbed its banks. On top were the claim posts.

She sat down. Dick Woosey had been one of the first to know about the body of ore; who had actually discovered it was unknown to her. Anyway, he'd ignored the whole thing; he would only search for gold. The wind whined in her ears.

She was alerted by the sound of footsteps on the stones of the creek she had just climbed. She grabbed her rifle and stood up.

A wide-brimmed hat emerged, then a ruddy face with its small grin. "I got worried you might be in trouble."

"You'll have to learn not to worry about me. By the way, why did you come up this creek and not the one near my canoe?"

"It came to me you were not where your canoe was left."

His sturdy cheerful person, his ordinariness struck her with a pang yet there was something a little strange about him. How strange and different she would find out later. "When did you say you first knew about all this?"

"Did I say?" He grinned cheekily at her. "It was Charlie Krug who first mentioned it though Billy Todd must have had a good idea—he was the first in here..."

She went to the nearest claim post. It had been renewed this year. "Do you know a Bill Knott?"

"He's a bloke who hangs about The Pas picking up bits of mineral information—not a real prospector."

"And hoping to make a killing on someone else's information."

She started down the creek and he came after. He asked if she was coming back with him. She was going to the end of the lake and if the weather held, farther.

"Try to be back by early evening," he said. "We're going to have a bad storm, even sleet and some snow." She raised her head; there was not a cloud in the sky.

She paddled past the wall of copper occurrences, measuring to find a break in the claims. There were no gaps. She went on up the still dark lake, the rock wall gradually diminishing, the banks becoming low and marshy. Out of the left shore was a trench overgrown by last year's vines, one of Dick Woosey's trenches, she was certain. But instead of following the trench she sat in the Duckling wondering at his energy, his optimism, hoping she was as sure of making a killing as he was. Trying to get the feel of the country round here, she watched as a pair of mallards fell out of the sky, swimming along the trench, talking busily to each other as they looked for a nesting place. The sun's brightness gone, the afternoon became grey and cold, and the wind rattled the dry reeds. In minutes the rain was pouring over her bare head and washing down her face.

Dick Woosey was paddling around Chisel Lake at the claim sights, waiting for her.

"Glad you're back," he called.

"Did you think I wouldn't make it?"

"You're new around here, new to pros..."

"You mean, I'm a fledgling?"

"You said it."

Taking the Duckling, he shouldered it to the lean-to where he kept his own canoe, his traps, old tin pails, all the accoutrements of a camp. Everything about the cabin was neat, an old soldier's neatness.

Inside the cabin a blazing fire roared in the fireplace, and on the little drum stove bacon and potatoes steamed. An old sweater, a shirt and pants were laid out on the bunk. While he was outside cutting wood, she changed her wet clothes, got into his dry ones, and hung her things near the fire to dry. He came back in, repeating an old love ditty he'd picked up in India:

> Come into the pawnee, love
> For the dark pagodas have flown
> Come into the pawnee, love—

"I don't like that song, it doesn't fit here. This is a different place and quite a different kind of people."

He gazed at her stern and beautiful face. He never repeated it again to her.

Tomorrow he was resuming his search for gold.

"You do hang onto gold, don't you?"

"And you pay too much attention to Mosher and his dogs' bodies."

"I told you I'm looking for sulphides."

"Then try Wekusko Lake—I've got an idea, got it from Mike Hackett." The advice was to have important consequences to both of them.

She slept in the bunk designated hers, one arm outside, her hand clutching her rifle. Every once in a while a flurry of snow pellets attacked the roof of the cabin.

The next day was chilly when they set out, the sun buried in cloud banks. Reaching the mouth of Squall Creek they parted and he gave directions:

"Push east through a narrow lake—it's called Snow—then keep on till you come to its draining creek. Push along now—by the way the creek's name is Snow too—and be bloody careful: it's fast. Keep on till it's no more than a thin neck of water and don't take it to its mouth, you'll get lost in rapids, small lakes and bays and the portages are just too hard for you, but at the neck you'll find a pretty little falls and there'll be a flat rock where you can stop, build your fire and make tea. Listen to the sound of water while you're resting and drinking, then take a short portage to Anderson Lake; it's easy to find, it's right in front of your nose. You'll see that Anderson twists south and east, you cross to its most southerly point and there you'll find a creek. Follow the creek along until you come to an open body of water. This is Wekusko Lake. For cripes' sake keep to the shore on Wekusko, don't push the canoe out into the middle or you'll be in trouble. The way Wekusko slants contrary winds meet in the middle and it's ruddy dangerous—people have drowned. Now, have you grasped this?"

She quailed under his exactness, thrust up her paddle to stop further instructions.

He hurled another warning at her, "Be careful all through in there...bears." He grinned and she was gone.

In the early afternoon she found high rocky sides rising above a large body of water. It must be Wekusko, she decided, and she beached the canoe, climbing to the top to a flat rock among sedge grass. She built a fire and stewed tea into which she dipped hard tack. While she drank, she trained her glasses on the lake, the middle rough though it was calm enough along the shoreline. She would take Woosey's advice and not chance her Duckling out there.

The glasses picked up two islands quite close to the shore; they were like fortresses, one long and thin and the other, separated by a narrow channel of water, a mere button. Both were heavily timbered with enough spruce of good size to build a cabin; the rocks were gabbro, favourable to the occurrence of nickel. They were hers, her islands; she vowed to come back and claim them. Her islands in her lake and she hoped they would contain a horde of sulphide. The smaller island had more gabbro than the long thin island and it dipped into the lake. She was elated.

The sun came out and it was warm, a benediction on her head. Lying back, she put her tin cup, glasses, and gun beside her and gave herself up to fantasies. She was so quiet that a nuthatch moved along one outstretched arm, skipped onto her shoulder, one bright eye examining her. When she spoke it flew away with a nasal yank-yank. She lay dreaming about her cabin on her fabulous island (she hadn't chosen the one on which she would build), the wealth of sulphides the two contained. Suddenly, she stood up, climbed down to the Duckling. "It's a dream," she told her little canoe, "and I must deal with reality."

But as she paddled back to the cabin on Chisel Lake she was still dreaming. She would return. The base camp on Chisel Lake, though large and comfortable as cabins went, she could not accept as her home because of the lake with its stakes of copper so close, a continual reminder of Dick Woosey's lack of imagination, his stubborness. The two islands were hers, her discovery.

The cabin was empty when she reached the wharf: Dick Woosey had not returned. In the evening with its still brilliant sunshine, there was hallooing from the lake. He drew up his canoe along the dock, his hat pushed back on his head.

"Come on down, I've got something to show you." Bending over, she gazed into the canoe. On a piece of canvas rested a row of rocks, one bright gold. She picked it up, a nugget of almost pure gold, the first she'd ever seen. "Put it back exactly in its place, each rock comes from a different place." He jumped out of the canoe, stooped to bring up the length of canvas but his foot caught on a loose board and he tripped. The rocks on the canvas became hopelessly jumbled together. He stared stupidly down, "Crikey, now I've done it!"

"Didn't you mark the spot where you found the gold nugget?"

"I'll go back tomorrow. You come with me."

The sun was already high in the sky when they set out in his canoe at four o'clock in the morning. He kept explaining he'd picked up the nugget the third from the last, then continued his searches but found no other samples with the same amount of gold. She writhed under his explanations. Why couldn't he simply say I don't know where I found it?

They worked all day, first along Squall Creek, a wide slow-running brown creek with low rock banks, then towards its source in the lake where it became marshy with small black spruce rooted in brownish water. "I looked there, see my scrapings?" Getting out of the canoe, they waded in, examining the water, the rocks, making more scrapings. "I'm sure it came from further up. I just picked it up on the shore...I had all of the rocks laid out in order..."

"If you just picked it up you must remember where."

"No, I don't."

"You were stupid," she said and couldn't help adding, "for a Regular Army man."

"I bloody was."

They moved on up into Squall Lake. "I just picked it up, it was just lying there."

"Here?"

"No, not here."

"Where, then?"

The rocks were quartz, the scrapings visible, the bright coloured lichen torn away. There were minerals here, exposed to the surface and in small fragments. The lake was large, laid flat on the earth with few bays, the rock surfaces level with the water.

"I kept always to the left shore, I remember that."

They paddled slowly along the western bank, searching for shearing, fracturing. The nugget might have fallen from a fragment of rock lying close to the shore or been washed down by the spring floods and found far from its original source.

It began to rain. They agreed not to build a fire in some sheltered spot but to make it back to the cabin. They spoke to each other in sharp, clearly enunciated sentences. In his ineptness she could understand with strange clarity his character.

Later, when they were drinking their tea, he said, "I can't fathom it."

"Oh stop talking about it."

The next morning he went back. He continued to go back but he never did find the source of the gold nugget.

The same morning she was urging the Duckling down Snow Creek. It was too rapid for her fourteen-foot canoe and she got out, taking the long portage. Her feet sank into the core of rotten trees, dead and fallen for twenty years; they collapsed under her and she waded through their sullen yellow dust. Black flies and 'no-see-'ems' rose from every leaf to attack her bare face and hands. No one had used the portage for years. Then in front, barring her way, was a black bear, standing on his hind legs, rubbing his muzzle against a tree trunk. She was close enough to see his suspicious little red eyes. Abruptly, she turned off, pushing through the mold, the spikes of dead branches malevolent and clawing at her body, as she made her way down to the fast-flowing creek. Here it was deep and silvery, gurgling omniously—a wicked chuckle but preferable to the portage and the bear.

As she launched the canoe, her partner's warning about Snow Creek floated up into her awareness but she had no time for regrets. The first moment in the water the canoe almost turned over and she had only just managed to right it when the current sailed her along, swerving sharply to the south where the creek broadened into a large bay. To her left was a narrow spit of land covered with old dead spruce, the water splashing and pounding its rocky shore.

The spit of land came abruptly to an end and she found herself out in the center of Wekusko Lake without protection. There was no clear pattern to the waves which came at the Duckling from all directions. The canoe kept tipping and shipping water. In front of its bow was a tiny island, a pile of rocks with hay growing out of its crevices. Just in time she made the island, the canoe now more than half full of water and beginning to sink. Removing her soaking moccasins and her socks, she rolled up the wet legs of her overalls. She was content to be here, safe for the moment, but soon she began to wonder how she would get to the mainland. There was no chance of anyone appearing to rescue her; she would be forced to swim to the spit of land at Snow Creek's mouth, one hand guiding the canoe. With her glasses she surveyed the land at the creek's mouth. It was farther than she could safely attempt and she swept the lake for other escape routes. The glasses caught a speck in the southwest; it seemed to be approaching from the direction of her two islands. The speck grew until it became a man in a wide-brimmed black hat and wide tan galluses. When he was close she shouted, "How did you know I was here?"

"Steady, boys," he shouted back, "I knew you were caught in Wekusko." And that was all he would tell.

When he stood on the island, he pointed across to the mainland in the east, "I've got gold showings I work on from time to time—I may as well have a look now."

"You have gold showings over there?"

He grinned cheekily.

Called Crowduck Bay, it was barren and rocky, the rocks being of volcanic origin. There were signs of scraping where he'd worked last year, the small veins of gold quite visible. He loosened the rocks with his pick, carried the pieces on a length of canvas to a large rock, then with the flat side of his axe struck the pieces of rock, picked up the yellow particles of gold and slipped them into a canvas bag, later to be screened at the cabin.

They set out for Chisel Lake at midnight. The water was calm, the sun a red orange ball on the line of trees along the lake's western shore, making black shadows of their canoes on the mirror surface of the water. When they reached their cabin, the eternal twilight had taken over.

She was full of thought. On finding gold he was unyielding—perhaps it was his British Army training and not altogether his own fault—while she was too single-minded, having listened too avidly to one man, Dan Mosher.

For three days more he continued his search for the gold nugget; on the fourth morning he said, "You want to get back to Crowduck Bay, don't you? Then you'll be closer to your two islands."

She didn't believe she'd mentioned the two islands to him. But she knew that living together in here he had developed a strange prescience, a kind of second sight with regard to her, which came to him just as easily as his far-fetched notions.

They set out with a tent, a shovel, a steel drill, a prospector's pan as well as the usual supplies of food. The Duckling was tied behind Woosey's big canoe.

He picked out a new place to work with visible gold occurrences. There were no deposits as such, only an erratic distribution of gold stringers. "Just enough to buy us some grub," he said.

Whistling as he worked, he used his pick to loosen rocks and the flat side of his axe to pulverize the gravel. She worked along with him, isolating the yellow gold grains from the dirt in the prospecting pan. When they operated the steel drill she turned the steel end while he pounded. Drilling down about six inches in the rock he shouted, "Now! I'm giving her hell!"

The leaves were full out on the poplars and birches, the flies biting hard, flocks of geese winging north on a strong south wind. But she stuck with him. Often towards evening she'd stand on the point of Crowduck Bay, raise her opera glasses towards the islands and get only a blaze of light reflected from Wekusko Lake. Here, the islands were nine miles away.

Once when they were taking their tea round the fire at night, she brought up the subject of naming them. Right off he said the small one should be called Rice, the larger one, Rice-Woosey but she struck off the Rice and called it Woosey. The islands had their names.

She'd begun to wonder at their relationship. It was more than a pure business deal; his prescience where she was concerned warned her of its closeness but what it actually was, she didn't yet know. She liked working along with him. It was backbreaking work but he was inevitably cheerful and good-natured though the findings were never more than a few grains of gold at a time.

One evening when she returned to Woosey and the fire from surveying the lake with her glasses, she found him lying on his back, stroking his right arm. "What's the matter with you?"

"I've got a bloody pain in my arm."

"Everybody has a pain somewhere."

"You've never heard of sweet charity, have you?"

"I don't let my aches and pains," she never had any, "interfere with my life."

"Behold, an iron woman!"

"I don't know as I'd call myself iron. I try not to think of myself." This was the arrogance of a healthy person and she knew it.

"What you say doesn't help this pain."

"Oh, forget it!"

She was to remember these words, long after.

He went to his sleeping bag. She waited for the aurora and made notes. It was still light when she rolled up in hers, her rifle in her hand, on the opposite side of the fire. "That gun," he called over, "when are you going to forget about it?"

The next day he was feeling better and under her promptings they started a makeshift camp close to a clump of black birch; it took them two days to finish.

Taking the Duckling the next clear day she admired the rocks, the trees, the land beyond the bay standing out in sheeny outlines of newness. She hugged the east coast of the mainland for protection, not for any close examination of rock formation. The rocks rose from the lake in squarish chunks covered with yellow lichen, black spruce growing out of its clefts, white birch maintaining a foothold on the narrow dirt shoreline. On the tallest point a bare-headed eagle held its back imperiously turned to her as she paddled past.

The lake appeared calm with only a slight swell. There were no outcrops of rocky islands where she could run for cover if the wind should rise and the waves toss. A family of pelicans skimmed the water in front of her.

Halfway across Woosey's big canoe was approaching, coming at her a little to her right as though to cut across her path; one arm was waving.

She stopped paddling, the canoe gently rocking in the swells. Across the stretch of water he was shouting, "We've made it! We've made it! I've found gold!"

He'd stopped paddling and gazed with an almost transfixed stare at her, "Didn't you hear? We're rich!" Rocking in the slight swell he garbled out his news. "After you left I threw aside my pick and axe, decided to take the day off too..." He was still shouting.

"Don't shout—I hear you perfectly. Then what?"

He was paddling along the east shore of Wekusko, not too far behind her, saw the boulders of quartz, thought it might carry gold and even as the thought came he saw the nugget of gold lying there on the shore.

She for all her claims of superiority had passed it by. She gazed over the water—were the swells slowly growing into small waves?

He'd followed the vein up the hillside, found three veins that could be stripped at once and went back to Crowduck Bay for his pick and axe.

"Did you put your claim papers on your find first?"

"Didn't have a thing on me."

Fine lot of prospectors they were.

"When I raced back I plied that paddle, I tell you..."

"Yes, what then?"

"The nugget was gone and there was a strange canoe..."

"You went to see what the fellow was doing?"

"I came on here to tell you."

A sickening sense of frustration made her turn on him. "Why come, build up my hopes only to tear them down?"

"I've got to get back there now."

When it was too late. A freshening wind was coming at the canoe from the northwest and a wave larger than the others thumped the bottom.

"I want you to come back with me."

"What's the use?"

He was paddling away from her. She followed slowly, what was the use of hurry now? A feeling of exhaustion came over her, settling down on her shoulders like a grey woolly pall. Everything was too much, required too much: too much energy, too much patience, too much know-how, too much of everything, just too much. Was this what she'd come into this country to find out? Only this?

She let him get ahead; when he was close to the shore, he pointed with his paddle to the canoe lying low in the water, an old greasy pack sack straddling the thwarts, weighing the canoe down. The owner, an experienced prospector, would know at once he'd made a find. Dick Woosey was getting out, climbing the sharp rocky hill, calling, "Hello...hello there..." Far to the left on his high perch was the bald-headed eagle, still with his back imperiously turned to the lake.

Angry and tired, she followed. Up here, where the veins of gold lay, it was snarly and tangly, a world of turmoil, piles of rocks, of dirt, dwarfed trees, dead trees, spindly unhealthy bushes and back beyond in the east was a vast area of burned-over land. "Oh God!" It was too much.

The man was standing there, sullen that he'd been found so quickly when he'd believed there wasn't a white man around here for hundreds of miles. Tall and beaky, surly and reluctant to meet the cheery friendliness of Dick Woosey. She caught the startled look on his face when his eyes lighted on her. A woman. She didn't like him and let Woosey carry on; he was good in awkward moments.

"Hello, my name is Dick Woosey and this is my partner, Kate Rice."

She knew he was thinking the two of them were shacked up.

"Howdee, name is Bill Campbell."

No more nor less.

"Looking around, eh? I was up here an hour before you came along...went back to Crowduck Bay for my pick and axe."

No mention of the gold nugget on the shore.

The man spat out a long stream of tobacco. "Looks like there's plenty here for two..." and changed it to, "three."

It was a kind of truce put forward against Woosey's honesty, his genialty. She was too upset to care. She picked her way down among the rocks, the dirt, Dick's invitation in her ears, "Look, it's late, why don't you come along to our camp? We can talk there..." How he loved company, a sounding board.

She got into the Duckling, paddled up to the makeshift camp and found a sliver of yellow soap, wondering what they would feed the unwilling stranger: they were running out of supplies. Going along a small trail she herself had made, she undressed and slipped into the green water.

When she came back she smelled moose in the pot. Evidently the man had some meat. She sat against a small black birch trunk, battling off black flies while Dick Woosey emptied a can of beans into the moose meat. The wariness of the stranger had been breached: he replied to Dick's talkativeness with a sentence or two of facts. He had a tent down on a small cove at the south end of Wekusko, had worked his way through from The Pas, hailed from Northern Ontario, a place called Haileybury, and had decided to try his luck in Northern Manitoba. It was all he gave out.

She sat apart from the two men, too aware that Campbell was trying hard to keep his eyes —and his mind—away from her. Dick Woosey was good at keeping the talk moving since Campbell had told all he was going to tell of his prospecting life. There was little he liked better than a roaring fire, some grub and plenty of tea. While the beans and moose meat bubbled in the pot they came to an agreement (not binding, she thought, but one of those phony things based on a gentleman's 'word') that they would help each other (this was Woosey's suggestion), and that they would prospect more or less in the same area (that too could mean future trouble but she made no comment). Campbell maintained he'd work two miles to the north of Woosey's property since he was there first (he'd had time to examine the ground—had he noted that Woosey's veins were small, ran out near the ridge?) Neither man mentioned the nugget of gold. No mention was made by Campbell of a partner, or partners.

Woosey served up the beans and moose meat, the tea. Over the tea he started on his life, reminding Campbell he'd once belonged to the old Imperial Army of Britain. He'd ended up in Winnipeg broke and had joined the Hudson Bay Railway as cookee.

She got up, went over to the green water of the bay, the red sun slanting down, piercing the water blood red, the lake bottom covered with old logs, green encrusted. A sturgeon swam lazily past until it was lost under a shelf of rock. She raised her glasses, sweeping the sky across the channel, an afternoon sky though it must have been nine o'clock in this land of perpetual afternoon. The furious sun was pushing at the trees, the bushes, the vegetation, urging them to grow and grow, to produce and reproduce more and more. And yet more. It was a jungle of crazy growth and soon men would be swarming over, tearing, killing the land brutally for gold. Campbell would have partners though he had said nothing (that was disconcerting) and they would come and they would bring others.

Bits of Woosey's voice floated over to her with a slight echo. "I owe everything I know of this country to an axe man in the railroad gang..."

She returned to the campfire and made some notes in her notebook. "Billy Todd was his name," Woosey was saying. "I live in his cabin now, it's my main base on Chisel Lake..." Campbell's face was turned towards her but his eyes wouldn't exactly settle. He'd want to know when she came into the picture and whether she shared the Chisel Lake cabin. She closed her notebook, picked up her rifle and went into the makeshift cabin. "Billy Todd took me in hand but he was a restless bloke, wanted to move about..." She got into her sleeping bag. Dick Woosey had never asked about her former life, knew only what he'd picked up accidentally. Where was the dream of Daniel Boone now? She had no time to think of him or his grandson Kit Carson either, so busy was she merely keeping alive. She was stuck into the mould of prospecting for copper, partner to a prospector for gold. What had become of her dreams of glory? She was too tired, too dead beat to care.

She fell asleep and wakened several times during the night; it wasn't dark but had a kind of silvery obscureness. Campbell was in the lean-to, on the other side of Woosey but unlike him he wasn't snoring, was wide awake. He couldn't believe that a man and a woman could form a pure business relationship, carry it into their day to day life. It was always going to be like this, people sniffing around them and she decided she might as well get used to it.

The curve of her life had always been a swing into the wilds of freedom but whether its curve had broken now, she didn't know and didn't know if she cared. As for Dick Woosey, he had simply accepted her as she was: he had a partner and that was all he wanted. Poor Campbell, with his narrow idea of the latent sexuality between men and women.

She would change but didn't know it, then.

She became aware of wind, snatching at the roof of the lean-to, vast mouthfuls of wind, ripping, blundering about camp like a big bear. Cans scuttled down the bank, splashed into water. Out beyond the canvas flap was broad daylight. The lake would be tossed by huge waves that would swamp her little Duckling, maul the big canoe of Dick Woosey if she attempted to reach her island. She got out of her sleeping bag. Campbell's mouth was wide open, his snores competing with the wind. He'd given up on her. Or had he? Time only would tell. She went outside, the wind catching her hair, standing it straight on end, its probing fingers cold on her scalp.

They started that cold windy day to work the gold claims. The wind took the half empty jam pails, whisking them over and over, down the rocks to the bay, prying and lifting the flaps of canvas sacks, everything in movement, trees, bushes, stones and rocks, picks, axes; everything had to be held down, steel drill, fry pan, prospector's pan, tea pail.

It was backbreaking work. Campbell's veins were on top of the hill; Dick Woosey's climbed the rocky hill from the shoreline where the rocks had to be removed. Tearing away moss, the overburden of bushes and small trees, they shovelled the dirt to get down to the bedrock and then take samples. It took them three days to reach the top, three days of the hardest work Kate had ever known. The wind had died but it rained, a torrential rain pouring over their heads as though the roof of the sky had opened.

Everything became mud, mud to their rubber-booted knees, mud in their eyebrows, mud in their hair, mud in their ears, they ate mud and it tasted of old rank vegetables, they drank mud and it tasted of metal, and mud was slippery, mud was mucous like glue, everything mud touched—and mud touched everything—it held fast. At night mud dried in great brown chunks, harder than granite. But her partner was always cheerful and chatty at her side, refusing to be discouraged. "What does it matter—this time next year we'll be millionaires and sitting pretty." Or, "This is nothing you should have seen the Hussars pushing camels over the Khyber." Or, "Tonight we'll stop early . . . cook us some good grub . . ."

She was glum these days and her responses would be negative, "You're too optimistic." Or, "I'm tired of hearing about your Hussars." Or, "We haven't any good grub left to cook." But she was glad enough to have him there, even though she would scarcely admit it to herself.

At the top, the main gold areas were found in the acid volcanic rock, highly schistose. Her partner's veins went as far as the ridge, were half a mile wide, often thin but here and there were abundant supplies of visible gold. The section to the north comprising Campbell's claims had been cleared; he'd done more work than the two of them together—he was a tough professional. The country was so forbidding it was a painter's dream of hell.

Campbell was so silent about his claims she was certain he'd found huge amounts of gold. He'd turned out to be grouchy and moody, almost always silent as though the relationship between her and her partner was an infringement on his conception of the roles of men and women.

She stopped work once, Woosey having gone off to explore the veins on the ridge, built a small fire and made tea. The rain had stopped the day before, the mud drying in great clumps. There were footsteps behind her. She waited, the tin cup of tea held up before her face as the footsteps came on. Out of the corner of her eye she saw a muddy boot so close it almost touched her body. She drank from the cup. "Ya're a good worker...been watchin'..."

"What is it you really have to say to me?"

"How about ya and me making a do of it together?"

"Do you mean partners?" she knew what he meant. "Mr. Woosey and I have signed an agreement."

"Wasn't thinking of a partner, maybe after we can fix up somethin' but right now I've found enough gold here to live in luxury rest of my life. Me and ya could live in Frisco..." He stopped, flung his arm about her waist and gave her flesh a little squeeze with his huge fingers.

She jumped up; his arm fell away. "You think women are created for your pleasure, don't you?"

"Sure are...what they allays round where men are, in minin' camps for?"

"I've got something to get into that small, snivelling head of yours—get out of my sight!"

He raised his fist to strike her but she threw the hot tea into his face. "Ya..."

But she was running down the hill and didn't catch what he'd called her. Whore probably.

It had taken only a minute and she had made an enemy when almost everyone in this place except her partner was a potential enemy. And uselessly. She got into Woosey's canoe. Before she could paddle away Woosey appeared. "Heard loud talking, what's up?"

She'd done him a disservice. Campbell's enmity would be transferred to him. Rather than explain she asked him how long the gold veins extended. "About six miles—we've certainly made it!"

Campbell didn't appear at their camp the next few nights and Woosey wondered about his absence. "You and he have a fight?" When she didn't answer, he said, "Campbell's a queer bloke."

3

She began to explore the country above Campbell's claims. She was finding gold occurrences here and there. She cleared the land of its overburden, tearing away the moss, removing the rocks and shovelling the dirt. She called the deposits the Pine Claims. Woosey was busy trenching every twenty-five to fifty feet to improve his gold showings.

Back in camp at night he brought news of another man, the partner of Campbell—it was Mike Hackett. Mike Hackett, friendly but wary (Don't come too close, I've important business on hand!) The two men built temporary quarters on their claims, naming them the Rex Mine. Each night Woosey brought more news; another partner had appeared, Tom Garth, then the word spread that there was gold on the east shore of Wekusko Lake, and one by one the prospectors appeared.

The story kept swelling, finally catching like wildfire. Tents were set up on the low grassy strip north and south of Woosey's claims and under the ridge that ran behind the gold veins. A shack reared itself on the grass to sell grub, buy furs. Woosey's property became known as the No. 1 vein. Mike Hackett and Campbell had disappeared. It was rumoured they'd gone to The Pas to form a company that would mine the Rex Claims.

There was a new quality in Dick Woosey. He was silent at night in camp, there was no cheerful rambling about the day's events, the new men, the new dance hall and saloon, the women. Kate knew what was the trouble. He had discovered a gold mine, had been responsible for bringing in prospectors (except Bill Campbell and his partners) and for the tent and shack town springing up, but now a totally different story was about to unfold.

Now he must let go. The first fine frenzy of prospecting was over. It was no longer up to him, to his intuition, to the amassing of all his energies to uncover the metal; all that was finished. He had no money for diamond drilling to satisfy the mining companies, give them secure data for negotiations.

He must go to The Pas, see a lawyer, form a company. He would have no idea how it was done. Kate had only a foggy one.

She was considering all these things as she cleaned up around the Pine Claims. Out of the trees some distance away, a stranger appeared, approaching without calling out.

When he was thirty feet off he startled her by throwing down a wad of bills on a flat rock. Nothing was said.

"Will you tell me what all this means?"

"I've got dough, plenty of dough."

She was angry. "What of it? Put it away. I'm not impressed by a show of money."

He picked up the wad, began counting hundred dollar bills, slowly, almost luxuriously, as though he could count on the cupidity of a seller. He'd done it so many times before and knew the results.

His showmanship began to fascinate her. She was being conned but she watched and listened.

The counting went on.

She began to change, was aware of the subtle break-down in her thinking. What was the use of pride, of pushing away this money he was offering for the Pine Claims?

When he reached ten, he started again, always slow, always languid. She marvelled at his expertness, his knowledge of the human mind. His voice went on but more slowly, more tantalizing. It stopped.

He was offering her a thousand dollars in cash, a thousand dollars in her hand. Neither she nor Woosey had more than a couple of dollars between them. He was offering her instant wealth.

He threw the wad carelessly down on the rock.

The claims were worth three times that amount.

She knew when she took her eyes away from the bills and lifted them to his face he had manipulated her into acceptance, thinking she was only a woman and a woman wouldn't know the real value of what she'd uncovered.

"I'll sell." She stooped for the money.

The whole transaction had been almost wordless.

He shoved some mud stained papers at her and she signed her name. He disappeared as silently as he'd come.

Long after, she heard the Pine Claims had been incorporated into the famous Laguna Gold Mine.

When she returned to their camp that night, Woosey was already there. He'd come out of his silence and informed her he was going to The Pas tomorrow to see about a company; he would take his gold nugget, his gold dust from his Crowduck Bay workings. He would bring back mine certificates.

"I'm the owner of the best known gold mine on Wekusko!" he boasted.

"Heaven help you!"

"What do you mean?"

"What I said."

"I'm the best-known man in the north!"

"Wait till the old Imperial Army man meets a smart lawyer in The Pas!"

"I can handle any lawyer!"

Then she told him she'd sold her Pine Claims for a thousand dollars in cash to a stranger.

He exploded. "They're worth ten thousand. You should have called me—I'm accustomed to handling men. The bloody blighter took you in because you're a woman."

"The bloody blighter did not take me in." She handed him five of the hundred dollar bills. "It takes five hundred to form a company."

But he wouldn't touch her money. "You're no better than the others!" After a debate he took two hundred but swore he wouldn't touch it. She hid the rest at the bottom of her sleeping bag.

They journeyed to Chisel Lake and he set out for The Pas at once, his hat level on his head, his black shirt clean. Standing on the sloping wharf she watched him disappear into the hot wind. Her sharp apprehension surprised her; she was by no means certain he could handle a crafty lawyer.

Alone on Chisel Lake she began to plan the new cabin she and Woosey would start to build as soon as he returned. Even the details interested her, the garden of vegetables, the strawberries she would grow. There would be three rooms in the cabin and it would face south; she began a list of the things she would need: a set of white china, a china cabinet, books, endless books. Her mind guzzled over the books: Trollope, Dickens, Thackeray, Scott, Shakespeare. But all the time she was planning and gorging on the books she would order she was scared, plain scared of her partner's meeting with a slick lawyer.

A forest fire broke out on the mainland, somewhere beyond the Herb Lake settlement, a mile from Woosey's gold claims. The Herb Lake settlement was located on the eastern shore of Wekusko Lake. The fire was driven by a west wind toward Chisel. The grey choking air increased and built upon her fears. Her partner was a good worker but dealing with businessmen and big corporations required special qualities. And he could be bull-headed and rock-stubborn.

Something else disturbed her; she would probably have to face the same problem, the same slick lawyer, the same businessmen with their big corporations and it would be infinitely worse for her because she was a woman.

It took days for the haze to lighten. The lake became calm with a yellowish sheen on it. Her supplies of flour and sugar and tea had given out. She made her way to Wekusko then paddled across to the Herb Lake settlement for more and to have a look at the little town rising bravely out of grass and rock and tangled forest.

The wharf was new, wide and short and protected by an island squarely in front; Woosey had told her the men called it Lucky. The log cabin store was on the left; the little town had two streets, one leading gently up from the wharf, the other at right angles behind the store across muskeg where a ramshackle bridge had been thrown up. A log cabin stood at the opposite corner from the store. The black dirt street—it was nothing more than a trail with a bridge over the muskeg—ended up in bush willows. To the north men were working on a new building, its rectangular scaffolding showing that it would be a church. A worn trail wandered off beside the church to a tar paper shack perched as securely on the earth as an old hat: the saloon and dance hall. Herb Lake settlement was a fact.

On the wharf a woman stood, tiny and roundish, her fair hair pulled back tight into a little knot, her round face cut into sharp wrinkles. When she smiled at Kate the wrinkles slanted diagonally up into her hair. "Tea? Give you tea."

Kate looked down at her. "Next time I'll take tea with you." She got into the Duckling, waving at the smiling face. A few yards out, waves began to pound the canoe; she was forced to turn back. The little woman might know of someone to take her across—otherwise she would be forced to wait, perhaps for days.

At the crossroads the woman came out of her cabin. "You come back," her face breaking into creases of smiles. "You fine lady, very fine lady."

"Nonsense."

"Now you take tea."

Inside the cabin was only a table and two chairs made by someone handy with carpentry. There was one picture on the wall, a coloured photo of a man in an oval imitation oak frame, recording no personality, only someone of male sex with a pair of eyes, a mouth and some hair (scanty). "Husband," said the woman with pride, "he from Greenland, Mr. Alborg."

"And you are Mrs. Alborg."

There was a smell of newly made bread in the house. "You wait," and she went to the room at the back, returning with a big black tin tray on which were two cups of black liquid and a stack of thick white bread with pale crusts. "You drink tea, you eat." She watched while Kate ate three slices of the bread and drank the tea that had boiled for hours.

Kate had to explain her small canoe could not manage the big waves on the lake. "Too small..." making motions with her hands indicating, she hoped, smallness and waves that rolled and tossed.

"Get husband." The little woman went out the door and Kate waited, waited until she became impatient. She left the cabin, walked along the dirt trail to the south, and then came back. Half an hour later the woman was pushing through the willows south of the settlement, panting for breath, her hair and clothes hanging with bits of leaves and twigs; she must have run a mile.

"Mr. Alborg prospect...go dock...he take..."

The Greenlander paddled up the wharf in his big canvas covered canoe, a large man with brilliant blue eyes in a tanned skin. "Get in. I take you."

The Duckling was tied behind with a rope that ran underneath and then was fastened to the thwarts. He went straight into the waves, dirty grey with white curling crests. Thump thump thump they pounded the canoe. It took two hours to reach the far side. When they came close he turned slightly and the waves struck with such vicious thrusts she believed the freighter would capsize and she would lose the Duckling.

During the crossing he was full of talk but the wind tore his voice away, and she had no idea what he'd been saying. She asked him if he was a prospector.

"Prospec', fish, work in Rex Mine when open."

"What about Woosey's mine?"

"Rex Mine better." Aware of the expression on her face, "You Missus Woos?"

"I am not Mrs. Woosey, I am Woosey's partner."

He nodded. "Yes yes, partner." He accepted her.

The Alborgs became her friends.

Dick Woosey returned when her calendar said September 2. The song birds had flown, the twilights lingered until nine o'clock when black fell suddenly on Chisel Lake and the forests surrounding it.

She was out on Chisel, fishing, had already caught six perch when the sound of a small motor ratatated among the rocks. She paddled over to the wharf; his big canoe rode low in the water from the weight of the canvas sacks.

"Steady, boys." He made no attempt to get out. "What do you think?" he asked and gazed at her as though something incredible had just happened.

"We're rich." He must have had luck to have money to buy one of the new motors.

"There's a war on."

"A what?"

"A war."

"What and where?"

"Old Blighty and Germany are at each other's throats and there's some cruddy awful battles . . ."

"But where?"

"We have six divisions in France. One of them's a cavalry unit. The Hussars went over with the first batch of Old Contemptibles. The Germans have big guns."

"But the gold mine and the lawyer?"

"We're trying to stem the German advance at Mons—it's pretty ruddy awful."

"But how . . ."

"A German Army is nearing Paris. I stayed on a couple of days to find out the latest."

"But . . .?"

"Oh, got two letters for you . . ." He pulled them out of his mackinaw pocket. "In the end the old Imperials will beat the tar out of the Germans but it's a sewer of a show now. It'll be all over by Christmas." Cheered by his own predictions he got out of the canoe, lifted one heavy pack sack. "It must weigh one hundred and fifty pounds. That thirteen mile portage almost killed me."

"Listen to me, I want to know how you got along with the lawyer?"

"Oh fine, fine."

"But how?"

"First you get a lawyer . . ."

She followed him up the path to the cabin door. "I *know* you get a lawyer!" His glibness, even his announcement of a war angered her. "I knew from the beginning you would get a lawyer."

"Calm down. First I got hold of the most important man in The Pas, he lends money, a man of the world, been in government . . ."

"What government and where?"

"I don't know—talk in The Pas was that he was a government man."

"Talk means nothing! He could be a crook."

"I told him I'd discovered a gold mine and he said I'd have to see a lawyer and he recommended one."

"Oh, did he?"

He didn't tell her he didn't like the first man, nor the lawyer, they both frightened him, but that had been afterwards on the long journey home when he'd had time to think. In their offices he'd found them friendly and easy.

"You saw this lawyer?"

"Sure, sure, and everything's turned out fine."

"You haven't told me anything fine yet."

"Calm down, will you? Mr. Stewart arranged the whole thing for me."

"And who is Mr. Stewart?" She followed him into the cabin.

"He's the rich wallah I went to see first." He threw down the pack and took a big breath. "I'm glad to get rid of that, I can tell you."

She detected an edge of fear in his voice.

"All right, all right, I'll tell you the whole bloody thing. Mr. Stewart introduced me to the lawyer, the two of them took charge of the whole affair. Mr. Stewart loaned me the five hundred and he has a portion of the stock . . ." he didn't tell her Stewart took forty-nine percent. . . ."the two got up a charter and transferred the title and claims to the company. I'm to have the majority interest in the shares—it's all in the lawyer's safe now."

"All this is in writing? You signed an agreement?"

"It isn't in writing—we were three gentlemen."

"Gentlemen!"

Had he handed over his gold mine to someone he scarcely knew? He was, like herself, only a poor prospector; the lawyer and this Stewart would be only too well aware of it. She gazed down at her hands, the broken nails, the dirt worked into the cracks of skin, the seams of black in the flesh that would not come out. A fine lady indeed.

"The name of our company is to be the Kiski Mining and Development Company—sounds pretty fine, what?"

"Did you name the company, or did this, this man?"

"Stewart did, and it's a good name."

She scorned his explanations and opened her father's letter.

It was short. She was to come home. He would arrive and fetch her if she did not. Neither he nor her mother liked the sound of her life. She was shocked. Had her mother finally ruined him? The letter could almost have been written by her. It was her father, that golden being of her childhood who had planted the seeds of love for the frontiers of the earth.

Woosey went for the second sack and threw it on the floor when he returned. "What's the rope doing down the center of the cabin?"

"I told you, one side is yours, the other mine."

"Are you bushed already?"

She opened Margaret's letter; it was a scrawl of bright blue ink covering twenty pages. She had persuaded her parents to take her on one of the Mediterranean cruises and afterwards she would coax them to leave her in Paris! Maybe she'd stay for a year or two. This crazy war should be over soon. Kate threw the letter down.

"There's a lot of good grub in those sacks, I can tell you . . ." He lay down on the bunk, but he was under a terrible compulsion to talk. "Ran into Hackett and his partner, Bill Campbell. They've formed a company, plan to start drilling at once, go down four hundred feet . . ."

"When do you start to drill?"

"Have to wait till Stewart comes."

"Why? It's your gold mine."

"We're going to make a million. We'll live in The Pas."

"Not me."

"I've made a deposit on a big plot near Christ Church, right on the Saskatchewan, we'll have as much money as we want."

Going outside and down the path, she got into the Duckling and sat dangling her hands in the water as if she could annul their record of toil. What terms described hands that dug ditches, graves, cesspools or cleared land for gold and sulphides?

He came out of the cabin, went down the path to the dock and leaned over the Duckling. "Blimey, what did you want me to do?"

"Stop acting like a gentleman with any promoter—you're not teaching officers how to play polo. This is a grim game."

He'd done his best. She must remember she'd taken on a partner who was at least half a gentleman. Both of them were ignorant prospectors set down among ruthless men. It was going to be tooth and claw.

"Why are you sitting there? Why are your hands in the water?" His tough black hair dipped to a peak on his forehead. They'd scalped him when he'd had his hair cut.

"I'll go and unpack . . ." his voice grating with weariness, "then I'll cook up some grub."

She withdrew her hands from the water, took up the string of perch and got out of the canoe. "When is this Stewart coming?"

"Week or two, soon as he finishes some business deal."

They went up the path together. "Wonder if it's just a few finishing touches on stealing someone's gold mine?"

"Kate!"

"Just a random thought."

They worked, stowing the supplies, the potatoes, flour, bacon, beans, rice, sugar, jams, butter, lard, salt, puddings, matches, candles, towels, a dip needle, three little scholar's black notebooks, a pair of binoculars for her. She took her new possessions into her hands. "Thank you, you remembered me."

"And I bought a brass bed. It's being shipped on the new railroad, the Muskeg Special."

"A brass bed? Whatever for?"

"I've always wanted a brass bed."

Woosey neglected to mention that in The Pas he met Tom Creighton just in from Phantom Lake and Tom let him in on a few secrets. An Indian named John Collins had come to him saying he'd found something on Flin Flon Lake. Following the Indian up to the lake, Creighton had seen just enough of the greenish stain where the snow had blown off the rock to know copper was there—but how much, he didn't know. He wouldn't be sure until after break-up. Creighton thought it was a big find of copper but he was keeping it hushed up. Leaving Woosey to wonder why it would be hushed up—it wasn't gold, after all—Creighton snowshoed over to Mosher's camp on Beaver Lake to alert him and the boys—the Dion brothers and a fellow called Dan Mulligan. Woosey was thoughtful: wonder if they'll squeeze out that Indian if anything comes of the deposits. For all the secrecy the town was buzzing.

4

Mr. Stewart did not come.

The wavies flew south early this fall; the ducks and geese disappeared from the rivers and shallow bays of the lakes.

Chisel Lake had frozen solid, then mild weather had set in. It snowed; the weather turned cold again. Kate stood for hours on the shore, gazing at the miracle of colour in the sky, finally pulling herself away to write in her notebook:

> To the esthetic appeal of the Northern Lights at this time of the year there can be no denial, when the intense cold has crystallized the snowy nights into a strange stillness that seemed to hold the very stars themselves in its spell. Then it is that the Aurora may wield its enchantment of colouring and graceful motion to shatter all this crystal immobility into dust of jewels that drifts in clouds before a soundless wind across the skyey spaces. I recall that upon one such winter night there appeared at the very zenith of the sky a golden bar of light, and knotted round it, soft folds of deepest red, like a scarf of fine tulle with lengths of free ends which lifted and gently wafted about as in a whiff of breeze—a beautiful emblem of the wonder and mystery of all things. A layer of ice whose surface is covered by myriad fine points from which the charge could escape into the air could account for the magnificent colour.

"It's more than time to set my traplines." She closed the notebook.

"Lay them west of Squall—that's what I used to do."

"I'm going to the Burntwood River." Travelling to the Burntwood would serve another purpose; she could explore a new frontier.

"You can't do that! The Burntwood's more than a hundred miles north!"

She set out for the Burntwood with three dogs and a toboggan.

5

He executed a little dance, holding onto his two front teeth. The pain, keen as a drill, cut through his jaw, up the side of his face and head, then subsided.

He was staring out the window, lashed by summer rains, icy snow, and streaked by sun and summer dust. The plank sidewalk below him was layered with mud and snow. A lame man worked his way through yesterday's new fall. The sun glittered like ice. The room behind him was fiercely hot from an overheated stove pipe and clogged with the odours of dust and unpainted boards. John Ewing longed for soft lights, bare sidewalks and pretty women in dark furs.

He was sorry for himself, sorry he'd left his beginning law practice in Selkirk to come up here, to The Pas, the end of nowhere, to practice two days a week. When he'd been a law student he'd had such dreams: he'd be a famous lawyer specializing in constitutional law (he had several books with him now at the hotel where he boarded but he was too discouraged to open them); he would dine in famous restaurants, the kind with potted palms, white tablecloths and big napkins, and waiters hovering in their tails; he would be accompanied by a woman in furs, a bunch of violets—his gift—pinned to her collar.

There were footsteps on the stairs and he turned, went back towards the desk. The pain drilled into his tooth and he danced again, holding his two front molars.

Dow Stewart opened the door, grinning, showing his false uppers. "If you don't get those two front teeth pulled, I'll carry you to the Doc's."

Ewing glared at Stewart. However big and fat and smart he was with money, other people's money, Stewart couldn't carry a feather; he'd have a heart attack if he did. He wondered moodily how this man's manoeuvering had brought him up here two days a week.

"Things working out?" The big man sat down, spreading open his muskrat-lined coat with its otter collar, pushing the otter hat to the back of his head. The fur shone like dull gold. The coat and hat were relics of his days as M.P.P. for Selkirk.

"Any clients?"

"No!"

"Hold on. You'll have more than you can handle." His eyes were slits.

Ewing knew the amiability was false. He'd been taken in by the easy assurance of a man of the world. As a young law student in Winnipeg, he'd been taken to the office of the M.P.P. for Selkirk and had been impressed by the Member's pleasing sociability, fascinated by the figure

he cut among the rich and powerful of the capital but even more important, his dreams had been fanned to white heat by dining with this man
and his fellow M.P.P.'s at the most famous hotel in the West, the Fort Garry.
The steel drill in his teeth eased and he remembered a little verse he'd
seen in the Selkirk paper.

> Little lines of railway
> Little grains of sand
> Make a certain statesman's
> Bank account expand.

"I wish you'd explain it all to me."
Stewart laughed. "We understand each other pretty well."
His admiration for Stewart had held until he became a buddy to the
Member for Rupert's Land, who no longer made an effort to hide his greed
for the riches of the north, all the gold, nickel and copper rumoured to
be hidden in the rocks and shores of its lakes and rivers. Stewart, he'd
discovered, had been making money on the side from the new railway
line to Prince Albert, had been bitten hard until now all he talked about
was gold gold gold.
"What's so funny?" Stewart wanted something and he'd have to wait
to find out what it was.
Abruptly, Stewart changed. "I'm having the gold from that Kiski Mine
assayed by a Toronto syndicate—they sent an engineer up to secretly assay
the property, and take extensive samples, and they report the veins are
narrow and not so well mineralized as say, the Rex Mine."
What kind of game was this? "You told me in the fall when you went
there on the sly that the value of the gold in the Kiski was not only maintained at a depth but at a greater width than the little Cockney prospector (what's his name?) believed. You said it would be a mine of 'considerable magnitude'—that's what you said."
"You've got too good a memory for your own good."
Was that a threat? He thought of a little verse:

> Life is hard by the yard
> But by the inch—life's a cinch

"I'm talking about the Kiski." Ewing was blunt. "You should have
taken out an option instead of forming a company on the word of that
little so and so."
"You just watch me . . ."
"I will watch." Ewing decided he could be tough also.
Stewart grinned as though he saw through Ewing's little gambit. "The
Rex has been taken over by a London England syndicate, they have the
capital but not the expertise to work it along the right lines. I'll provide
that, I've been made manager. Then there's the Laguna. A little salting

from the Kiski will help increase the value of its certificates."

"You don't own the Laguna or the Kiski."

"I will."

Ewing was sharply uneasy. Manager of the Rex, scheming to take over the other two.

Stewart shifted his eyes to the big third-hand Cary safe, its small wheels set on two narrow boards to keep the huge piece of steel from falling through the floor to the Gateway Drug Store below.

Pain shot through Ewing's teeth and he twisted in his chair.

Stewart rose, pulled together his coat and lowered the otter hat over his forehead. "Look after the Kiski!"

It was a command. This was what he'd been brought to this godforsaken place two days a week for: for dirty tricks.

From the landing outside, Stewart called, "I'll make an appointment at the Doc's, pay him too . . ." Feet were going down the stairs.

Holding his left hand over his front teeth, he went to the red Cary safe, managing the combination with his right hand. The huge door creaked open. Would he do it? Why would he do someone else's dirty work for him? He turned the knob of the steel inner door slowly and with a series of reluctant jerks reached out for a certain pigeonhole and drew out the portfolio of the Kiski Mining and Development Company Certificates. Sitting down at his desk, he opened the folder. The envelopes were unsealed, the certificates were street type, without names. That Cockney didn't know that, wouldn't understand what street type meant. But his hand refused to move. He began to dream again: he was a famous lawyer, a specialist on constitutional law (he must get on with those books in his hotel room), more famous than Stewart, dining at the best hotels, (no more Rupert House in The Pas for him), a maitre d' hanging over the table, lights soft, his companion a pretty woman in dark furs.

It'd be easy, the easiest thing he'd ever done.

6

Mr. Alborg's unwillingness to make a map of the Burntwood country was only a part of the disastrous trip.

Woosey warned her of the tales he'd heard of the Burntwood.

She reminded him she'd ridden the rapids of the Sturgeon-weir.

"Luck was on your side."

Alborg was willing to sell Kate three dogs to travel as far as Setting Lake where she could lay her traps. But Setting Lake was too close to Herb Lake settlement and the swarms of people deluging the new town in their search for gold—the miners, prospectors, surveyors, government geologists, engineers, corporation men, storekeepers, saloon keepers, the Rector of St. John's Anglican, the girls. A new rooming house had been built in town and another at the cove on the southern part of the lake where Campbell had pitched his tent and still another run by a woman called the Diamond Queen at Mile 82, the stop on the just-completed railway line, so-called because it was eighty-two miles from The Pas.

With or without Alborg's map she was going to the Burntwood.

He agreed to draw a simple map for such a complicated journey. He made a line through Crowduck Bay to the Grass River, turning sharply south and then east into Pakwa Lake, then following the creek at its northern end to Setting Lake. His stub of pencil stopped. He was hoping she would change her mind. She did not. The line twisted north through a series of bays, shoals, and rapids into many small lakes crowded with islands and difficult channels before it re-entered the Grass River again. The line stopped at Pisew Falls and when she was not influenced by his caution he moved it on to Paint Lake—a lake with more arms than a devilfish. It paused, waited and went on again round a long point of land and up the west shore of Paint through muskeg until it joined an open body of water which Alborg claimed was not a lake, went on until it ran into the pretty Ospuagan Lake (pretty only in July) then it headed straight north into a creek named Manasan and followed the Manasan until the Burntwood swept in fury across the northern perimeter of the whole area. The line stopped.

Beyond the rock wall of the Burntwood she would find plenty of silver fox, black fox, ermine and marten. She would find also plenty of wolves and moose on both sides of the river.

It took a week to reach the Burntwood. She lost her way twice, the land and waterways being covered with snow and lacking any trees to mark the separation between them. She wasn't as concerned about the loss of time as by the amount of frozen fish, her food supply, the dogs consumed.

She'd started happily; in open country she would jump onto the runners, in the bush she'd run behind the toboggan. She was free, she was exploring on her own, dependent on her own powers. It was what she'd come to the north to do.

The dogs began to give her trouble. The lead was a handsome long-nosed brute with slanted, cunning eyes. He howled every night, upsetting the small male and female. She was forced to crawl out of her sleeping bag, shoot her flashlight into its eyes, and order, "Shut up!" The tawny wild eyes regarded her with malevolence. She had always prided herself on getting along well with dogs, but a mistrust, even hatred was building up between them. She renewed her fire, crawled back into her sleeping bag, the howls starting up as soon as she settled down. The two small ones answered with short snapping barks. Getting up again, she cracked her whip in the lead's face. The yellow eyes glared back, unblinking and savage; she hadn't the heart to lash the whip over its beautiful creamy coat. She renewed the fire, made a pail of tea and sat down. The lead began to howl. This had repeated itself for six nights. She was surprised at her uneasiness.

She was running into uneven, hummocky snow and her feet sank into hollows. The dogs whined continually. She might have reached Ospuagan Lake but was by no means sure. She camped early, tying each dog separately to a small bush willow. They howled. There must be wolves about, though she had not seen any nor had she noted their tracks. All night she alternated between sitting down, drinking tea and moving about to keep the dogs quiet, and the next day she found herself becoming fuzzy and unaware of the terrain through which they were travelling. She was half ready to turn and go back to Chisel Lake. Suddenly, the lead dog stopped. She ordered him to go forward. Turning his face away, he did not move. She brought the whip down with a vicious thrust over his creamy coat and where it struck the fur was a curved line; the dog bared his teeth and the slanting eyes raised to her seemed in the tawny second to be alive with savagery.

His feet and the feet of the two other dogs behind him were sinking into pools of water. Her own were soaking. She raised her glasses to take stock of her surroundings; about a hundred yards ahead was a dark streak of open raging water; it must be the Burntwood. She had gone farther than she'd thought. She swept the binoculars about the horizon. Almost resting on top of the black spruce were rolling black clouds—a winter storm was on the way. She pulled the lead dog towards the bank.

It was not a place she would have chosen for camp. The land was low and covered with large boulders and a scrimping of timber, small thin willows, tamaracks, alder and tall dry reeds that keened in the high wind. Behind her was a ridge of rock and in front the rocky cliffs of the Burntwood. Unleashing the dogs, she tied each to a willow, the lead dog giving one long wail as he sat on his haunches, his cruel eyes following her. The other two strained at their leashes. It was going to be an uncomfortable camp; she should have turned back.

She set it up against a boulder, using two willow poles and a length of canvas for a roof. The wood smoked when she made a fire so she threw on more tamarack; it flared, then died to a smudge. She warmed a can of beans and made tea. When she sat down, the dogs howled; she was too tired to care.

With twilight came the cries of wolves, one long oo oooooo oo from the direction of the ridge behind her. The dusky shapes of two wolves slunk away but they would return. The dogs went wild; the willow holding back the lead dog bent almost to the ground with his efforts to get free. She went to tighten the rope when there was a clatter of hooves on the rocks and the great antlers of a bull moose were silhouetted against the sky.

No one could withstand the slashing cut from the hoof of an angry moose. She ran for a partially uprooted tree, her rifle forgotten. Some of the roots still clung to the hollowed depression in the ground. Plunging her body in amongst the roots, she covered herself with leaves, branches, twigs, stones—anything she could grab, barely managing to finish before he trotted up and sniffed about the hole, his dangerous hooves perilously close. He was curious, not angry, and kept on sniffing. She made little noises, scraping her finger nails over a stone, whistling softly to keep the moose interested and away from her camp and also to keep the wolves away; they would hardly attack a full-grown vigorous male.

The moose, through protecting her from the wolves posed a threat of his own. He could easily put one of his hooves through her skull. On the other hand if he ruined her camp she could starve or freeze to death. A tree snapped. The lead dog had broken free and raced past her to join his wolf relatives. Losing interest in the leaves and twigs of her hole, the moose moved off until she brought him back, alert and watchful, by scratching and whistling. She wondered how long she could keep him here. He gave a snort and trotted off to sniff and root about her camp. Two objects rolled over the rocks. The noise surprised the moose; he snorted again and his hooves clattered away over the rocks and stones. He had gone.

The dogs had stopped howling. She crawled out of the hole. Her legs fast asleep, she was forced to sit and rub them back to life. Even in the blackness she could make out the devastation; the canvas roof, having caught on the moose's antlers, was gone and might be anywhere. She crawled about, feeling for her rifle, the first time ever she'd made a move without it. Perilously far from her camp, she found it among a clump of tamarack and hugged it to her. The rest of her equipment would have to wait until daybreak. Fortunately her matches in a tiny bottle were in the breast pocket of her mackinaw. She built a small fire.

At daybreak she found her pack sack tossed as far as the rocks sheltering the river, the canvas roof draped over a bush willow where it had dropped from the antlers of the moose, her binoculars in a stony hollow, one lens cracked, the can of beans and her pail pitted and crumpled but still able to hold water. The first scurry of snowflakes fell as the wind soughed through the scrimp of trees; the blizzard was upon her. The two remaining dogs were asleep.

With a sudden scream of wind and driving snow it fell and she knew it might last three days or even a week. Against the overhang of boulder she built a small fire and crouched over it. Before the day was done the canvas topping, serving again as roof, collapsed with the weight of snow.

It was no longer a question of laying traps for silver fox and ermine. There was only one need now: survival.

She was lucky—the blizzard only lasted another day, or what she believed to be a day, having lost all sense of time. The dogs were two lumps in the snow but they began to stir and whine for food. She was very low in supplies and gave them half a frozen fish each. If the snow ceased and the wind dropped she would make a start for Chisel Lake. Once, when the wind died down she thought she heard a dog howling and wondered if it was the lead dog returning with his wolf relatives to plague her; in the next pause there was nothing and she convinced herself she was imagining things.

Again, the howls came, over towards the creek and she knew then she wasn't imagining them because the two dogs, shaking off their snow, howled back. She stood up. A voice was calling.

"You didn't half get yourself a good way off!"

Pulled by five dogs, Dick Woosey ran his toboggan almost into her fire.

She did not ask him how he'd found her in this country almost untrod by white men, not until after her father had come, and had gone.

7

She rode the long way back on the toboggan, wrapped in furs. They reached the cabin on Chisel; five dogs and a toboggan were drawn up on shore—Stewart's?

Inside, Kate's father rose from a chair, straight and unflinching in his dark, seemly clothes. He looked like a Methodist parson about to deliver a stern warning to his robust and uncaring parishioners.

The thin body, parchment-coloured face did not belong to the golden person she'd believed in; she was devastated.

"Hello there, I'm Dick Woosey and this is my business partner."

"Father." She went to him, took hold of his shoulder, the bones under the cloth skeletal. "Father." He was a sick man.

She had mentioned only once in her letters home that she had a partner but he would have set up barriers against believing the partner would be a man; that she shared a cabin with this man would be impossible for him to conceive.

"Father, I've been away to the north . . ."

The blue green eyes, still brilliant, were sweeping over her tangled hair, dirt-smeared face. His mouth was twitching.

"I went to trap but mostly explore . . . there was a bad storm, I got caught."

"I say what—this is your father and he's here to visit us?"

An Indian, pulling at the butt end of a cigarette, sat on Woosey's bunk. Back against the wall was a brass bed, a bear rug hiding its springs. The rope down the center of the room was gone.

"I have come to take you back with me." His eyes flicked over her hands, black with smudges from reluctant fires, fingernails like claws, grown long and curved.

Kate sat down. Where had her father's dreams gone, his dreams of the frontiers of this continent he had told about? Had he fed her on fairy tales more terrible than the wicked witches of her mother's stories, had he planted dead seeds in her five or six year old mind?

"Your daughter is co-owner of a gold mine," Woosey boasted. "We've made it, we're rich!"

"I must return today, Kate."

"Father, father—this is my life now." What had happened to him? "You will not return with me?"

"Can't you see?" It was you who pointed the way, you! she wanted to shout.

It was a stalemate. Neither of them would give in.

His lips trembled, the sharp blue green eyes filmed over. His disappointment was too terrible for her to see.

"I'll come later, I promise. I'll come this winter."

"You must stay a few days, now that you're here," Woosey said, "I'll make a feast. I shot a cow moose and her calf while Kate was away."

"I bought supplies in The Pas—they will do us." He glanced at his Indian guide, "We will leave, now."

He couldn't change his mind: he'd changed it once when he'd married her mother and the marriage had destroyed him.

He picked up his black coat with its black velvet collar. The Indian got up, gathered the pack sack in his hands, swung it onto his back.

Oh father. She sat there, remembering her mother and their old hostility. "How is she, my mother?"

"Your mother is not well. She was looking forward to your arrival." He started for the door.

"Here, here—you can't go all the way to The Pas in that, you must have something warmer..." Dick Woosey pulled off his mackinaw. "There's plenty more where that comes from," and he draped the red and black mackinaw over the tall thin figure.

There had never been anything more unsuitable to her father than the gaudy red and black checks hanging from his shoulders. Walking carefully, neatly along the path to the toboggan, he sat himself down, gathering his black coat about him. The Indian threw a fur robe over his body, cracked the whip and shouted, "Mush!" With a swirling of snow the runners glided over the frozen lake.

Dick Woosey shouted, "Good-bye, good-bye. Come again!" His voice rang along the rock cliffs.

"Dear father, good-bye," Kate murmured. The last she saw of him, he was sitting bolt upright on the toboggan, the bold plaid mackinaw flapping about his spare shoulders. He never turned, an alien figure in this frontier country.

She went back to the cabin. She was convinced she'd never see him again.

"Cheer up, you'll feel better after you've had a bath. I'll get the pails of snow and you can heat the water."

"How did you find me at the Burntwood?"

He was enigmatic. "I borrowed the dogs from Alborg, took them out on Wekusko and they took off. I simply followed them, that's all."

He was an unusual man.

There were spectacular auroral displays on Chisel Lake these early winter evenings. Every night she was out standing on the shore with her binoculars.

> . . . a barrage of bright green searchlights along the western horizon while over the whole northern half of the sky sheets of green light played like summer lightning amid amethyst and emerald and silver. On that occasion, so intense was the force, of whatever nature it may be that causes the lights to appear in the sky that at the moment of brightest, most concentrated, white light, it was suddenly transformed, by some miracle of the ether, into the most vivid colours of the spectrum. Fluted white ribbons of vibrating light rays one minute became in the next instant processions of sharp tongues of flame, violet in colour along their joined bases, a flashing green at their tips, and the lot of them chasing one another like madcaps athwart the milky way . . .

The fact that so many of the finest displays I have witnessed followed upon a day or days of high gales of wind leads me to account these gales as the source (in part) of the static charges, *i.e.*, built up by friction which in the dry air of the north result in the beautiful discharges we call by the poetic name of "Aurora."

8

He had no intention of letting Kate know he had spent part of the time she was away lying on a bear rug in front of the fireplace with the old pain in his arm.

During intervals of pain, the thought of Stewart's betrayal boiled in his mind and compounded his illness. On the fourth day following her departure for the Burntwood the pain had eased and he was walking about the cabin, noting the diminishing wood pile and the lack of animal meat. The sound of dogs barking at the wharf brought him to the door.

It was Alborg with a message: a brass bed had arrived at Mile 82 and had been picked up by the woman who ran the new boarding house at the railway stop of the Hudson Bay Railway's Muskeg Special, now running as far north as Mile 241. She was known as the Diamond Queen.

Alborg had become the Herb Lake settlement's handyman; he was a miner, carpenter, prospector, commercial fisherman, land realtor, dog raiser and supplier of bread (his wife's) to the new rooming houses. He entered Woosey's cabin, aware at once of the shrunken wood pile, the jaundiced colour of Woosey's usually florid complexion.

"Been poorish last couple of days."

Alborg cut wood, brought it into the cabin and would have cooked up a batch of grub but Woosey said he was better and quite capable of looking after his own needs. He had never cottoned to Alborg the way Kate had. Alborg worked in the Rex Mine.

The next morning Woosey snowshoed over to his Kiski claims. It was a lonesome, deserted place with a flutter of snow hiding, yet in a peculiar way emphasizing, the untidiness of torn-up earth and rock. On the horizon was the bright new shaft of the Rex Mine, reminding him of Stewart's perfidy. Rage made hotter by his own fears about Stewart and the lawyer Stewart had recommended sent him hurrying back on snowshoes to Herb Lake. He'd felt rocky and weak on his way over, but now raw power surged through his veins and quickened his muscles and he felt fine. He was brash and overbearing as he marched into the saloon. Why he'd come here, he could not have said; it was merely the first place he'd reached.

It was empty of customers. The smell of stale beer and cheap whisky had seeped into the wood leaving a pungent odour of sourness, its strength and acidity affecting his breathing. The saloonkeeper stood at the bar, wiping glasses. He had never seen Woosey before.

"Where's everybody?"

"Rex Mine. Everybody here works at the Rex."

White lights flashed across Woosey's eyes. "I'm the man who brought everyone to this place. I was the first to find gold. I'm the owner of the Kiski mine!"

"Talk is, not so much gold in the Kiski."

He was incoherent with rage. "I'm an officer of the old 18th Hussars Cavalry! I stormed Chitral in '97. I tell you the Kiski is the richest gold find..."

The saloonkeeper believed the man in front of him had no money and was, besides, some lunatic prospector. He disappeared into a back room.

Woosey lost control. He pounded the bar with his two fists. "You come back here, you! I've got something to say to you! There's gold and plenty of it in my mine! There's a million dollars worth of gold, I tell you!"

The saloonkeeper did not come back.

His shouts crashed in his own ears. He strode out. Not enough gold in his gold mine! At the door he shouted back into the room, "Just wait, feller!"

Down on the dock he glared at the frozen lake with its black spruce fringe, and his fury drained away. His knees trembled. A bitter wind raised the brim of his felt hat; when he stooped to fasten on his snowshoes, the effort was painful and he gasped slightly for breath. Then, he turned into the wind, sniffling at the thin rim of clouds resting low, almost to the tops of the trees. A bad winter storm was building up somewhere above the Burntwood River. And Kate was up there.

But he snowshoed south away from the storm and towards the cove at the bottom of the lake. Slowly at first, because he was still weak, and then faster until he was moving with a long loping stride.

It took him an hour to reach the cove where the new rooming house, a chinked log house with dormer windows on the second floor, set almost on top of the wharf. He ignored it and mushed along the trail to the south, through a thicket of alder, tamarack, black spruce, white and black birch and poplar to the railway line. He figured he had about an eleven mile trek before he reached Miss Sophia O'Ryan—the Diamond Queen—and her new rooming house.

The trail had been widened, a swathe cut through the woods to allow the passage of a wagon, its tracks leaving ribbons of soft dirt, old brown leaves and snow. He kept looking back over his shoulter at the bruise of blue black that rimmed the tree tops as though he was pursued by demons. Above him the sky was grey, with a screen of light cloud through which the sun tried to penetrate.

He stumbled often on this part of the trail and his way was slow; the rocks and tree roots were still working up to the surface. It was dark when he opened the door of the rectangular log house. It was a plain room with a large brown bear rug on the floor and a long table with a lamp on it, but it was hot and smelled of food.

A woman rose from a chair by the large cooking stove. She was small and roundish with gold-coloured hair pulled back tight into a bun at the base of her neck.

"Allow." Her voice was high, with tones of silver; seeming to him the way an old trouper of the London musical hall stage would speak.

"The last time I saw you was at Bacon's, in The Pas."

"Good evening."

Her eyes were small but of a lovely hazel colour; even in the man's old grey sweater, her rounded form was seductive. But tonight he had little use for her too-evident charms. He felt aggressive, cold, wondering cruelly if she was still living with the blacksmith she'd taken away from his wife and nine children.

"There's a brass bed here."

The brass bed was in her shed. Mrs. Hale kept the rooming house at the cove and her man ran a wagon service from Mile 82 to the cove and on to Herb Lake; he would deliver it to Woosey's cabin for a sum.

"I can pay. I'm the owner of the Kiski Mine."

"Some of t' men were saying t' gold is scarce..."

That rumour again. It made him feel weak and he sat down, abruptly.

"Don't you bover luv, I'll bring you a wee dram. We don't serve spirits but keep a bit 'andy." The h's disappeared naturally in her speech.

He drank the brandy she put into his hand.

"You sick, luv?" Her arms in the rough grey sweater came about his shoulder, dropped to his waist, then he was being half lifted from the chair, helped as though he was an invalid (her strength surprised him) to a sofa behind the stove. He closed his eyes and almost immediately was asleep.

Later, he stirred as two men and the woman talked about battles with strange names. The name Ypres kept appearing. Ypres? What was it all about? He'd never heard of Ypres. He sat up.

At once, she was beside him. "'ungry, mate?"

He stared at her. She brought him a plate of deer meat, cabbage, carrots and potatoes and a cup of strong tea.

In the yellow lamplight the black-bearded man, the blacksmith and a young man with blond hair and a handsome sharp face that reminded him of Kate were speaking of England's old Imperial Army being withered away under the big German guns. He ate the plate of food, drank the tea. The War, the War, it followed him everywhere. His comrades, Green, Walker, Wilson must all be dead or rotting on French earth.

He gazed out of the small window above the sofa at the black, slow-wheeling sky, full of nostalgia, carrying his melancholia into the dawn; it was leaking everywhere, up into the silky white cobweb gently swaying from its hold on the rafter, onto the table where the three people sat, placidly discussing the War and drinking their tea—they could easily sense it if they stopped only a second to listen and wonder at the silence behind the stove.

The Hussars had been his life, his secret life, now. He'd started at fifteen as a band-rat, been promoted at 'Shot to a soldier of the line, then after India and Chitral made an NCO. He would never stop being an Army man so what was he doing here, lying safe and warm in this room? Dying for one's country was a kind of success; he was only a straw man.

In the morning he had only a vague idea of the night before, of the talk, of his almost insane dejection. He had one compulsion: to get out of here fast.

"It's only dawn, luv, wat's your 'urry?"

The sky was still black with night. "I have to leave."

She served him breakfast at the table, bacon, potatoes, bannock, raspberry jam and tea. The black-bearded man and the young fair-haired one were nowhere to be seen.

It was five dollars for the night and the two meals. When he'd paid for Mr. Hale to deliver the brass bed to Chisel Lake, he was surprised how little he had left.

Setting out in the darkness, he judged the storm to be one day away. She accompanied him a short distance, why, he didn't know.

"Do you live alone?"

"I live with my partner."

"'andy, wat?" When he didn't answer, she persisted. "You prospect toget'er?" Her voice changed, was harsh now, echoing among the bare trees and grating on his ears.

"My partner goes her own way."

"'ave seen your partner in The Pas, ver' tall, wi' severe face."

"Kate is tall."

"Brass bed is for 'er or you?"

"Kate makes her own arrangements."

The coldness, the aggressiveness had come back; he refused to answer any more questions about Kate. He'd often wondered why she'd accepted him as partner when she believed herself superior to him. She had a way of diminishing him yet he admired her, her coolness, her self confident audacity and her beauty. He would show her she'd made a good bargain when she'd taken him as partner, he would!

Miss Sophia O'Bryan fell back. "I'm English, too—I know you're a gent."

"Yes, ma'am."

"Ask me Auntie she knows a toff when she sees one, mate."

"Good-bye." He did not turn. He'd show Kate! One of the Old Mob would show Kate Rice yet! And he strode sturdily on, a Hussar on the march. "Hey, cheese it! Cheese it!" he heard again the troop sergeant's voice splinting the air, the quinine soaked, sun-baked wallah, that pukka bloomin' soldier! "Have a go, mate! Let's see a bit of something! Let's see some fireworks! Lep! Ri! Lep! Ri! Lift your feet! Double! You knock-kneed bunch o' jumpers!" Are they all dead? All? Mist covered his eyes; he stopped. But something of the Diamond Queen's curiosity communicated itself to him and he turned to gaze back at her. Light was just breaking through the limbs of the trees, her round soft English face looking towards him was sharpened by pity.

"Take care, luv!"

He went on. March. March. What was he doing here, here in this ice-coated land, here alone without his buddies? Why, he should have been there, there with them on that field wherever it was, whatever its name. He had deserted them, that's what he'd done! He thought back to that day after the battle of Chitral, the blood pouring down the Sar-major's blue tunic and him yelling, "That man in the rear rank there, do your bloody collar up! Who gave order to fall out? What the bloody hell do you think this is? A picnic?"

Then he was stretched out on his pallet of straw, all his regimental fellows round him, straining his eyes to the sentinel of stars up there, too weary to sleep. And the sound of the muezzin, the eternal chatter of native voices and afterwards the reveille, silver and sweet in the morning air. And the bull voice of Sarge, "Take all blasted day! Hungry gutted lot o' perishers!"

There was a lump in his throat and his eyes were moist. Stopping, he gazed down at his snowshoes, up to the great black lump of cloud waiting above the trees. What was he trying to do? Why go to his partner who never in her sweet life wasted a single thought on him?

All of them, all his old regimental fellows must be dead, knocked off their mounts by German guns. He was just an old trapper and prospector to the rescue of his partner. He was off again. March. "Come day—go day—God send—pay day." March. March.

Hurrah for the gallant Hussars!
Hurrah! Hurrah! Hurrah!
When the trumpets are sounding
And the big guns are pounding
Who is it who stands steady
Alert at the "Ready"?
Why, the gallant old Umpteenth Hussars!

March. March. On. On to the Settlement and the Alborgs.

He requested the loan of his dog team from Alborg; it wasn't what he'd have done normally—the offish feeling still persisted—but this was an essential journey. His partner was in trouble.

Driving the borrowed team to his cabin he had a stroke of luck, sighting a cow moose and her calf within easy range. He shot the cow in the right leg, the calf as it was running away, and skinned them on the spot, cutting them up and making a cache. The livers, hearts and a big hunk of the meat he packed in an oiled bag to take on his journey. To pacify the dogs, going wild with the smell of fresh meat, he tossed a chunk of raw carcass to each.

The storm caught him at Pisew Falls.

9

She went out the last day in January to see her father. At the Northland Hotel she changed to the only women's clothes she possessed, her 1906 graduation skirt, the high-necked lace blouse, the long black coat with the gathered sleeves; on her head was a high black bearskin hat and over her hands, extending beyond her elbows, a pair of bearskin gloves. They shook hands with great solemnity at the train steps. To Woosey, she was going out to a place as far away as England and he wondered if he would ever see her again.

The tall figure with her food supplies, her tea pail slung from her back, disappeared into the train. He turned away, shouted to the dogs and set out on the lonely trail back to Chisel Lake. Taking her seat, she sensed his desolation and was surprised at the strength of his feelings.

As the train moved across the snowy land, over the shaggy little frozen lakes, the creeks and the rivers, sitting in the colonist car in her old-fashioned clothes she caused a sensation. Passengers from the first class found reasons to visit the car where she sat, reading a mining manual or making notes in a little black notebook, or eating hard tack and drinking tea. Rumours spread: she was a Russian Princess, she was a spy—"they say the country is full of spies"—she was a Belgian refugee from the war. When the train pulled into Dauphin, she got out and walked to the end of the platform, gazing over the cold white farm land that had given Hardie Jones goose pimples when the sun had released the rich oozing, steaming earth from its shackles. She spoke to no one, kept her own counsel.

At the station in Toronto, passengers, red caps, people waiting for trains, people getting on trains, put down their bags to gaze after her as she strode past with her fine free-swinging walk, her canvas pack sack slung over her back. People speculated about the telegram she stopped at the telegraph office to send.

She wired her father that she was taking the five o'clock train to St. Marys out of Toronto; she did not leave the station. In the women's waiting room, heated to tropical temperature, old women sitting comfortably spread-legged among their valises and their bundles stared while their sleepy minds sniffed around her. Oblivious, she ate the hard tack from her pack sack and read a newspaper, but the headlines about Kitchener and the King of the Belgians made no sense to her.

Four hours and ninety-eight miles from the city, the train drew into St. Marys. Her father and mother waited, standing aloof and isolated from each other, the only ones on the snowy platform. Her father, stiff and judicial in black, his thin eyelids half-closed over his brilliant blue green eyes, his face even in the poor and yellowish light even more parchment-coloured than when she had last seen him; her mother, short and too fat, wearing a blue velvet hat with a wing spread like one of the new aeroplanes, her hot black eyes jutting out from a rouged white powdered face. Her mother reached her first.

"You'll have to go shopping first thing in the morning, Katie—you can't be seen..."

Her father said, "You've come, Kate," gazing round for her bag.

"It's on my back, father."

Both her parents believed she had come home for good.

During the night she was unable to sleep, kept rising to open the window further. She was unable to eat the breakfast—the soft rolls, the heaps of butter, the rich doughnuts—or to drink the coffee laden with thick cream.

Two mornings later she was striding towards the flour mill on the river in the lower part of the town, where her father worked. On the walk next door stood a little girl whose head swivelled on her thin neck, her eyes jerking as she passed; Kate swept over the brow of the hill, still conscious of the eyes reaching after her. She was accustomed to stares.

She must tell her father she could not stay, that she longed to leave at once. She could not sleep at night, nor eat the meals, nor spend hours shopping with her mother. In truth, her home suffocated her, the old red brocade hangings which had "come down" in her mother's family, the fireplace mantel decked with useless china, the water colours of static red roses and sheep; she rejected them all and longed for the cabin, for lobsticks, tamaracks and rocks, for the free-moving air, for plain grub and good cheer, her partner's kind of grub and cheer, for his strange second sight, even his imperial arrogance.

She'd streaked about the house in moccasins, opening doors and windows, her mother running after her, the fiercely black died hair fly-ing out from curlers, "Katie . . . you're letting in air . . ." The black satin screens embroidered with long legged golden herons crashing about her ankles, she picked them up in a burst of exasperation and carted them to the attic, her mother screeching after her, "Katie, they've always been there!"

The reception yesterday had been the worst, passing and repassing sugar and cream, the cream too thick with butter fat for the pudgy women in their creaking corsets, the mincemeat tarts, her mother's friends gaz-ing blankly at her moccasins, her outdated graduation outfit, at first with astonishment and later as though she was merely outlandish and freakish. By the time they were drinking their last cup of coffee, consuming the last tart, tonguing the last crumb about their pale mouths, they had turned to the more familiar and easier topics of death and tragedy, the growing lists of the war-dead posted each day on the bulletin board of the newspaper office. They forgot her in outdoing each other reporting calamities and catastrophes.

But to tell her father she could not stay was the toughest thing she'd ever done. There was a small core of resentment lurking inside her mind that his life had become so impoverished that he hung all his hopes and yearnings upon her. He sat at the paper-strewn desk in his office, the room shaking with the rumble of the giant wheels grinding the wheat into flour. On top of all his papers was a Bible, open to Revelation. Had he started at Genesis for his class at the church and now reached the end? The reports from bankers, lawyers and creditors were covered over with his notes. Oh father, father, she whispered.

He finished the sentence he was writing, methodically put down the period and then he lifted his face to her. "You've come to tell me you are returning." She gazed at a death mask. It cut her to pieces.

On her way back to the house she ran into Emily, her old classmate. The small figure pushed a sleigh with a spread-eagled child on it, a child at each hand slowing her leisured progress up the hill as though she were forced to drag her body, bloated with yet another life.

"Emily, it's you!" An ancient child face clutching his mother's hand pointed his face up at Kate. "You got what you wanted, I see," Kate said.

Emily's face, too thin and tight, changed from instant recognition into old worn dismay. "It's not what I thought . . ."

"But Emily, it's all hard."

In the sleigh the youngest child straightened his small body, throw-ing out rigid legs in protest against this delay. Emily's attention dropped to her son, the two others bawling as if they liked the sound of their voices echoing up the winter street. Her face closed against Kate.

"It's all right for you to talk, you always got what you wanted, anyway."

"You're wrong, Emily. I haven't got everything I wanted."

Still, Emily felt she had been completely rejected. "Well, it's nice to see you . . ." Emily's face suddenly put on a kind of copy of her old eager self. "Remember Carl?"

"What about him?"

"Well he's married, has two kids and goes around with a high school girl. Imagine." Catching at Kate's non-acceptance of her words, she looked down apologetically. "Well gossip's about all there is."

"Oh Emily."

Her father was the only one to see her off, the only one on the snow-starched platform. A great red sun rose above the hills in the east. She was sick with heartache and would never witness a sunrise without remembering the bitter sting of seeing her father, the golden satin father she had known as a child, now so frail and so completely destroyed.

In Toronto she did not go to the women's room at the station cloistered with its old women and their interminable bundles, but instead walked the streets oblivious of their names or where they led, of their character or the stores that lined them. People stared at the commanding and beautiful woman in her old-fashioned clothes with a pack sack slung on her back.

Kate was torn with anxiety about her father when she wasn't asking herself questions: what had happened up north since she'd been gone? Had Stewart shown up? Had her partner heard anything more about his gold mine?

She walked until she was stopped by a large gnarled hand, reaching out from a fine black coat with a black velvet collar. "Not so fast!"

She pulled away but the strong, old hand held firm. It was a prospector's hand; the face that belonged to the hand was dry and seamed with wrinkles, the banker's tie of navy and white stripes had a grease spot squarely on the four-in-hand knot.

"What ya doin' here?"

It was Campbell. Bill Campbell who had sold his share of the Rex Mine and had made a fortune. He was living like a rich retired banker.

"Never forget ye."

She was being propelled across a street, down another by the old prospector's grip.

"How's that man o' yurs?"

"Are you referring to my business partner?"

He chuckled and pushed her along. "Guess mebbe there's other names fer it." Up a step. "Live at the King Eddie now."

Inside, he tucked one arm securely under hers, the other sawing the air as he gazed around the lobby, showing the bellhops, reception clerks, hat check girl and cashier what an old-timer who had struck it rich was bringing in. They smiled back indulgently; he tipped them well.

She was led to a table with a drooping white cloth where a large menu was put into her hands by a waiter in black canonicals. Campbell wanted the best, the most expensive meal the hotel had to offer for his lady friend.

She sat bemused, her mind swirling with thoughts of her father, the bleakness of Emily's life, and her own; but at least she had freedom, her life held prospects of promise. And her partner's life, what of it?

She became a momentary captive of Campbell's, wondering where was his beakiness, his surliness? Was this what happened when a prospector struck it rich? He was now plump and soft in the middle, self-satisfied with fat living. They were brought lamb and she hated its blandness, its pale taste.

"One thing ya can't get at the King Eddie, is moose meat." He roared with laughter, struck his fist on the table, the sugar and creamer, salt and pepper shakers dancing, his false teeth clicking.

How would her partner react to making a pile of money? He claimed he would build a house in The Pas, raise Indian ponies, but she wondered. For the first time since they worked together she realized she knew little about him; she knew some facts of his life, but she didn't know him. It occurred to her now he was a lonely man living in a vast, unfriendly bushland.

"Ya look a bit peaked, isn't he feedin' ya?"

"I feed myself."

"Haven't lost a bit of yur vinegar."

How would she react if suddenly she had thousands of dollars on her hands? What would she do?

"Where'd ya say ya were holing out?"

"I didn't say."

He roared again.

Buying books and china wouldn't be the answer. She needed to be free to go, to explore—there'd always be land.

"Ya still with him then?" There were grease spots on his banker's pinstriped navy vest.

"I am still Mr. Woosey's partner." She would go far beyond the Burntwood River. But what of her partner? He was sociable and would go to The Pas or return to England.

"My pal Tom Garth went to Frisco but I had a mind to come here." He waved his hands, the nails yellow horns that had plucked out roots of trees, pushed aside rocks, and torn bushes from the reluctant earth in search of gold. "Don't know where Hackett is."

They got up from the table, the head waiter and all the other waiters waving his passage into the lobby. They all had shared in his largesse; his hands with their yellow horn nails responded happily.

"Feel as if I owe yur something . . . want to buy an outfit...guess ya could use one, eh? I owe yur man fur the gold float I picked up on Wekusko—reckon he saw it furst." He was puffing at a cigar. She expected him to spit; he did not.

"You are correct, my partner did see the float first."

"Said so, didn't I?" His breath was fusty and smelling of cigar as he leaned towards her. "Ever thought a leavin' thet man o' yurs?" The strong old prospector's hand was propelling her along the street. "Jes' thought as how I'd ask. No harm in that." She was led into Eaton's and up the elevator. His eyes that could read a rock for its mineral content could not distinguish the floor numbers.

They stood in an elegant grey and white department, its quietness almost ecclesiastical. "Mr. Campbell, I do not wish a new outfit—where would I wear it?"

A woman with high arched, disdainful eyebrows made a few tentative steps towards them. "Want the most expensive outfit ya got." He indicated Kate with a graceful arabesque of his cigar.

When she regarded herself in the navy blue French suit with its white silk tucked blouse, the narrow navy shoes that pinched her feet, all she could see was the tragic figure of her father on the frozen railway platform and another far from here, turning away to begin the lonely journey to his base camp. She gazed down at her scarred hands.

"Take them back!" The lunch, these clothes, the whole thing was crazy.

With a sure instinct the saleswoman knew Kate's male friend would buy the clothes. "Madam will leave her old things here—they will be given to the Salvation Army."

"I am wearing my own clothes out of this store!" She strode from the dressing room.

Campbell's christy set at a jaunty angle, he opened a wallet swollen with bills and received two discreetly elegant grey and white boxes.

They waited for the elevator. "Ya ain't goin' to stick to him?"

"Mr. Campbell, Woosey is my partner and we signed an agreement."

The elevator glided down and they stepped in. Setting down the boxes, he removed the cigar from his mouth. "How 'bout Frisco if ya don't like the Eddie?"

"Mr. Campbell!" They moved onto the crowded street.

"It's simple, jes' don' go back."

"Listen, Mr. Campbell..."

They were butted apart at the corner, his old calloused prospector's hands clutching the grey and white boxes. Half a block away strode a tall figure in a black bearskin hat, a pack sack swinging on her back, long skirts flying high over a pair of miner's boots. Alone on the curb, nursing a dead cigar, he stared after her.

One week later the train pulled into The Pas.

On the platform to meet her was Dick Woosey.

10

Mr. Stewart did not come that winter. Kate warned her partner it was a scheme to keep him off-balance, make him so anxious that he'd agree to anything; even to a takeover. Woosey denied that Stewart had any such plot in mind (though not very forcefully); he made excuses: new ore samplings needed to be taken, there'd be more stripping ordered and then there was the War of course, communications were slow, difficult. None of these arguments convinced Kate.

He held a theory, he never lost it, that most of the mineral occurrences in here followed a triangle lying on its side, the base running roughly between Wekusko Lake and Mystery close to the Burntwood River, the apex being west of Wekusko, roughly at File and Elbow and Cook Lakes. Part of his theory was right.

Woosey was a hard worker and always genial. Although she would never admit it, under his aegis she began to lose some of her terrible arrow-pointedness, her inflexibility, her practicality; toward the finish of her life she would even lose much of her fine, reasoning mind, but by then other causes were at work on her. Now, geography played a part also; she began to relax into the timeless pillow of the north, into its slow sure swing of seasons. But it was hard for her to let go completely. There were times when she was too aware of her superiority to Woosey: she was an honours graduate in Mathematics, she could write clear and succinct English which he could not, she was keen at realizing the nature of the promoters he must deal with while he was easier and slower, more inclined to make excuses for them. Then she would scoff at him: "What do you know about the sulphides, pyrrhotite or chalcopyrite?" Or, much closer to the bone: "Why do you let Stewart get away with it? You think they're all good fellows, just bleeding with the milk of human kindness..." He took it all, but he had problems that claimed his secret self, unknown to her. He was dealing with psychic troubles in his soul.

As the year passed, Stewart wrote to say that he could not come right away. Other business demanded his attention. The mine would have to wait.

Kate was slow in noticing other people's feelings, not given to heeding moods in her associates, or if she did, ignoring them. But events were not slow.

Woosey went to The Pas, the town ablaze with the news of the fabulous find of copper at Flin Flon. Tom Creighton and Jack Mosher, (brother of Dan) by late summer of '15 had established the copper showing and rushed off to round up their partners: Dan and Jack at the camp on Beaver Lake, the Dion brothers and Dan Mulligan off prospecting. Together they staked sixteen claims. The rush was on. In the very vanguard of the rush was a railroad man called Jackson; Jackson went south of Flin Flon with a man named Reynolds and found a big deposit of copper on the shores of a small lake named Schist, only ninety miles north of The Pas. It was Jackson's first trip out and he'd stuck it rich. His find became the Mandy Mine. Other bits of information were on everyone's tongues: a wagon road was being built between Flin Flon and Schist, a thorough testing would be made before drilling began but because of the war little time would be wasted. The gossip was that Creighton was working with a man named John Hamill or Hammell (no one knew or cared how the name was spelled) who had connections with Boston mining men, the firm of Hayden Stone. Hayden Stone was definitely behind the development of the Flin Flon copper mine.

Woosey was unimpressed. It was copper. And who wanted copper? One year slipped by. He hadn't told Kate, not thinking it worthwhile. But by 1917 she'd heard and remembered her two islands; she'd let them slumber in their antique trance long enough. She returned.

From the angle she approached the smaller island it seemed more than ever the fortress she recalled. Confirming her first impression, the growth of tall trees rose up sentry-like, protected by nearly vertical rock cliffs. She did not bring her canoe in too close. A quick glance brought a tightening of her heart—the rusty weathering schist, the exposed quartz gabbro meant minerals. She circled the island, her heart beating faster. The gabbro ran a few feet under the water on the southwest side and that rock contained minerals. The cliffs opened, there was a place to land her canoe; pulling up, she climbed over the rocky protusions, small bushes, stones and dirt to the top. Tall sedge grass and this year's hay crop waved about her knees. It was a flat plain up here with a thin mantle of moss and drift, the trees standing in a clump on the southwest shore. She examined the rocks under and around the trees. The schistose gabbro carried copper and nickel—how much she could only guess.

For a long time she was quite still, lying flat out, the enormity of her find, its consequences to her life and the life of her partner having a strange effect on her. She was completely matter-of-fact. Her island—it was bound to happen. Ever since she'd first seen it, she had known, subliminally, at least. She tried to think how Dan Mosher would accept the find, then getting up she gave a shrug of satisfaction.

She set up her claim posts, four claims for herself, four for her partner and three for dead Indians.

While she was gone, more news of Flin Flon had seeped through to Woosey in his forest and lake wilderness. The copper ore taken from an open cut was being hauled by wagons and later by sleighs to Sturgeon Lake and stored there until it was shipped in open barges down the Saskatchewan River to The Pas and then by rail west to the Trail smelter in British Columbia. Even with these expensive transfers the ore paid great returns.

Rushing into the cabin, Kate announced to Woosey her discovery with a kind of suppressed excitement. "I've discovered a large showing of copper and nickel on Rice Island," expecting from him a show of jubilation. When he took her news so quietly, so tranquilly, she burst out, "Aren't you going to say *anything*?" It was then she was alerted to something almost inert in him. When had all the cheer and the talkiness gone? When had he ceased his tales of the cavalry in India, his life in England? The realization struck her now as though hit by some blunted object. "What is the matter with you?"

"Matter? It's the bloody war, that's the matter. I know the Americans are in it but it'll take a year before they can get their army over . . ." The last time he'd been in The Pas he'd learned of the terrible losses of British men in their trenches, waist deep in mud, and of the comparative comfort of the Germans in their higher, drier ground.

Was that all? "But it isn't any concern of yours."

His eyes went small and hard. "That's all you know."

She'd made it worse.

He went about preparing the meal in silence. Afterwards, by the fireplace, silence. It was the last week of October 1917. After their evening meal, he said, "I'm returning to The Pas. I'm going to enlist in the Strathconas—it's the cavalry."

The shock was too great. For the first time in her life her tongue was tied, she did not know what to say. But she knew it was useless to try and keep him; she'd rammed hard up against something iron in his life. Lamely she tried, "If you've made up your mind..."

"I'll leave for The Pas at daybreak tomorrow." There was a new, vital quality to his voice.

Reasons why he shouldn't go crowded like a host of harpies into her mind: what about the unfinished business of the gold mine? And Stewart, what about him? What about the nickel showings on her island? What of it? What about the cabin she planned to build on the larger island? What about...? The list would not stop.

"What about our partnership?"

"I'll sign over my interests, everything to you..." his voice was commanding, with underneath a note of great joy, "you're so great on signing...till I return."

"You're going to remain in England, after...?"

"I might get..." He didn't say it.

But she knew. There was a chill in his words, just as there was cold in the high-heavened night. She moved closer to the fire.

She said good-bye to him in the morning.

On the dock he clicked his heels smartly. "Steady, boys!" and was gone.

After he'd left she was surprised how little heart she had for prospecting, or for journeying in the Duckling. She clung close to the cabin as though some of his presence was there in the one room.

Her first journey after his departure was made to The Pas for supplies. At the store she found Woosey had left a note for her.

Dear Miss Rice: I have found a man going south to 'Peg. He is in the cavalry, the Strathcona's like me though I've not yet signed my attestation papers. We travel together will write from barracks. yours R. Woosey

The coldness, terseness of the badly put together letter stabbed her to the quick. At first she felt she couldn't go back to the lonely cabin in the forest; she'd go off on her own somewhere else. He could be gone for years; he might be killed or lose an arm, a leg or both legs; he might remain in England. All kinds of possibilities assailed her as she walked the muddy plank boards of the little town. She was surprised at the strange responses the letter evoked. Then, listless and without heart she started back to the cabin.

Around the end of December during a mild spell she was back in The Pas with a catch of raw furs she'd trapped. With the proceeds she bought a dog team. There was another letter from Woosey, as cold and terse as the first, almost past understanding to her sharp and lucid mind, the English was so slack. He didn't know when the Strathconas would leave for England and France and the fighting. During the winter Mr. Alborg who'd gone for supplies to The Pas brought her another letter containing a photograph of Woosey in his uniform. In it he was a different man, a real soldier, standing straight at attention, ceremonial sword in leather-gauntletted gloves, spurs on his shining boots, brass buttons gleaming, the spit and polish showing clearly, tall bearskin hat. How proud he was! He was a soldier again, ready to die for glory!

She continued to trap and prospect. As freeze-up continued on its certain course and the long days of summer came and then they too began to wane she grew so accustomed to silence, to loneliness that she came to believe it was the natural way for her to live. Days would pass in which she didn't give her partner a thought. There were no more letters; she was sure he'd gone to France.

He'd become almost a memory when on the first of October, 1918, she was fastening her canoe to the dock in front of the cabin on Chisel and her eye caught a curl of smoke weaving up from the chimney into the branches of the jack pine. Inside by the fire stood Woosey, a pot of potatoes and bacon stewing on the fire; he was dressed in his old prospector's clothes—no fine uniform, no polished, spurred boots, no gleaming buttons, no bear skin cap. She stood still.

"Hello," he said. His eyes gazed at her, dead and almost fawn-coloured. His face had lost its ruddiness, was a kind of bilious grey.

"Where's your uniform?"

"Been discharged."

She was resentful at his sudden intrusion into her life; she'd learned to manage on her own again, to handle the prospecting in the summer, the trapping in the winter, the trips to The Pas, the loneliness. Now, it was all changed. Now, she must accustom herself to another human being, make way for him in her life.

"They discharged me...medically unfit for combat. My regiment's gone, gone to France."

She was about to say, Well, pull yourself together, but she stopped herself in time; it would have been too cruel.

"You were about to say, 'Pull yourself together,' weren't you?"

And she, honest, said, "Yes, forgive me."

It took several months before they could get back anywhere near to their old relationship; she was too resentful of his presence and he was too dejected to notice. He remembered too well the afternoon in the infirmary: the big partly opened window looking out on the field of ragweed, the bitter choking smell of it, the Doctor coming into the room, his Captain's uniform a little slack, the belt slipping just a fraction. He was a tall older man with greying hair—all the young smart ones had gone. Woosey had brought his heels together, lifted his arm in a smart salute, the old 18th Hussar, but the Captain deflated him. "Don't bother," he said leafing over the sheaf of papers in his hand. "I see you couldn't finish the stint with your squad this morning...complained of a pain in your heart?"

"Not my heart sir, my arm."

"But your heart, you had a pain in your heart?" He gazed down at Woosey over his small gold rimmed spectacles.

"No sir, it was my arm, the pain I mean." His eyes, his whole senses were dulled by shock, staring out at that bloody field of ragweed, the choking, piercing smell of it.

"Take your shirt off. Lie down." The Captain opened his black bag.

He had kind eyes, but these Canadian Army types had nowhere near the smart efficiency of a British Army officer, Woosey thought. Yet he lay down on the thin, much washed khaki blanket with foreboding. He knew what was about to happen. He was about to be discharged. He lay with hard, stiffened muscles.

The Captain was not so stupid. He stepped back from the hospital bed. "You'll have to relax my boy, or I can't examine you."

He tried, but his muscles were drawn tight as steel. He lifted his head. "Sir, I can't . . ."

The Captain looked at the papers in his hand, again. "I see from the medical certificate when you were attested last November they gave you a fit A2—and only eight months later you're unfit. Must have been a medical officer in a big hurry."

Woosey couldn't answer. He closed his eyes, the stinking ragweed still in his nostrils.

"You look older than your thirty-seven years."

He could feel the Captain bending over him, feel the breath on his face. "I've given you a couple of minutes to relax, now."

"I can't, sir." Can't was an ugly word for a soldier.

11

He stayed close to the cabin, oblivious of the passing seasons, the long silky evenings of summer, the short boisterous noons of winter, never venturing far, neither travelling to his still dormant gold mine, nor inquiring after Kate's nickel showings; he was content to do the small necessary tasks about the camp site, splitting wood, hauling water, doing a bit of fishing. Kate shouldered the real burdens, laid the traplines, prospected, went to The Pas with the raw furs, returned heavy laden with supplies.

Kate did not press him. Perhaps because of the many times he'd come to her rescue she now unquestioningly did what was necessary. But when months grew into years—they had now entered the 1920s—and still he did not snap out of it, her anger and frustration boiled over. What was he going to do—sit on his backside close to camp till he died? Let the gold mine fall into the hands of Stewart? Let her nickel mine languish or be taken by another schemer or the same one? The new cabin they were going to build on Woosey Island, what about it? She'd had enough of inaction and was leaving at once for Woosey Island to pitch her tent and start clearing the land, then she'd dynamite the rock, get Alborg to help with the actual building.

Startled, he stood up, gazing about him as though he'd awakened from a long sleep with fearful dreams. Perhaps during the years the trauma of his discharge from the Canadian Army had closed over, been healed. "I'll help you with the clearing and digging. It's a little late though."

She would not listen. That night they started planning the new cabin. The cellar must be large and deep, the cabin must be snug and warm to take care of the winds sweeping the lake; it would be big, three rooms, a bedroom for each, a roomy kitchen.

It was November and it had turned mild, the snow on the big island blown off by the high winds. At first he tired easily, his muscles lax, but gradually his strength returned, his muscles tautened. He became genial and talkative. But he never spoke of his service in the Canadian Army.

They felled trees on the island for the floor. She was in a hurry for the thick hand-adzed boards to be laid before the big snowstorms began. Alborg would help them. Woosey schemed to have the biggest housewarming the lake had ever seen; half a moose roasted in the fireplace, he'd bake real bread, there'd be fruit and candy and brandy. What did it matter that his money had almost run out?

It mattered to Kate. She mushed out on snowshoes west of Squall, as Woosey had long ago suggested, to an old Indian trap cabin and laid her traps, leaving the dog team to him. He took the team to the island and began collecting stones for the fireplace.

In three weeks she was back with a small catch of rat, marten, mink and one prize, a beautiful silver fox, to find a great heap of stones collected by Woosey to start the fireplace, enough to reach the grate up from the cellar. It had begun to snow, a swirling of large dry flakes, but there were no blizzards yet. Woosey took the dogs to Herb Lake and brought back the cement and Kate, staying at Chisel, arrived each day to help lay the stones.

It was close to Christmas when she returned to her traplines. When she came back Woosey would go out to The Pas, sell the skins, and also see Stewart and the lawyer.

Stewart was on his mind constantly. His gold had lain dormant all through the war and the years that followed. Now that he had come out of his melancholia he felt a renewal of his hope—and also of his apprehension about Stewart's involvement. While he worked, he talked out loud: "You're a double crosser, you're tricky, I don't like you. If you have defrauded me and my partner out of the gold mine, I'll . . ." He never could decide what he'd to to Stewart.

Kate returned with a catch of the usual rat, some mink and marten, five wolves, red fox, black fox and beaver. She had not caught another silver fox.

It was a skimpy pack of furs Woosey took out to The Pas.

12

He sat in the crowded, stifling office of John Ewing. Every chair was filled with clients in old bearskins and sweaty woollens over unwashed bodies; the hot sour essences choked him. Fighting for breath, he was too conscious of his heart; it seemed to be missing beats and he was fearful it might stop altogether. He threw open his mackinaw, pulled at the neck of his sweater, and even that show of energy brought on a series of short tight then missing heart beats. He held his breath.

He didn't attempt more than a nod of greeting to Tom Creighton who'd just entered and sat down on the opposite side of the room. He would be gone before Creighton was served and he wouldn't wait, though he preferred the blighter to any of that whole gang at Flin Flon—he had decent manners and was well-spoken. There was another prospector beside Creighton, an old fellow, somehow familiar, with a great matted grey beard, old mackinaw with the elbows out, boots with cords for shoe laces; he was a troglodyte, exotic and alien even in this office.

Ewing had a constant frown down the center of his forehead, two missing front teeth cancelling out the frown and giving him a clownish appearance. He seemed much older than Woosey remembered.

Creighton stopped chatting with the old man and came over. "Hello Cockney, glad to see you!" Standing squarely in front of Woosey and absorbing all the air with his big, broad shouldered body, he whistled, "Hear you discovered a gold mine a ways back. You must have made a pile by now."

Woosey could only make a grimace for reply. He'd made nothing. He'd made slightly more than three hundred dollars from the sale of his skins and by the time he bought supplies there'd not be much left. He'd have to make out till he saw Stewart.

"Come on over and see our outfit at the lake. The new camp buildings are something to see, I can tell you. We're in full production, bit of a slowdown there for a while but going great guns now. I'm building a race track with all my money—Ewing's drawing up the deed. I hear that the

Free Press in Winnipeg figures we'll see 200 million dollars."

His eyes followed Woosey's frantic pushes at the neck of his sweater. "You're good with ponies, come on in with me. Afterwards, thought maybe I'd race dogs—maybe greyhounds."

Woosey wanted Creighton to go away.

Creighton half turned, attention drawn by talk between the lawyer and the old prospector who had sat beside him. "Can't you understand? I tell you Stewart is not in town, won't be back for a week."

"He's on some beach, eh? Sunning hisself on other gent's money, eh?"

Woosey recognized the old man; the voice belonged to someone he once knew, someone who'd once hung about The Pas picking up any prospects he could find. Old Bill Knott.

"Want him to buy my gold claims, eh?" Knott said.

"You'll have to wait," said the lawyer.

"Don't feel good, eh? Maybe scurvy, eh? Want to go out to hospital, need money, eh? Need help, seein' things in bush, hear voices in trees, eh? Sell fer anythin', see? Enuff to get me out, eh?"

"Bill's bushed bad and he's sitting right on top of a gold mine, cabin's right on it, up on Elbow Lake," Creighton explained.

Poor old bushed cove. "Thought he was dead . . ." Woosey had no more breath left. Creighton's face was fairly bursting with pink and tan good health while he and Knott were sickening with some kind of putrescence.

"Rot!" The lawyer slammed down his fist.

Creighton winked at Woosey. "Wager Knott's right—he is sunning on some beach. Could be Hawaii? Or else he's in hiding right here . . ."

"Want him to buy my gold claims, eh?"

"You'll have to wait."

"Don't feel good, eh? Need help, seein' things . . ."

"He's bushed real bad."

"I'll try to get Stewart . . ." Ewing's eyes flicked over the waiting clients as if he'd like to sweep them all out of the room.

"Wager he'll get him, even from Hawaii?" Creighton winked again.

Woosey got up before they were ordered out and passed round Creighton, trying to drum up his old fighting spirit. Steady, boys! But he wondered if his breath would completely fail him as he stood at Ewing's desk.

"What's your name?"

"Woosey here . . ."

"Woosey?"

"Owner of the Kiski Mine." And, struggling for air he continued, "I've come to look at my certificates of ownership." He'd planned to say much more, to sound commanding and powerful but he had scarcely sufficient breath left to meet the shrewd eyes (was it cold calculation?) levelled at him.

"Kiski, you said?"

"They're in that safe."

"That safe is full of mining certificates . . . Kiski, you said? There's nothing happening at the Kiski—it hasn't been worked . . ."

"You listen to me—it's a going thing. I saw you put those certificates in two envelopes . . ." He was forced to put both hands on the desk, to lean on them for support.

"Look, I've got to leave. Come back in a couple of weeks."

"You get those envelopes now!"

Ewing went to the safe. The big door clanked open, the inner door creaked and Woosey itched under the whole slow process, looking at the pigeon holes, the bit of red and blue carpeting like the floor of a church, the hands hovering, finally drawing out a portfolio, bringing it to the desk—the *bhisti* was so cruddy slow—opening the portfolio, drawing out the two envelopes.

His heart gave a lurch. "The envelopes are unsealed! What does that mean?"

"What are you suggesting, Woosey?"

"Anybody can take them out . . ."

"What's the stew about?" Ewing removed a bunch of certificates from one envelope, waved them at Woosey. "They're all here."

"How can I tell if everything is all there?"

Ewing was returning the certificates to the envelope. But he'd seen. "There's no certificates with my name on them!"

The lawyer was putting the envelope back into the portfolio. "I have to close up."

"My name, feller!" It was a cry for help. No one heard, no one paid any attention.

Creighton was talking to Bill Knott who was pouring out his troubles. "See, need help, eh?"

"I'm not giving you any more of my time." Ewing stood up.

Woosey grabbed his lapels as Creighton was breaking away from Knott, "Look Ewing, I have to see you!" Ewing shook off Woosey's hands. Woosey was gasping for breath.

He grabbed his bearskin cap and rushed from the office. "Wait!" Creighton called after him. "Wait for me, Cockney!" Woosey was pelting down the long narrow flight of stairs. He had to have air. He leaned against the frame building, sucking in the clear, frigid air through his mouth. His heart's racing quietened, its queer palpitations stopped.

He walked back to Bacon's and lay on his cot. The cubby-holes on either side were empty; partitions went up six feet and ended. He slept through a drunken quarrel, a rowdy card game, a fire in a straw mattress. He dreamed his name was sharp before his eyes: 51% of the certificates of the Kiski Mining and Development Company the property of the said Richard Woosey. Afterwards, he came to believe the dream was true.

At dawn he was awakened by a shot. Getting up, the only man in the flop house to rise from his bed, he went down to investigate. Bill Knott lay dead in the frozen mud outside the door, killed by his own hand. "Poor blighter, poor old bushed sod."

Kate had used all the stones Woosey had collected. The fireplace stood five feet above the floor level. If her partner returned before Christmas or even after, they would celebrate by cooking a meal in the new chimney. She was happy, happier than she'd ever been. She came back to Chisel; he appeared three days after Christmas with a great snapping and yelping of dogs.

He brought sacks of supplies, only necessities with one item of luxury, an English plum pudding. He seemed his old talky and cheerful self but she soon discovered he was a sobered man. No, he had not seen Stewart, he informed her; he had seen the lawyer and had accomplished nothing. He'd met Creighton and the usual blokes and sewer types that filled Bacon's. He told the story of Bill Knott, how he was bushed and seeing faces and hearing voices, how he'd killed himself in front of Bacon's while all the time he was sitting on top of a gold mine. Now Stewart would step in and get his hands on it, by hook or by crook, mostly crook.

Kate remembered seeing Knott's name on the claim of black jack on Chisel her first day at the lake. She had little feeling to waste for someone who'd shot himself—being bushed was one of the hazards of this game. Woosey chided her, "Poor ruddy cove, anybody can be bushed."

She wouldn't be put off by her partner's vagueness about his visit to the lawyer. "So you didn't get anywhere with the lawyer?"

"I did not." He refused to say more.

His energy seemed inexhaustible. The day after his arrival they took the dogs over to their island for their celebrations. The stones of the new fireplace were damp and cold, the fire hissed and smoked but the day was rather mild, the sun peering though lacy clouds with the north wind sweeping down twenty-five miles of open water forcing them to crouch for protection in front of the fire; Woosey had finally coaxed it into a blaze, a good cooking base for bacon and potato stew. It was their first Christmas celebration in the cabin, their first housewarming, even if the hearth was exposed to the sky, so haunted by their dreams, their leaping aspirations. They had never been more cheerful, more bursting with plans.

Even Woosey was optimistic, proclaiming "We've made it!" sensing no contradiction with his former attitude.

Over the plum pudding and the brandy he made his plans: he would go to the traplines, lay double the usual number of traps. It was night when they mushed back to the cabin on Chisel Lake. In the morning Woosey was off to the traplines.

The Alborgs were the only people in Herb Lake she trusted. They came to the Chisel Lake cabin early in the New Year to celebrate, a bitter night of fifty degrees below zero. Their five huskies set up a howling at Woosey's three, and no amount of pounding would stop them. The Alborgs brought meat pies with strange Ukranian flavourings, bread, tea, brandy and a great rarity, four oranges. Woosey and Alborg drank too freely; they drank to the Kiski Mine, to Kate's nickel and copper showings, to Alborg's enterprises.

Alborg fell into a doze; Woosey swaggered about, bragging about the wealth just outside his grasping, bombarding the sleeping man and his little smiling wife with details of the fine brick house he planned to build in The Pas. With each of her nods he added another brass bed to a new bedroom. "You have five already," Kate said, "how many bedrooms are you going to have?"

"I have a liking for brass beds."

She shut him up. He became passive and resigned.

At two in the morning, Alborg roused from his sleep and left with his little wife.

The evening had hardly been a success. Kate complained her partner's boasts were downright tiresome. But it had been a break in the relentless toil and the oranges were a great treat.

The day after, a young engineer mushed in with his dog team to inquire about the metal showings on Rice Island. He represented Ventures Limited, an exploration company belonging to Falconbridge Nickel and he wanted permission to drill. If the findings warranted, the company would take an option, drill further and within a stated time, say ten months, they would make Woosey an offer. It was to Woosey he made his bid, though Kate was present.

"How many claims do you have?"

"Miss Rice, you mean."

"I hold four claims, four for Woosey and three of them in the names of dead Indians," Kate said. It was a common practice among prospectors though a dishonest one to use dead men's names as owners of claims. The dead could not easily be traced.

"Is this right?" he asked, turning to Woosey. "You're sure the Indians are dead?"

"The claims are Miss Rice's affair, feller!"

"All right. We'll say they're dead. Remember, a hold-up on even one claim can gum up the whole works."

"You're speaking to Miss Rice, sir!" Woosey reminded him.

When he'd gone, Kate said, "Who does he think he is?"

"He thinks you're a woman—*you* tend to forget."

13

Dick Woosey set out for the traplines west of Squall Lake.

Ventures Limited had not returned. She did not know if their interest in the nickel content on Rice Island was justified or not but it seemed prudent to keep an eye on the property. It was still too cold to set up her tent; each day she snowshoed over. When the weather allowed she would work on their cabin, Alborg helping when he could take the time.

They raised the logs, fitting them into their proper hollowed-out niches at the corners. When it began to rain and rained for four days, the logs were as high as she stood, six feet from the floor.

Woosey returned at the end of the first week in May. He was thinner, his face grey and pasty, but she reasoned it might have been the pale aqueous light everywhere. Or was it worry over his gold mine, and the perfidy of Stewart that gnawed away at his mind and heart? It was more important for him to make money, make a lot of money, than it was for her. She resolved not to speak to him about it. But later she knew she was bound to; he was an intensely private lonely person, not as outgoing as herself for all his sociability. That sociability might be a shield to protect his inner self.

He brought back mostly rat which did not bring in much cash, some beaver, mink, marten and another big beautiful silver fox—silver fox was in great demand in Europe and brought fancy prices.

They were cabin-bound, forced to wait till the ice was out of Chisel and its tributary creeks. Kate chafed at the delay: she wanted to work on the cabin, keep an eye on the nickel claims. It was a hopeless kind of life she'd chosen. It had its own laws and they were not the laws of freedom as she expected but of disappointment and hopelessness, and she was compelled to learn them. The grievances were many: they were running out of money, out of supplies—they would be forced to borrow, anathema to her soul; the weather made it impossible to travel; their house on the island was far from completed (an exaggeration); they were surrounded by broken promises—there was Stewart, there was Ventures Limited, though Ventures had promised them nothing. It was too frustrating and she could no longer bear it.

Woosey's almost constant cheerfulness angered her, then finally became an insult. She quarrelled with him over the slightest excuse and refused to apologize.

"You have to be careful, life in here in the bush is not wholly a thing of energy and bravery and know-how. There are other ingredients needed—you have to keep a level head. You can't exaggerate, for the worst tragedies occur unless you keep levelheaded," he lectured her.

She snapped back, "Thus speaks the old Imperial Army."

"You forgot something."

"What did I forget?"

"You forgot, 18th Hussars, Queen Mary's Own!"

She stormed out of the cabin.

He followed her to the door. "All right—what's your alternative? Go back to your mother and father?"

With the rain running down her face she thought of the destroyed man down in Ontario. If she went back she wouldn't wither away slowly but would go insane quickly. Still, she wouldn't give in to her partner. "I could go back to teaching, you know."

But could she? Could she go back, knowing in herself she'd failed at the very thing she wanted to do?

When he left in his canoe with the bale of furs the first day after Chisel Lake and the creeks draining it were cleared of ice, she was on the wharf, waving him off. His simplicity and good humour had saved her.

Setting up her tent on the big island, she worked feverishly with Alborg's help to fit the last logs into place. She would be forced to charge the tar paper for the roofing at Herb Lake, along with half a pound of tea, half a pound of sugar, half a pound of flour. She had only a little money left from the sale of her Pine Claims.

She was alone, laying the tar paper on the roof—Mr. Alborg had gone prospecting on the Burntwood River—when Dick Woosey appeared below the cabin.

It was the first of June.

"Steady, boys! You won't believe what I got for that fox. We've got supplies and we don't owe anyone a red cent!"

She owed for tar paper, half a pound of tea, sugar and flour, she told him.

His face changed slightly, a dullness coming over his eyes. "You've got money stowed in the boot of your sleeping bag."

"For emergencies." But she came down to welcome him.

She was standing on the big island, her binoculars at her eyes, watching the stranger on the small island. He wore a grey felt hat and a mackinaw jacket and he was on his hands and knees examining the rock. His clothes, his absorption meant he was a promoter of some kind. She picked up her rifle, went to her canoe and paddled the few yards of water between the islands to a small cove. A spanking new canoe with a powerful motor was drawn up directly before the steep path. She beached farther down, walked the ledge above the water like a cat, and without a sound climbed the hill. She stood behind him.

"Who are you?"

The man spun around, getting to his feet with difficulty, "What do you want?" dusting the twigs and dirt from his knees with irritated motions. The mackinaw rippled open about his soft, heavy paunch.

He was a windy desk man, the worst kind. "What's your interest in the rock?" she asked.

"I have a right to be here."

"Who gave you that right?"

"I did."

"That does not constitute a right in my eyes." She raised her rifle.

"Wait a minute, woman!"

"No minute allowed." She aimed the sight just above the grey felt hat. "Get off this island!" and shot. The bullet sped one inch above his hat and crashed among the rock cliffs.

"You blinking fool."

She shot to the right of him.

He was sliding, scrambling down the path to his canoe, gawky and insecure, a landsman, along his canoe to the motor. Before it took, he lifted a large, puffy face, eyes darting fury.

She raised her rifle; his fist shook at her.

The motor spluttered in his inexpert hands. He was off.

Her partner returned from Herb Lake in the afternoon. He'd paid Kate's bill for the tar paper and her skimpy supplies and he now had little money left after buying expensive packaged English biscuits to serve Stewart tomorrow. He'd been told that a Mr. Stewart from The Pas was looking for him and had left a message he would be at the Chisel Lake cabin the next day.

Both of them returned to the cabin. While she washed the floor and beat the bearskin rugs, he mended the sinking wharf. In the morning she dressed in her graduation clothes; he fished for rainbow trout. He was anxious and hurt about Stewart's long delay, feeling he'd been kept waiting on purpose—but what purpose? Stewart had said it wasn't as easy as he thought to put a mine into operation but Woosey had seen no evidence of Stewart's work on the mine's behalf in the years since it was discovered.

He took out his anxiety on Kate. "You should put some powder on your face."

"Why?"

"It shines like a mirror."

"A mirror isn't so bad."

"It reflects."

"What's wrong with that?"

"Use some flour, why don't you?" To his surprise, she dipped the tips of her fingers into the sack of flour and rubbed them over her face.

"More."

She rubbed on more.

"More."

"That's enough. Now who's in trouble, now who's worried and taking it out on me just because I'm here?"

She went out to the back of the cabin to gather violets. The flowers were not yet open: next week she'd fill the cabin with their perfumed bloom.

There were voices down at the dock. Stewart had come. She waited for her partner and the promoter to settle themselves in the cabin before appearing. At the door she had a sudden seizure of fear and listened but the voices were friendly enough, Stewart's oddly familiar. Opening the door, she went inside. Stewart, whose back was turned, wheeled, his face sharp with instant recognition. She knew him as the man she'd fired at yesterday.

"This is my partner, Kate Rice."

"I don't give a damn what she is to you, she has no part in our talk."

"Miss Rice is my business partner."

"If she stays, I get out."

"All right, all right but I'd like to know what all this means?"

Stewart was going out the door. "We can talk on the dock."

"We expected you to have some grub with us."

They ate the food prepared for Stewart. Woosey's mood had changed; he could not suppress his excitement. Operations at the mine would start at once, the Kiski Mining and Development Company was a fact. They would drill forty-five feet for the gold. In three months' time he'd be a rich man, Kate a rich woman. Over the tea and biscuits he talked and talked about his mine, the spectacular amounts of gold they'd unearth, the house in The Pas he'd build, the ponies he'd raise.

"I've struck it rich! At last, I've made it!"

There must have been a time when Campbell, even the stolid Dan Mosher had talked like this, and she was persuaded, despite her canniness in dealing with promoters, that he stood a good chance of becoming a rich man, that the desires of his heart would be fulfilled, that he would build his house in The Pas—or return to England. As for herself she would keep the cabin on Woosey Island and from it set out to explore beyond the Burntwood River.

"I've met Stewart before," she told her partner.

"You have? Where?"

"On his knees examining the rocks on Rice."

"And you shot at him." His second sight was always close.

"Twice."

He sobered at once. "Stewart won't forget that . . ."

He became interested in the nickel and copper deposit on the small island for the first time. He went over the rocks on hands and knees. The whole southern part would need to be cleared of trees and overbrush; the two of them could do that. Then he would take over, shovel the dirt down to the bare rock and dynamite. The veins ran along the southwestern corner and down into the water—he understood the difficulties a company would face in drilling straight down through the rock into the water.

The work of clearing the trees was done after he returned from the Kiski. Fitting in the windows of the cabin and finishing the roof was forgotten for the time being.

The engineer from Ventures Limited returned. He ordered drilling of the deposit to begin.

PART III

1

 925 was the best of summers; a summer such as never was. Every plant, every bush and tree secreted its juices; every leaf, spear of sedge grass, every living thing glistened and grew sleek and succulent with the oil and marrow of earth's golden essences.

The rowan trees on the banks of the Grass River entering Wekusko Lake from the west bore great green clusters of fruit that would ripen and glow red; the wild cherry trees blossomed among the dark banksian pines; the violets behind the cabin on Chisel Lake carpeted the ground with blue; the marsh marigolds, wild iris, purple gentians softened the high grim shores of the big island; grass and hay grew tall and multiplied on the smaller island. The ground in front of the new cabin was yellow with buttercups, their petals smooth and shining as satin.

The air sang with the sounds of loons, ducks in great flocks, chipping sparrows, flickers, red-headed woodpeckers, nuthatches, white-throated sparrows and the warblers, the Wilson, the Yellow, the Myrtle.

Kate made notes constantly, filling three little notebooks with her observations. Two of the best Auroras she'd ever witnessed took place over Wekusko Lake.

She felt a glorious sense of freedom; she would do a bit of roofing, then take off in the Duckling, riding along the western reaches of the Grass River, using its mossy portages, gazing at its three falls, its quiet pools, once or twice camping overnight, feeding on the wild rice in the small bays, returning to the big island with sacksful to share with her partner.

The wall of black jack on Chisel was sold to a New York syndicate; there was trouble about some of the claims but that was cleared up and the sale had gone through. Drilling would begin soon. She was so content with her life that the development of ore close to their cabin meant little. Woosey had never cared about the black jack.

She finished the roof of the new cabin and they moved in. It had no windows but in these warm days it did not matter. The big island was known in Herb Lake and on all the maps now as Woosey Island.

They lived like princelings and needed few supplies from the store in the settlement. Kate gathered the wild rice along the creek sides that opened into the Grass; she picked the succulent and tart red and black currants, the blackberries under the overhanging limbs of the rowan trees, the red raspberries that hung plump and perfumed from their bushes growing everywhere in the clay-covered country on the mainland. She fished for fat whitefish, perch, trout and walleye on Wekusko Lake.

There was no time for the celebrations they had planned with the Alborgs. Woosey was busy until the long twilights at the mine site; the new mine shaft had gone up as Stewart had promised, yellow and raw in the sun. Kate ceased her lazy canoe trips along the Grass River and hurried to plant her garden, digging in the incredibly rich and shallow island soil, putting in potatoes, carrots, cabbages, onions, green peas, beans and strawberries.

The sun never ceased to shine. The bushes, reeds and fruit bounded out of the black earth. It was a very dry summer. Forest fires blossomed west of Chisel Lake, starting like an explosion of thousands of firecrackers and sweeping over the land before it was left to die out in the muskeg. Thousands of acres of prime white spruce disappeared; their old cabin on Chisel was spared but the development of the black jack was set back.

It was Woosey's summer of flowering and he brought forth great branches. Canoeing back to the island in the long twilights, the chimney of the stone fireplace on his cabin was clearly visible for miles, a testimony of his success. And he gloried in that success, in his new notoriety, striding about the mine and Herb Lake conscious he was being pointed out, one of the prospectors who had made it.

There were eight miners at the Kiski, hired to bring up the ore in spectacular amounts and of finer quality than Stewart believed was possible. Stewart had warned Woosey he was in for disappointment; he was forever warning him of something or other, always attempting to intimidate and humble him. Woosey refused to cower. He had put all his hopes on his dream: the owner of 51% of the certificates of the Kiski Mining and Development Company.

Almost overnight he was famous as the original prospector round Wekusko Lake, responsible for the settlement at Herb Lake being built, a real old-timer. Engineers, geologists from Ottawa, promoters from almost everywhere visited the cabin on Woosey Island, sat at his table, seeking advice or information or help in making maps. Ventures Limited had two engineers camping on the small island with Woosey's permission while they drilled and occasionally shared his and Kate's grub.

By midsummer money was pouring in. Stewart gave him fifteen hundred dollars, but after seeing the gold brought up and its quality, Woosey thought it should have been much more. He demanded to study the books. With great affability Stewart brought out an old scribbler from a drawer in his desk, fingered a few pages and pushed it across to Woosey. The words and figures were written in pencil, already scruffy and partially rubbed away.

Assets, notes payable, accounts payable, reserves, current liabilities. How were the figures beside the words arrived at? They meant nothing to him; he had never before read a business statement and he became lost in intricacies, combinations of words he never knew existed, such as: *net working capital, tangible net worth, gross sales less allowances, net sales less cost of sales, raw materials, labour, depreciation.*

"What does depreciation mean?" He thought he knew that word.

"Why, the mine is bringing up less and less gold, you know that."

"I don't know that—it's bringing up a pretty showing."

Gross profit less administrative profit less expenses, exploration. The gross profit semed to match the less administrative profit.

He knew and understood what exploration meant. The figure beside it read ten thousand dollars. "You'll have to explain that ten thousand for exploration! I've explored the rocks, no exploration was needed to the tune of ten thousand!"

"Look you—every mining concern worth its salt sinks money into exploration."

Loans: "What about loans?"

"Forget I put down the original capital to form this company? And I've poured out my own money to build the mine shaft, pay labour costs before any returns came in—all this plus interest. Forget all that?"

"You must have charged about 23% interest!" His eyes ached, his head swam with frustration. "All I know is, I'm not getting enough out of this operation. Blimey if I know who put you in charge—I didn't!"

"Look fool, you came to me, I didn't come to you. You borrowed the money to set up the company, offer the certificates, then it had to be run. You depended on me—it's simple."

But it wasn't so simple. He handed back the scribbler. Arguments always ended in Stewart's favour; Woosey was more confused than ever and underneath the sense of all his success was a gnawing fear. He told Kate his feelings when he returned to the cabin; he and Stewart were bound on a collision course, and the longer delayed, the worse it'd be.

"I want to have a look at that book."

"No woman could make head or tail of it."

"I'm going to look at it. In spite of being a woman, I can tell what's wrong."

She took Woosey's canoe across the lake. She did not knock at the door of the shack Stewart had set up on the Kiski property but pushed open the door and marched in, rifle raised.

"Show me that business book."

Stewart jumped to his feet. "Git out! You git out of here!"

She brought the rifle up to her eyes.

"You put that down! I'll call the Royal Northwest Mounted Police—they can deal with a nosy whore like you. I'm a law-abiding citizen . . ."

A shot pinged an inch above his head, entered the wooden board and made a neat round hole.

He rushed towards her, face purpled, a scream between his teeth, "Git! Go on git!"

The door slammed behind her. No one had ever before said "git" to her. The words rang in her ears, drowning out the comforting put put putaput of the little motor.

She did not tell her partner that she'd shot at Stewart again. She would not need to tell him; he would know.

Ventures Limited were now prepared to do business. The nickel and copper had been assayed; the ore was found to be mostly nickel of a very high grade but there was the question of the amount that would make it worthwhile to mine. However, they would take an option and at the end of six months, or sooner, they would either make an offer, or back off. They paid Woosey a thousand dollars for the option.

Kate was very angry about their attitude. The two engineers had been friendly when they took their meals in the cabin, openly showing their admiration for her, but when she complained that all business relating to the nickel must be conducted through her, they were astounded.

The elder, a man named Lindsey, said, "But Miss Rice—you're a woman and we can't do business with a woman."

"Why not?"

"You don't know anything about business."

"Then you have no business with that mine!" She leapt to her feet. "You drop the option and go back to your company. Tell them a woman refuses to bargain with them."

"Miss Rice, it'd be useless to tell them."

She knew he was right and turned to her partner. "You see this thing through. Every detail must be in writing and signed by you and me. No gentlemen's agreement!" She left the room, furiously angry.

Woosey handed over the money afterwards. She went off to The Pas and spent the entire amount, recklessly shelving all her old caution. She bought china, a china cabinet to hold the hundred-piece set, a telescope, another pair of binoculars, half a dozen pairs of moccasins, a black light for studying fluorescent metals, and a mattress for her partner's bed. Remembering the Trollope book she'd seen at George Martin's camp, she ordered books with leather covers and a book case to hold them.

She was returning with the Duckling low in the water, the heavy purchases being sent by the railway to Mile 82. Forgetful of her recent frustration, Kate paddled idly, enjoying the fine banksian pines on the riverside with the red currant bushes, like numerous offspring, clinging for safety under the mothering boughs. She was only half aware of the pull of the Grass River along the bottom of her canoe, the increasing swiftness of its flow to Wekusko Lake and the sound of white water ahead. Dreamily her canoe reached the start of the first portage on the way back, the slightly tramped earth of the landing place she and Woosey used (they were almost the only people who did use the Grass route to The Pas); she realized that she didn't give a hang for her purchases, that this was her moment—she was completely alive now, without worry, almost without heartbeat. Her body, her whole being was floating. In that languid second it was too late. The Duckling poised on the edge of the ten-foot drop. "Don't you try those bloody falls!" Woosey had warned.

"Why not?" she called out in exultation, rejoicing in her responses, the quickened nerves, the sharpened muscles. The canoe dived, smothered with spray and foam.

There was a wrenching, tearing sound. The Duckling's bow had struck a rock and began to take water, a lot of water, fast. If she didn't jump, it would go down; she jumped. The river funnelling between high banks was viciously strong and carried her along as though she was a bit of flotsam. The lightened Duckling ran up a rock in the center of the current and hung teetering back and forth in the waves. Twice she sucked water into her lungs, and managed to get her head out. Unable to swim, both arms flailed the air to grab a stone, a half submerged tree, anything. One hand struck a slippery slime-covered rock and clung, her trunk and legs jerking forward with the strength of the river's flow. She was trying to get her other hand to the rock but her grasp was loosening. She clutched with desperation, gathering all her strength to place her other hand onto the rock, her breath tearing out of her lungs, her heart bursting. Now she needed strength to throw herself over the rock, swim to the bank.

When she reached the portage on top she was frightened, each breath requiring a struggle, each beat of her heart striking at her chest as though it would fly out of its nest of arteries and muscles; she had escaped death by seconds. She lowered herself onto the mossy portage, legs angled, and lay an hour perhaps, her eyes tight shut until gradually the heartbeats softened. The sense of strain in her body lingered, a subconscious memory, she who'd never been bothered by aches or pains or physical stresses. She did not try to get up.

It was a portage of trees and leafy green shade with little sun and she was becoming chilled. She knew she must get up, light a fire and get out of her clothes. The Duckling would have slipped off the rock, taking with it all her supplies; she felt for the matches she always kept in a small bottle in the upper pocket of her mackinaw; it was gone. She shivered but did not try to get up.

A tremor on the ground alerted her that someone was coming along the portage, and, she could tell by the heaviness of the earth murmurs, carrying a loaded pack sack. She was trying to rise to her feet, trying to control her shaky leg muscles when she heard, "Steady, boys! Remember the 18th has the Maxim gun and the Pathans have not!

Remember the unhealthy state of the Tin Camp at Ladysmith, all that sickness—we marched to the Mooi River in March '99—we camped in high ground this time overlooking the railway . . ."

"You!" She sank back on the ground. She didn't ask how he knew where to find her. He knew.

"Thought you'd be lying somewhere near the falls on the third portage from Wekusko, it's bloody well more than ten feet, that drop." His body was hung with sleeping bags, a blanket, canvas packsack; his belt held a tin tea pail, a fry pan, a pick, an axe. He was removing his burden. "Get out of those wet clothes, it's chilly here—you'll catch pneumonia." He unrolled the blanket, felt it for warmth, "It'll do. Roll into that and get into the sleeping bag. I'll get a fire blazing."

"How did you know I'd need a blanket?"

"Always carry one, for emergencies, you know."

It wasn't true. He'd known she'd been thrown into the water, had known she'd taken on the falls.

"Move—or I'll strip you."

She tottered when she rose and he grabbed her. She protested, "I'm quite strong."

"I'm well aware of it."

She leaned against a poplar and peeled the half-wet clothes off her body. After, she lay in the sleeping bag, wrapped in the blanket.

He was crossing sticks carefully, starting the fire, hanging out her clothes to dry, putting the tin pail of water almost on top of the flames, throwing fistfuls of tea into the water. All his movements were quick and sure, bred of a thousand campfires.

"It's wonderful!"

At the unaccustomed praise he turned to her, "What's on your mind?"

Knowing this man had come when she needed someone, had taken control of her life for an hour or so, gave her a sense of complete renewal. She watched him build the fire, pouring the scalding tea into the tin cup, reaching down, and she, stretching out her hand to receive it, "Watch out, it's ruddy hot!" Ordinary words, ordinary actions but now lifted by the extraordinary acuteness of her senses into pure sensual pleasure.

"You're too good." It wasn't at all what she wanted to say. She wanted to identify what was undefinable for her. Another woman, Margaret for instance, would have done it easily, naturally, but to put into exact words this sensual feeling released into her body was too big a hurdle for her to take.

"Oh forget it."

She laughed, remembering her abrasiveness in another context long ago at Crowduck Bay. She didn't know whether he'd understood her inept words and in order to cover up for her, he had made her laugh. He possessed a delicacy that was almost beyond her ken.

He put the hare stew at the edge of the fire and went in search of her canoe. He was gone a long time, so long she began to fuss and fret;

something had happened to him. He came finally, head buried between the gunwales, oozing water to his waist.

"She was stuck against a fallen tree . . . has two gashes . . . couldn't find your pack sack."

"Where did you leave your canoe?"

"At the first portage."

He put the stew in the center of the red ashes and reheated the water for tea. She noticed something she'd never observed before—he used a spoon rather than his finger to mix the lard and flour, baking powder and water for bannock. He was too much of a gentleman for the prospectors and promoters he lived amongst, hard men like Mosher, Campbell and Stewart—Creighton was more the gentlemanly type. The nice ones, like Charlie Krug, always died.

"What are you thinking?"

She didn't want him to know. "Your intuition ought to tell you."

"Come off it, I'm no cruddy mind reader."

"All right, I'll tell you—you're too much of a gentleman for this kind of life."

"But I chose it."

"You also chose me."

"Blimey, so I did."

Before he dished up the grub, he disappeared. Bringing back a spray of red currants, he handed it to her.

"Thank you." She ran her fingers dreamily among the translucent circles of red as though he'd handed her a gift, something valuable and lavish. It made up for the casualness of his last remrk.

It was a long blue evening with the sound of white water, the soft drift of pine boughs, the hiss of fire, her partner extended full length at her side (they'd always taken opposite sides of the fire). His head was held in one arm, the bronzy shadows capricious and fitful over his face, his familiar black shirt and tan galluses, his closed eyes and his silence. He looked physically powerful, thick wristed with a strong short neck, but there was something feminine about his intuition. Dreamily, she stroked the red clusters of berries and green leaves.

The time came when he usually stirred, and rising to make a fresh pail of tea would begin to tell as if he must keep forever green the adventures of an old cavalry man in Afghanistan. She had been the restless receiver, either indifferent or outright unwilling; now she waited, wanting him to rise, to make fresh tea, to begin his tale of old, far-off events. It was another of those moments of perfection that come unsought and rare in the north. He remained silent as if he had closed her out from the slogging soldiers of the Raj among their alien Himalayan passes.

"Talk to me. Tell me . . well, tell me about your wife."

He opened his eyes. "May? You want to know about May?" He gazed at the fire, the shadows of pines, as though this place, this moment was the last place, the last moment to tell about May.

"Yes May, I want to know more about her."

"May lived in the village near my home in a cottage called Rose Cottage. She always did take to roses scrambling over a cottage front, 'dresses it up,' she used to say. Her mum worked as a countess' lady's maid and she'd read far too many romantic tales of milords falling in love with an upstairs girl, or some such thing. My mum employed her from time to time when we had hunt guests. Mum was a romantic, too but in quite a different way: she read romantic poetry—Keats, Shelley, the Frenchmen, Lamartine, the whole lot. She used to call May's home "Rosedene." May must have set her eyes early on me when they should have been bolted on some groom, then she could have made entry into a mansion through the back door where she rightly belonged. She wrote me in India and S.A., many little stiff and self-conscious letters and I so anxious and lonesome for my mum that I read and answered them eagerly. It was May who told me of mum's illness and later, death. Pater wrote me only once, to announce her death and time of funeral.

"I can't remember how May got round me because I don't want to. When I came back on leave from India she and I got married and this rigid girl of the lower classes, very knowledgeable on all the arts of enticement (from romantic novels, I suppose), became pregnant. She refused to return to S.A. when my stint came up. I was an innocent, I can tell you. I was too young. Anyway, out of the Army I worked for a sporting gentleman who had a string of polo ponies and I hated it. Always, 'Yes sir, no sir, Yes your son is making excellent progress, sir, he'll make his mark on the polo field, sir.' At this time, we lived in a cottage. I hated that too, was too accustomed to the big draughty rooms of our mansion. The cottage was called Rosedene. How I hated that name! I was never and never would be the gentleman May wanted."

He stood with one swift movement from his recumbent position. "That's enough of May."

He was outlined in a ray of sun, still golden, sifting through the pine boughs and the greening twilight. He drew a long unsteady breath as though he could not bear to talk about his married life. "I'm here, that's all."

"What about the scar then, how did you get it?"

He ran his hand along his left cheek where the scar began its gradual ascent to his hairline. "Hand-to-hand combat with a Pathan tribesman," was all he would say.

After her rescue on the portage of the Grass, she believed their day to day life together had reached some turning point. Certain subtle changes did occur; she listened when he told his stories—only occasionally now of people, places, events and tribes, of inaccessible peaks of the Himalayas, nonetheless scaled by the 18th Hussars, of battles too dim to reach history books, all mingling with the crackle of auroras and the hiss of campfires in the infinite twilights of the subarctic nights.

But no big changes occurred immediately. As he'd always been proud, he was proud now to introduce his guests to her, and there were plenty of them, men from The Pas, Winnipeg, even Ottawa. He boasted about her, her mining exploits, her notebooks full of information on the aurora borealis, the vegetation of the country, the migration of birds. He spent lavishly as he'd always done for those who shared their table. And he was always full of talk, full of poetry:

> They say while we have any sun
> We ought to make our hay
> And India has so hot a one,
> I'm going to Bombay.

His tales were always colourful: "The Pathans were a supple, savage lot. There were one hundred and twenty miles of Himalayas between us as we debouched from the railroad at Nowshera. It took us twenty-six days to reach them—we crossed two great mountain ranges, one of them twelve thousand feet high where we could find no way except a single unused track where no horse or camel had ever trod. There was sheet ice and snowdrifts and we had only our army greatcoats for warmth. The next year we were at the Mooi River in South Africa and the worst thunderstorm we'd ever known burst over our camp. We were just watering the horses—they stampeded and the camp was nearly levelled to the ground. After a stint in Natal we were ordered to Ladysmith, a chip from Dante's Inferno . . ."

"I don't think the gentlemen are interested."

"We had terrible casualties at a place called Adelaide Farm; those not killed, wounded, or missing were made prisoner. I was one of the few who escaped, but three thousand of the enemy were out on the Newcastle Road looking for us.

> We always are ready;
> Steady, boys, steady!

"Your guests!"

> Why, don't you know me by my scars?
> I'm Soldier Dick, come back from the wars.

"This soldier Dick has looked into the eyes of Mr. Kruger."

While the guests listened politely to Dick Woosey, they were plainly fascinated by Kate though except for objections to her partner's talk she remained aloof, a small smile tucked into one corner of her mouth. They regarded her as a beauty but so unlike the women in their lives she seemed to be a new breed of female, even a new sex and they were slightly wary of her.

After they had gone she scolded him for the lavishness of his table fare. She chided him for talking too much about her and about his old Hussars. "I don't mind, I want to hear them but I'm sure those men don't."

"You ruddy well do mind, and I'm trying hard to stop."

"I say again, don't stop because of me."

"By the Lord Harry, you've always said exactly what you meant. I tell you I'm trying to stop and there'll come a day when I've forgotten about my old comrades and the battles we fought." This would never happen and he knew it. And what was just as important, she did too.

She was sitting outside the cabin, Woosey in what had now become his favourite pose, stretched out beside her, head held in his hand.

He'd built a small fire to brew their tea; the grey smudge rose frothily into the air, warding off the few black flies and 'no-see-'ems' that braved the island (it was tolerably free of them). She asked what she'd wanted to know since the incident on the Grass River. "Tell me about your life before you went to India, your mother and father."

"You asking me?"

"Would anyone else?"

"Not a cruddy one."

He finished his tea, his face turned from her, and gazed out across the lake. He took so long she thought he'd refused.

"My father was a younger son of a younger son, we went like that right down the line, we never had any money and lived in some relative's forty room house near Liverpool, as ugly a place as you'd find; the rooms had lofty ceilings and there was a great deal of light-coloured fumed oak woodwork, but I loved it, loved its bigness, even its ugliness. Pater never worked, spent all the money he had on horses, and he had some nailing good hunters, I'll say that for him, and spent all his time riding to hounds or at some point-to-point. My mum rode to hounds too, rode sidesaddle. I can see her just before riding off, gazing down at me, a little duffer, and through that veil around her bowler, I saw tears. She didn't want to leave me but she was a proper lady and knew what was expected of her. They were accepted, poor as they were, as County. The Vicar dined with us," he chuckled, "that's proof."

It was so at variance with his life here, the lake, the rough but snug cabin behind him, the little fire with his tin pail of tea sitting on the ashes, the hushed blue twilight, the whole wide universe expanding around him, free and beauteous and dangerous, a place where Dan Mosher's maxim, *Best shoot to kill*! was a postulate. She wanted to stop him, these beginnings of his were too painful for him; she could understand why he talked so much about India and South Africa and his army life there—it had been different from his upbringing, from May and her snobbishness, from everything he'd known. In a way it was like his existence here, the danger and the adventure.

"I never had any education, never attended one of the schools for gentlemen's children, or had a governess. We had no money, it always came down to that, you see. My mum taught me reading and writing, a bit of geography and history, hardly any arithmetic—she couldn't subtract and divide and that's why I find it so difficult, but she never had much time. She accompanied my pater to the meets but somehow she managed to teach me. We had jolly times together, she used to kiss me a lot, imagine a teacher kissing her pupil, and I loved it. I loved it, you see. I was twelve when I knew I'd have to join the Army as soon as they'd take me. I joined up as band-rat at fifteen with the Hussars; we trained at Aldershot. At sixteen, the Old Sweats left for India. The pater was off at a point-to-point in a neighbouring county, he never said goodbye but my poor mater . . ."

"Why do you call her poor?"

"She wasn't happy and she was a naturally happy, jolly woman. She came to see me off at Portsmouth, her face lonely and scared as I watched, growing smaller and smaller until it was only a blot as the vessel eased away from the quay. Oh, I'll never forget that day, it's engraved on my mind forever, bands playing, flags snapping briskly in the breeze, me in my Pompey, that's the pith helmet, my new uniform and her face growing smaller and smaller. I was ready to cry, I rubbed my face on the sleeve of my smart new uniform and a Sarn shouted, 'Steady there, boy!' pushing his red, leathery face into mine.

"I never saw her again; knew I wouldn't, that's why I was so close to weeping. She died of typhoid, drinking bad water from a well at some meet."

It must have been the beginning of his strange power of intuition. "And your father, what happened to him?"

"Still alive when I came to Canada, still living in that big draughty mansion, full of the smell of dust and with all his ribbons and trophies decorating every mantel, and cursing roundly because his rickety bones made it hard for him to mount the slippery saddle of some expensive chestnut gelding, seventeen hands tall. I never liked him but I couldn't hate him. He was caught in a system and took advantage of it; my mater was a victim. May used to like to visit the house after mater's death because her father-in-law was gentry. She'll be there now with my boy."

Oh yes, May. But she was not important to him, never had been. Kate was a little surprised at her feeling of relief.

He got up. "That's enough." He wandered off to the far side of the island.

She waited for his return; when he did not come she got out of the chair and walked over. He was standing at the edge of the cliff, looking towards Herb Lake and his gold mine.

"What are you thinking about?"

He turned as though it was a strange question for her to ask.

"Are you thinking about your son, turned into a proper little gentleman and riding to hounds, and perhaps already a good cavalry officer—or do they have cavalry units anymore?"

"I've put all that behind me." His tone was impersonal as if his thoughts couldn't possibly concern her. "Do you really want to know what was passing through my mind?"

"I wouldn't have asked if I didn't."

"I was thinking about the gold mine and how I'll have money, plenty of it, one of these days."

"Don't you think it should be watched day and night?"

"No one can jump the claims now."

She recalled again Dan Mosher's warning. "You don't know who's snooping about. Stewart may be bringing in some of his pals to take a look . . ."

"What can he do?" He moved away. "And yet, I don't feel right about the mine."

He went back to the cabin.

She followed along, picking up the binoculars beside her chair.

"Good night," he called.

"Good night."

It was no more or less than their usual parting but tonight it sounded flat and stale. Walking over to the path leading down to the water's edge, she lifted the binoculars toward the hay and rice smothered mouth of the Grass River and brought them down again. She wasn't interested in topography.

Certain phrases would not leave her. *She used to kiss me a lot . . . her face was lonely and scared . . . I was ready to cry . . . we had no money, it always came down to that . . . I was thinking about the gold mine and how I'll have money, plenty . . .*

Until the Grass River incident she had always regarded the speaker of these words as someone to whom she gave about as much attention as a temporary camp, a shelter for the night in time of need, a kind of non-person, and never as a man with needs and feelings, a man of fires well banked, of warmth, of sufferings. The sense of pure sensuality that had swept over her body that evening on the river alerted her to a new awareness of herself and her relationship to him. Never could their life together be the same. Whether he was aware of the change she did not know. He'd given no sign.

A streamer of white light flashed across the northern perimeter of the sky and was suddenly blotted out as by a huge hand; now the hand played with a sprinkler, dazzling heaven with blue stringers of ice.

She turned her back and moved to the cabin. His need for money came first in his life.

Ore came out of the Kiski in golden nuggets. When he strode about the Herb Lake settlement, talking to his guests, it was always there, the homage given a man who could pull himself up by his own boot straps and grow rich, and make all his associates rich, too.

2

"I want some movement on this mine!"

"Stick to your part of the business, Woosey, and stop giving advice— you're making a plain ass of yourself."

"That's debatable."

"Look, once and for all, I don't give a damn about your complaints about the way I'm running the mine. Gold isn't so damn important, it's copper and nickel that count since the war."

"What does that mean?"

"It means exactly what you think it means."

After one of these encounters with Stewart he'd get into his canoe and make for Herb Lake, a mile away. He'd end up in the saloon; the saloonkeeper knew him now and always welcomed him. He would order a brandy; his ego would be upheld by the friendliness and the drinks. Afterwards, he would march into the store to the left of the wharf, buy English biscuits, tobacco, jellies, custards; all the most expensive items.

He was never completely taken in by his success in spite of his seemingly arrogant reaction to it; some part of him remained ever thoughtful, another self looking on in judgment. One night after his last cup of tea he told Kate, "I think I'm overdoing it."

"If you are asking me and I don't think you are, I'd say plainly, yes."

The summer of great content ended brutally. On August 26, the first of many killer frosts took place.

The birds, the ducks and geese, the small feathered songsters had mysteriously disappeared—the lake was not on any of the great flyways south—and only a lonely quack-quack sounded in the cove at the foot of the big island's cliffs. The marsh marigolds, the iris, the purple gentians raised blackened stalks above the earth; the vines of Kate's beans hung twisted and crisped. She was able to retrieve one large cabbage as curled and beautiful as an enormous green rose from her ruined garden. She worked all that day, August 26th digging out the potatoes, the carrots, the onions. The strawberry bed had shrivelled into dark brown powder. The sky above her turned as black and blue as a bruise with a line of sour yellow above the spruce on the mainland. Below the cliffs, the lake heaved like an ocean. Coming inside, she lit the fireplace for the first time since last May.

By the end of August, Woosey and Stewart were thoroughly tired of one another. Stewart never came to the cabin on Woosey Island; if he wanted to talk over current running problems of the mine he summoned Woosey to the hut he'd built and used as an office halfway between the Rex and the Kiski mine sites. It made Woosey angry to be ordered like some lackey—he was the owner of the Kiski, wasn't he?

When a miner, an Indian, brought a message to the tent Woosey used for an office this first day of frost he shouted, "What does the bloody cove want?" He stormed into Stewart's hut and slammed the door behind him.

The one room was walled with raw wood, roughly thrown together, not yet mellowed and smoothed by time. One large Hudson Bay calendar, opened to June, had been nailed to the boards. Stewart sat at a new varnished desk. His white soft face—it never tanned no matter how long exposed to the sun—winced as the door banged but the eyes did not lift from the page.

Woosey was kept standing in front of the desk, like an ordinary foot soldier before his commanding officer. It reminded him of that terrible afternoon with the Strathcona's as he waited for the medical officer, the stench of ragweed in his nostrils. "I say, what do you want with me? I should be ordering you!"

"Yes?"

He always had something unpleasant up his sleeve. "What is it now?"

Stewart smiled. "I only want to remind you of certain facts."

"What are *your* facts?"

"Facts that concern the future of the company: it's too far from a railway; machinery's too costly to get the gold out; the mine is too inaccessible."

"Most mines are not situated in cities or even near them, don't you know that?"

"Another thing, we can't get good men to work up here."

"I'll hire Indians. There's a lot of them north of The Pas, they don't belong to any particular bands."

"What I'm getting at is, no great expansion can take place."

"What of it? We do the best we can." The cove was holding something back.

"Sure we do the best we can, but I just don't know how much there is left, whether it warrants . . ."

"Why, the finds have been spectacular!"

"There's nothing yet to complain about, but remember the Rex has over-extended itself and will close down."

"Close down? The Rex close down?"

"As manager I always doubted there was that much gold."

Woosey was so disturbed about the news he was speechless. He knew that Stewart had sprung the surprise to produce the effect it had.

"Now the Laguna Mine . . ."

"What about the Laguna?"

". . . has been salted and there's to be an investigation."

"What's going on here?" Had the gold been stolen from the Kiski and then added to the Laguna findings in order to raise the stock price, he wondered. It would be an easy matter for some miner to steal the gold, put it into his hat and bring it up.

"You think about all this."

Woosey slammed the door on his way out, his mind swirling with suspicion and, worse, more fear.

Back at the cabin, Kate made tea for him.

"I'm sick and tired of Stewart. He's giving notice about something. It has to do with gold. I think he's pulling out of it, has his eye on copper and nickel. Watch out for our nickel property."

They both were aware of the value of the claims; Kate had always known what the rusty weathering schist meant. Ventures Limited would be returning and would give an offer or ask how much was wanted for the property. They must have an answer, be ready to accept or reject.

Each night over their cups of tea they would discuss the amount they would ask, until it became a kind of game with them. Kate said they should ask a very high price, then there'd be leeway to manoeuver.

"One million dollars!" Woosey surprised himself; it was an unheard of sum since a thousand meant riches.

It was inconceivable. What could they do with a million, what could anyone? "Smaller," she said.

"One hundred thousand."

"Try again."

"Two hundred and fifty."

"Try the top price again."

"One million."

Such a clear cool sound. She had an inspiration. "Did you ever hear how much Campbell got for his share of the Rex?"

"It was rumoured—but you can't tell the truth of it—seven hundred thousand and his partners the same. More likely seventy each."

Kate, remembering the money he spent in Toronto, believed the larger amount.

"I don't think either of us knows the difference between a hundred thousand and a million, that's the cruddy truth of it."

It was not quite freeze-up. The lake was not yet frozen over although in its sheltered bays and creek mouths a thin layer of ice had formed. The small lakes on the mainland were frozen but the ice was not thickened.

She was hard at work setting her traplines west of Squall Lake; she took a new route, following a creek as it twisted its way north and west. The first night was sleepless, spent in the old Indian trap cabin, lying in her sleeping bag on the hard clay floor; for some reason her mind kept returning to her father, not the destroyed man but the beautiful silken personality of her childhood. Her ears pounding with the howls of the wolves, she began to wonder if her imagination was not playing tricks— had he ever been the genteel and cultivated person she had pictured to herself? Perhaps she would never know, and it saddened her.

The wolves were becoming bolder and moving in closer each night. One night they were especially troublesome, their cries more eerie and chilling. Working her way out of her sleeping bag, she tore open the door. There was the classic picture of the northern night; four animal shapes, outlined in brilliant moonlight, their heads raised. She shot one through the mouth, another in the hind leg; as it turned she shot again and it fell.

When the others raced off she dragged the first two back to the cabin.

She continued to lengthen her traplines to the north and west. She was aware that she was working up towards the possible source of the Burntwood River. Ever since her doomed visit she had dreamed of finding its source, of exploring the frontiers beyond. There was something about the Burntwood that brought back her sense of power and freedom. According to Mr. Alborg, its shores had been for eons of time a favourite trapping ground for the bush Crees as far away as Norway House, far to the east.

One morning she left at daybreak to make a run for its source. It was overcast; she followed the creek where she'd laid her traps. Meandering through a forest of tall frozen reeds whose roots were buried in snow, the creek fed into a small lake, slanting north and west and she was alert for the stream that led out of the lake. She'd raced the dogs for two hours and they'd begun to loll, tongues hanging out, their whiskers covered with ice. At an easier pace she ran them along the stream bed as it twisted and turned, searching for an opening, the entrance into another lake. She'd decided to stop for a rest, build a fire, make some tea. For the lead dog she'd brought some cake. A female she'd named June, she seemed always to be smiling and Kate had discovered she loved cake. The two others turned their long noses away in disdain.

Suddenly, the trees parted from their closely defended banks of the stream, drew back until they were part of the horizon. She was entering the wide expanse of a lake of considerable size. It could be the source of the Burntwood. But something more exciting made her whip on the dogs. Ahead of them the snow was furrowed with snowshoe tracks, sharp tracks, made by new snowshoes, the tracks of white men, two white men.

They had come this far out of the north and after reconnoitering and consultation had turned and gone back. Who were they? What were they doing? She followed their tracks; they led finally to an old Indian trap cabin, and then out again into the horizon.

She went inside. Boxes, some of them torn open with cans of stew and jam spilling out, were lying next to two rough bunks along the walls over which new and expensive down sleeping bags had been thrown. She was reaching for two cans of beef stew when a notebook on top of a carton fell to the floor. Opening it, she leafed through the pages. No uneducated prospector had made the notes, they'd been done by a geologist with a canny and knowing eye as to rocks and to possible ore sites. The Burntwood River was being investigated.

She sat down on a box and read. One name and one company kept appearing; Canada Nickel, then initials, D.S., then Dow. A queer first name if it was a first name? As she was closing the notebook, a full name: Dow Stewart. What did this Dow Stewart have to do with Canada Nickel?

It was becoming dark in the cabin. Jumping off the box, she grabbed two cans of beef stew, two tins of raspberry jam and ran out to the dogs.

For a time it was easy to follow her own trail but the short day glimmered to a close, a faint moon came out above the black army of spruce and it was difficult to see. She was apprehensive that she'd lost her tracks and had missed her way. The black army of spruce came together again and she mushed along a creek but whether it was the right creek she did not know. She ran along beside the toboggan, talking to the dogs and wondering if she should stop, build a temporary camp among the shelter of trees, but the dogs after their rest at the geologists' cabin seemed keen and fresh; she would keep going and stop later. The sled slid jerkily among a forest of stiff reeds and she knew where she was. She'd reached the trap cabin where she was camping.

Her run to the source of the Burntwood cost her dearly: on the day she'd gone, one silver fox, one ermine, and one marten from her traps had been eaten by wolves. She stayed close to the cabin and her traplines now; her existence became a vigil of visiting the traps, picking up the animals, skinning them, laying poison, shooting wolves and eating lonely meals. Each night she put her sleeping bag on the ground sheet close to the fire and gave herself up to a host of disturbing thoughts.

The real discovery of her visit to the Burntwood's source was something else. The trapline, hers and her partner's, was being threatened and ultimately would be destroyed. Canada Nickel and a man named Dow Stewart would see to that.

The Burntwood would have mine shafts and smelters along its desolate shores, just as Chisel Lake would have its mine and smelter. She could prepare herself to move on, go far beyond the Burntwood, but what of her partner? The country of Cook and File, Chisel and Squall and Wekusko was his country; without a shadow of a doubt he would refuse to move. He was an Englishman, a stubborn British Regular Army man and he would think giving up was a sign of weakness, of yielding to the enemy, though once after his service with the Strathcona's he'd almost given up—but that was a peculiar thing, something she'd never understood. She would be forced to make a choice: stay with him or make a move into the unknown, alone.

Their partnership had become so vital to both of them, so durable, she could not conceive of breaking it. There was also something else, something she would be forced to face. Sleepless in her bag, wolves howling on the ridge above the cabin, she faced the question squarely: did she actually love this man who was her partner, this person she'd barely acknowledged in her innermost being, or did she not?

She could not answer the simple question. She could not.

One week after the Burntwood trip, unhappy and exhausted, she returned to the island. Her partner was full of good cheer and had prepared a big fish stew to welcome her. "How did you know I'd be back?" A useless question.

"How'd it go?"

"It didn't."

"Had a feeling . . ."

"Tell me—what is Stewart's first name?"

"His first name . . . blowed if I remember. Why?"

In the end it wouldn't make much difference what his first name was, the Burntwood was threatened.

Two weeks before Christmas, Stewart handed Woosey a thousand dollars in cash. Being handed money that came from *his* gold mine, which he had uncovered with his own hands and strength, enraged him.

"Who the bloody hell do you think you are—I should be settling my own accounts, withdrawing my own money, not getting it handed to me like some trooper of the line!" He demanded to see the books.

Assets, current liabilities, net working capital. It seemed in certain instances such as *current liabilities* and *depreciation* the figures were much larger and in others, such as *raw materials* and *assets,* much smaller than the figures he'd seen before. The amount for exploration had doubled. Instead of ten thousand it was twenty.

"You've doubled the exploration amount, why?"

"Look, you fool—you aren't capable of running anything, let alone a mine."

He was being brow-beaten into submission. He could not tell Kate; it would make him look a bloody fool as Stewart had said.

But Kate had reached certain conclusions of her own. She'd become so sensitive (she who had paid small heed to the feelings of others) to any change in her partner she could divine the cause with exactitude. *We had no money, it always came down to that.* Money meant his gold mine, money meant Stewart and his lawyer.

She was certain there never had been a gentlemen's agreement between the three of them; on her partner's part yes, but not on Stewart's or his lackey's, the lawyer. She knew there must be stock certificates and they must be in envelopes or folders; Stewart must have control over those envelopes by having control over the lawyer. The lawyer was a mere cat's paw in this game, hoping to gain some profit, enough to quit with a tidy sum and set up a respectable law practice in Winnipeg, or heaven forbid, Ottawa.

She had no expertise in business, could only guess and surmise. The lawyer was a crook.

One of these days she was going out to see him.

Christmas 1925 came; the Alborgs spent it with them. They brought meat pies, white bread, butter, oranges, blueberry jam; Mrs. Alborg had been busy during the summer gathering berries shimmering blue and warm from the hills and ridges beyond the settlement. Woosey and Kate supplied the fish and bacon stew, an English plum pudding and brandy. It was bitterly cold with no sun, the wind never letting up its gale-force sweep down the lake. But the cabin was hot and snug, the walls having been chinked with cement during the summer and the windows fitted in.

Mr. Alborg was quieter than usual. He spoke of his commercial fishing, which was not going well; Herb Lake was no longer a thriving community; men were slipping away to greener fields and the few remaining at the Kiski did their own fishing. Mrs. Alborg still spoke little English and was content to let her husband do the talking. When they were eating their oranges, Kate asked Mr. Alborg if he knew anything about a Canada Nickel Company. He did.

"Coupla man come, say from Canad' Nickel, say big company, everythin' big." He spread his hands wide, his amazing blue eyes snapping and gold gleaming in his mouth. "Say wanna buy my claims on Burntwood, say claims too far north, too far everythin', ver' smart man, good talker, say never git to mine, too far, too far ship out nickel, whole damn thing too far—we give you fifteen hundr'."

"If everything is so far, why were they so anxious to buy?" Kate asked.

"That talk sounds familiar," Woosey said. "Don't you sell."

Alborg made a clicking sound with his hands as though golden shekels were falling from them. "Short of dollar . . ."

Woosey nodded. He was unusually sober for a Christmas celebration.

When it came time for the Alborgs to leave, little Mrs. Alborg was blown off the steps of the cabin into the snow, and so they stayed the night with Kate and Woosey.

Christmas was depressing this year.

3

John Ewing raised his hand to the left side of his face, his fingers gently massaging his jaw bone. The gnawing pain of his teeth hurt and he was not a man who could stand pain with grace.

"Take your hand away, I can't see your face," Stewart ordered. He was testy.

"Look, stop nagging me, will you?" He kept his hand on his jaw.

"You make me nervous, always having teeth problems."

"You, nervous!"

"Why in heaven's name don't you have them all out, once and for all? I did and I was younger than you."

"One of these days . . ." His eyes were leaden. He had a feeling he was in water beyond his depth and was drowning. He'd thought himself to be a cagey fellow but Stewart was always one length ahead of him. The way he'd flung that fur-lined coat open he could tell new and big things were in the offing, big for Stewart. Where was it all leading to—for him?

Stewart sat by the door where he usually plunked himself down, his coat spread open, showing an ornate gold watch chain looping over his paunch, a diamond tie pin stuck in his expensive dotted tie. He didn't buy that tie in The Pas; the only kind you could buy here were already knotted in a four-in-hand and attached to a celluloid collar.

"What's in it for me?" Ewing knew that to catch up with Stewart you had to be as cunning as a fox. He had too many ways of manoeuvering.

"Big things." For the first time Stewart smiled, pushed back the otter hat and relaxed his body.

So he had been edgy too. "Yeah, let me be the judge of that." Ewing dropped his hand from his jaw.

"I plan to sell the whole caboodle of gold property on Wekusko—there's more money in nickel."

"You don't own the Rex, you only manage it, remember?"

"Sure. I wrote the London people last summer that I had new and more extensive samplings taken from the Rex and the results were as I thought; there just was not enough gold down there to pay the cost of drilling and bringing the ore out, let alone the cost of transportation."

"Why, forty-five ounces a day came out of that mine—you told me so, yourself."

"The veins were shallow, they were running out and the lack of regular railway service didn't help, either. I wrote them in London that I'd been in touch with Thomas Bird, M.P. for Nelson riding about getting better service, trying to press for some action and I was told it'd be ten years before the Feds got round to providing regular and daily service. I passed that on to them in London."

"Stick to the subject. You had fifteen men this summer mining the Rex—you must have thought it paid."

"I had to transfer them from the Rex, put some on the Kiski—the rest are gone."

"Gone?" Everything was already accomplished. It was like sticking your finger into a can of worms.

"The London outfit want to sell. I knew they would. Just got their letter."

"Just a minute—how did you get control of the Rex?"

"Listen, will you? You don't listen, that's one of your problems. The London people decided it'd be a good idea to get out. They want to sell. I knew they'd want to sell."

"How did you know?"

"Know-how, Ewing."

"Yes?"

"I bought cheap. Sometimes you just have to wait, just sit on your ass and wait, make the other fellow sweat a bit and then the plum will fall—it's simple."

"Not so simple." Some other lawyer had been conned in on this. Ewing felt self-pity. He'd given up his Selkirk practice and was in here, the world's most godforsaken place, and it looked like for good. He wondered at the change in himself; once he'd have withdrawn his mind from a man like Stewart and his schemes and found pleasure in some odd bit of poetry, or daydream about women, but now he was unable to remove himself from what Stewart was saying.

"And since I already own the Laguna and the Kiski . . ."

The Kiski? Oh yes, the Kiski and the certificates that had been taken out. "The little cockney hasn't caught on yet?"

"He's stupider than I took him for."

There was going to be trouble; he could feel it in his bones.

"Anyway, I'm selling the three to McKeever Brothers of New York, that'll make a little productive property for them."

"I don't care what their names are."

"You'll be handling the deal, better know their names, eh?"

It was robbery, pure and simple, and he was stuck right in the middle. His muscles, his brain screamed panic; he sat blinking at Stewart.

"I'm going into nickel in a big way—that's where you come in. Vice-President of Canada Nickel, nice, eh?"

No, No, Ewing pushed the title away from him. He didn't want it, he didn't want anything to do with it. He found himself asking lamely, "But I don't know of any nickel deposits around."

"I know of plenty. There's a nice deposit on an island in Wekusko—I hear Ventures has taken out an option on it but I'll find a way to get hold of it. Meantime I've got experts out on the Burntwood and up above Flin Flon. They cost me plenty, you better believe. What I got out of the Laguna and Kiski, I'm spending on exploration—it'll pay me . . ."

"With a few diamonds on the way?"

"Sometimes, Ewing, I almost like you."

Ewing put up his hand, ran exploratory fingers along the left side of his jaw. The pain would not go away.

"Have them all pulled," Stewart stood up, "sooner the better."

Ewing wondered if in some way the pain wasn't a body response, a physical reaction for allowing himself to be party to a robbery. That wasn't so far-fetched. He'd read an article lately on breakthroughs in medicine which had used strange, new words—that one, psychosomatic, was a stunner.

"Pay attention, you're handling my business!"

"Not all of it." He hadn't written that London letter.

"Remember, I plan to build an immense nickel industry! With my experience and ability to develop and work it along the right lines, I'll be in control of an empire no less!"

"No less." How was he to get out of this mess? His mind refused to help, wandered away to the druggist's daughter who worked in her father's store downstairs. He'd just lately become aware of her; he'd take her out tonight to that new Hawaiian restaurant—The Pas had discovered Hawaii. She wasn't the woman in dark furs of his dream but she was presentable and available.

"You know, Ewing, you're losing your edge and it has to be sharpened to a fine hone to handle a great industry—I might have to get someone else."

"You already have, haven't you?"

"You're basically smart but your mind wanders," Stewart was buttoning up his greatcoat, "and you always have some physical problem," adjusting his otter hat. "I've got to have a man in The Pas in one hundred percent condition. Now I've got to give you some thought."

"That's right, you think."

Stewart glowered and went out, banging the door behind him.

Ewing listened until the steps on the stairway died away.

"Oh God!"

4

Ventures Limited returned. The man tying up the dogs was unknown to them and they were not sure of his business until he stated it. He was older than Lindsey, the first man who'd come. He came in and sat down, refusing the biscuits and tea offered.

He ignored Kate and turned his attention to Woosey. "How much do you want for your nickel claims?"

Woosey was prepared. "One million." It slipped off his tongue with an ease that surprised him.

"Ventures are prepared to offer one hundred thousand."

Kate spoke up. "We couldn't let the claims go for that."

"Do you agree with that, Woosey?"

"One million is the figure we have agreed on."

"You won't reconsider?"

"No," Kate said.

"It's your say, Woosey."

"No."

"I'll take your answer to the company and will return, either with a new offer to you, or what is more likely, another option and more drilling."

It was left at that. Neither knew whether they had done the right thing or not; both were united in their hatred of this part of the prospector's life, being forced to leave the question of money to another's judgment or good will or greed.

She was doubly angry because this representative had been even more obstinate than Lindsey in refusing to recognize a woman as fit to do business. "It's hateful and I'm spineless to put up with it!"

"I'd hardly call you spineless—that's one thing I would not call you."

5

The weather was mild, the snow deep and soft. There were no dog or toboggan tracks round the old Indian trap cabin nor smoke from the smoke hole but when she went inside she knew they'd been there. The fireplace was full of partially scorched and fire-twisted cans of opened moose meat or beef, and bits of burnt paper. She took all the paper, the burnt and crisped pieces as well as the clean ones, and laid them carefully on her canvas sheet. She lifted out the opened cans; there was still enough beef and moose meat stew left to make a meal. These men were extravagant. She sniffed at the contents and decided not to touch them.

After she'd built a fire, heated a can of beans and eaten, she examined the pieces of paper; some were so badly burned they crumbled in her hand but there were others. *Sweetheart.* It was part of a letter to a wife or friend. Another piece gave a whole sentence: *I want to get out of this.* What was *'this'*? Searching for nickel, or did he want to get out of the bush? or, and more important, out of irregularities in Canada Nickel and Dow Stewart's policies? A larger fragment read: *does Stewart get the money? Gunning Man. govt to spend dollars opening hydro-electric power plants. Fed govt to run a bi-weekly railway line along Burntwood.*

She mushed back to her own trap cabin. Spending a whole day on a creek to the east and north, laying traps along the snake-like course, she found where the snow had blown away, traces of samplings the geologists must have taken. There was an apple green stain on the rocks that meant the presence of nickel arsenide, but how much was another matter that would have to wait until after break-up to be determined. On her way back to the cabin she picked up a silver fox, still alive in the trap, and a dead marten in another. Her mind was so busy with the words she'd read on the scraps of paper she ignored her good luck.

Wolves were coming each night; each night she would go out with her rifle and kill one or two, the shots ringing and echoing over the deserted land in the clear, frosted air. Still the wolves came. One night there were six; lifting her rifle, she wounded one wolf in the leg. Crying with pain, it ran off with the others, leaving a trail of blood. She went after the injured animal, bound to kill it outright, but the snow, crusted on top and soggy beneath, slowed her; she shot again but missed and the wolf kept on running. She returned to the cabin, following its path in her mind, full of anguish, knowing it would end its life alone, a lingering agony in some lonely hole. But she was free of wolves and slept for the rest of her stay to the eerie hoots of the great grey owl.

She had planned to be away a month but she was so eager to return with her new knowledge of Canada Nickel and Stewart she packed her furs after three weeks. It was the best catch she'd ever had—it was like playing the horses: when you didn't care, you won. She hadn't cared, her attention having been directed to the Burntwood, and the animals simply came to her traps: two silver fox, four black fox, five ermine, one mink, three marten and something else, a surprise, two wolverine.

A moose meat stew awaited her at the cabin. She was no longer surprised at his prescience concerning her. When they were drinking their tea he told her the news. Tom Garth, one of the partners of Bill Campbell, had returned from San Francisco broke and wanting work at the mine. Woosey had given him a job and would have to pay him out of his own pocket since Stewart refused to take on any more men. He had news of Campbell also: he was living in San Francisco at a hotel for swells, but his money wouldn't last much longer, Garth had confided, wagering he'd be back, looking round Wekusko again.

She began her story of the burned letter, telling Woosey that Stewart had people examining rocks along the Burntwood for nickel, that he was going into nickel in a big way and that he was so sharp with other people's money and goods he could persuade governments to spend theirs to enhance his own projects.

She expected a strong reaction from her partner but he rose, stretching. "Yes, I've known all along he was up to something," he yawned.

"Don't you see? We've got to act right away!"

"Not this minute, Kate . . ." He yawned again. "I'm going to kip in. In the morning, we'll think . . ."

"No, not in the morning!" She was tired of inaction. "I'm going to The Pas tonight. I'm going to see that crook of a lawyer—if it isn't already too late to do anything. I may be able to get somewhere with him. Anyway, I have those furs to sell."

He was wide awake now and sat down. "No Kate, no. It's not a good idea. Let me handle him."

"You've already handled him and nothing happened."

"I've had to learn. I've had no business training except what my mum and the army gave me which is nothing. And there's a real reason why I think you shouldn't go . . ."

"What is the real reason?"

"You'll go in there with your rifle and start shooting up the place."

"I've more sense than that—I learned my lesson with Stewart."

"I don't doubt you, but still I wish you wouldn't."

"I'm doing it for you, too. Anyhow I've made up my mind."

"And you always do what you've made up your mind to do, don't you, Kate?"

Her brilliant blue green eyes locked with his intense brown ones. The talk had changed subtly. "What are you driving at?"

"I'm talking about you."

"Any dolt would know that."

"You have all the North American impatience and because you have a university degree you believe you can handle everything, plus an added factor, you're rather prone to scorn."

"You're making a catalogue of my faults—what else is on your mind?"

He gave her such a peculiarly sweet smile her heart was pierced but she had no patience to listen to her heart.

"You know, don't you, that you're the type that's apt to get bushed?"

"Go on . . . while you're at it."

But he continued to smile at her with such sweetness and warmth she moved to the far side of the room to be away from him.

"I admire you greatly, Kate."

She knew he admired her and she also knew his admiration was no longer enough for her. Somehow, the talk had edged away from the subject in a way she didn't quite understand.

"Despite all this, I'm going to see that lawyer."

"You would say that. I can't and won't stop you—and I doubt if even Dan Mosher could."

"I won't take my rifle."

6

She started for The Pas with the dogs at daybreak. The weather had changed; slanting snow driven by a hard wind out of the north followed her all the way. It took four days.

She left her rifle and the dogs at the Northland. She hadn't planned on the cost of staying at the hotel but it was night with the blizzard still blowing by the time she'd sold her furs; it was of a severity that usually came in the early spring season. She was tired; the tiredness came from alarm about her partner's gold mine, about her own nickel showings. It had not grown less during her journey.

The door at the top of the narrow stair was open, a furnace of hot air blasted down the stairwell. She closed the street door behind her and was enclosed in stygian darkness except for a small field of light from the open door on the landing above her. She climbed quickly and quietly and stood a second in the open doorway.

Facing her sat a man, almost certainly the lawyer she'd come to see; one hand touched his jaw, the other rested on some papers cluttering his desk. His whole pose was slack, his face softened as though some dream rolled him towards a gilded object. She'd expected a much harder, tougher looking invididual; the softness surprised her.

A big red safe occupied the center of the side wall. Its heavy steel outer door had not been clicked shut.

The lawyer shifted his gaze, conscious now he had a visitor, his eyes travelling upwards over a pair of long legs in trousers thrust into miner's boots and up to the blue plaid mackinaw, to the face, his mouth gaping slightly, the woman's face. The most beautiful woman he'd ever seen. He rose from his chair.

"Who are you?"

She moved to the safe. "Does it matter?"

"I think so—yes," he replied, his voice still carrying filaments of his dreaming.

"The gentlemen's agreement must be in here." Her hand went to the big round knob of the outer steel door.

He watched lazily as her hand turned the knob and the door swung open. "What's that?" He made a step towards her. "What's that about a gentlemen's agreement?"

"That's the nub of the problem." In her bearskin hat she was a full head taller than he.

His hand reached for a chair, brought it forward for her. "Here, take a seat."

Her hand was twisting the knob of the inner door. It opened with a creaking noise.

A smile spread over his face, slightly quizzical but more amused at this beautiful woman making free with his safe. "Who are you, anyway?"

Manila folders in their dozen or so pigeon holes were exposed before her. She clasped one. Which would contain the Kiski certificates?

"Look, you come in here, talk to me about gentlemen's agreements— tell me what you mean." His voice sounding reasonable, even pleading, he went on, "I don't go in much for riddles. Tell me."

"You're better at robbing, aren't you?" She would be forced to pull out the lot unless she was lucky to land on the right one.

He was still smiling, the smile confused, a little startled by a woman dressed like an old prospector, not his dream of a beautiful woman but surpassing it. "I wish I knew what you were talking about."

The folder she'd pulled out bore the legend: *Canada Nickel.* "You don't know anything about removing certificates of the Kiski Mine from Dick Woosey's envelope and putting them into Dow Stewart's, do you?"

She put the folder back and pulled out another.

He moved closer. "Look, this joke is going too far . . ." He put out his hand towards her shoulder. "I might lose my temper, and then?" His voice was more pleading than angry.

Another folder: *Rex Mining and Development Company.* "Whether you lose your temper or not is your affair."

He grasped her shoulder with firmness. She was stronger than her slightness indicated and did not flinch. "Now, you tell me who you are and your business here!"

"Take your hand off me and I'll tell you who I am."

He removed his hand.

"I'm Dick Woosey's partner."

"Woosey, Woosey . . . that little son of a gun . . . that Cockney!"

"That gentleman."

"You! You sharing his sleeping bag?"

Now her hand seized another folder.

"Stop this!"

"Try to stop me!" *Kiski Mining and Development Company.* She had it.

"Right now!" His hand pushed at her shoulder. She didn't move. "You hear, stop!" He grabbed the folder out of her hand. "I don't care for your riddles." His smile had gone, his face turned sallow. Long lines ran from his nose to his square chin. Though he had never been a good looking man he could hardly be called bad looking, but at this moment he was ugly.

"You only care about making a pile. Hand that folder over!"

"You've got your nerve coming in here, helping yourself to my private papers." There was admiration in his voice.

She was warned by his face. "That's one thing I have plenty of." She caught hold of the folder by a corner.

He twisted his body away from her, "Oh no you don't . . ."

The corner came away in her hand, a jagged triangle of brown paper. She was going to have a knock-down fight on her hands.

Still with the folder held in one hand, his face was turned to her, a sour little smile about his mouth.

He was daring her to come on, take it from him, making their struggle into a kind of sexual game. She picked up the chair he'd brought for her, raising it high, "Hand over that folder!"

"Come an' get it!" He turned completely away from her.

She swung the chair above him. He ducked, the folder dropping to the floor as his hands went out to save his head. The chair came down, hit flesh, and there was the sound of bones cracking. She threw the chair across the room. She'd hit him but didn't know where.

"She's killed me. My gosh . . . my gosh . . ."

She stooped to the folder, one hand out to take it. A figure appeared in the doorway.

"What's going on up here?"

Her one hand was still reaching down for the folder. It was the druggist from downstairs.

"Miss Rice, you all right?"

"Oh my gosh . . . my gosh . . ." Ewing was holding one hand.

She stood erect. She'd always loathed wounding or maiming an animal, now she'd injured a man. She'd had enough of violence.

"I've hurt him." She went towards the door. "Do something please, fix him up."

The druggist gazed at her in astonishment.

The moans intensified, or seemed to, as she went down the stairs, like a child's cries when the attention of the listener is withdrawn.

Outside, the sun was shining, flooding the new snow with glitter. She drew a series of jerky breaths. What now? She turned towards the Northland, sick at heart.

A man was walking towards her; the old vigour of his body, the movement of his shoulders and arms struck her. It was someone she knew. It was Dan Mosher. She stopped.

He drew up. "You livin' here?"

Dan Mosher so changed in countenance and body as to be almost unrecognizable; where at Beaver Lake he'd been a big man without an ounce of fat and in the prime of life, he was now a skeleton and old, his face sewn with deep lines and each line seamed by threads of dirt. "They left me, the bunch, Tom and the bunch . . . took off . . ." The mud-coloured eyes fell from her. "Spend money . . . don't care . . ." Hawking and spitting, making pits of red brown in the new snow, he went on,

"Livin' lone cabin 'bove Flin Flon . . . no good, livin' lone."

She moved after him. "Mr. Mosher—I want to tell you . . ."

He was leaning over to bring up the red brown liquid from his lungs, "Go 'way, go 'way," He was walking on talking to himself, "Go 'way, go 'way," the snow bank slotted with pockets of red brown to mark his going.

This was the man who'd taught her what she knew of prospecting: *Shoot to hurt*! and if someone was jumping his claims, *Best shoot to kill*! It was Dan Mosher who'd taught her violence and she'd been too apt a pupil.

Her show of violence had got her nowhere. What worked for Mosher didn't work for her. And what was worse, she'd made the problem harder for her partner. Her sense of defeat was so strong it was chemical; even her mouth tasted bitter and acidic. On the way out the dogs caught her distress; they bit and strained and snapped, poking when she ordered them to push on, racing when she wanted to stop for tea.

Along the portages of the Grass River she kept expecting her partner to appear; she wanted his welcome, his easy acceptance of her and her failings. There'd be no questions, no how's, no why's until she was ready to give them, no, "I told you so, didn't I?" when she did give them. And she would tell him everything, the whole sorry story.

But there was no Dick Woosey. When she mushed out of the mouth of the Grass, above the battlements of the island's rocks there was no welcoming smoke from the chimney.

The cabin was still warmish with a haunch of moose meat on the table. Recklessly, she fed it to the dogs. She stayed, wating for an hour, making tea, eating cold bannock, waiting. He did not come. She mushed over to the mine, a compulsion to ask his forgiveness lending wings to her going.

He wasn't at the mine. It was more desolate than ever. She took off her snowshoes and tramped about looking for signs of his presence, sinking to her knees in the scruffy snow. The sky was hard, a brilliant blue bitterness. Mine shafts of the Rex and the Kiski, her partner's canvas tent, Stewart's cabin, the snow, the bushes, the slag heap of stones and dirt running nakedly down the steep hill to the lake were in various tones of grey. With their terrible secret power the black spruce waited in a silent semicircle round the clearing to take over. The minute man let go they would send out their shoots and begin again to reclaim their own. No one was here; even Stewart had gone as though for good, as though he'd let go of the gold mines, and the black spruce by some earth-sorcery knew it.

She snowshoed over to the settlement at Herb Lake. Her partner must be there. But he was not there. The snow about the Alborg's place was well-worked with dog tracks and dog droppings but no dogs. The cabin was empty of the Alborgs. Going down to the store at the wharf she adked for her partner; the owner thought he'd seen him passing the window sometime earlier, could give no more information. She bought some sugar and candles. She was vaguely uneasy. He'd never done anything like this before, he'd always been in the cabin when she returned or she knew where he'd gone, but there was always a first time.

Tears blinded her eyes, ran along her cold cheeks and she let them come, occasionally brushing the moisture with a bearskin glove. The air was breathlessly still except for the ceaseless mush mush mush of her snowshoes ploughing the grainy snow of the lake. Her head was bent, weeping gushed out, a bounding source; something in her had given way. A sob tore out of her lungs and she stopped. Who was she weeping for? Her partner? His gold mine? Her nickel mine? Herself?

A faint remembrance rankled in her mind; it was something the Cree schoolteacher at Budd's Point had said once. Lifting her head, she tried to recall, blinking round the lake's white circumference, its ring of black spruce as though to find her answer. She found she'd gone miles off her course, having headed south and west toward the cove while her two islands were five miles away to the north and west. Somewhere was a faint sound of dogs howling.

When she reached her island, she found two teams, her own and her partner's, and one she'd seen before but couldn't remember when or where; they'd been tied too close together and had set up a furious enmity, howling, straining at their leashes to get at each other's throats. Inside the cabin a fire burned and it was warm. A tall figure rose from a chair. He was the man from Ventures.

"Miss Rice . . ." He was gazing as though there was something strange about her red eyes, her dirt-streaked face. "I want to see Mr. Woosey, I have some business with him."

"Do you?" She was listening to the howls of the dogs and in the second they were quiet to the first faint crackle of an aurora.

"Is he around?"

"Around?" She was alarmed; it was too unusual for her partner not to be here.

"Around, yes?" The man watched her. "He'll be back shortly, I trust—a few hours?"

"Yes, a few hours . . ." She was totally alarmed now.

The man rose and nodded good bye.

He returned much later that night. She'd been out many times in the moon-lit landscape searching the whole perimeter of the lake with her binoculars. Where was he? The last time she'd come inside she went for her notebook to jot down some observations on tonight's aurora: it had started with long ribbons of green fire and then had abruptly ceased and the moon had come out. The notebook was already open with a scribbled message on its pages. *Borrowed dogs from Alborgs on way The Pas maybe meet you returning on portage or river you gone long Steady boys.* She turned the words over in her mind to get their feel; she detected panic.

Later, there was a knock and the Ventures man returned. "Woosey not back *yet*?"

"Not yet."

"Then you tell him when he comes the company abides by its original offer to pay one hundred thousand for his nickel claims."

She surveyed him coldly. "I abide by my original demand. I want a million for my claims."

"Will you give him this message—Ventures Limited proposes to take another option on refusal of their terms. They will pay him one thousand and drill seven more holes—do you understand all this?"

"I'm aware that I still own the claims and that is the important thing to know."

He stared as though she had not taken in what he had been at considerable trouble to say and then he closed the door and left her.

She was scarcely aware of his leave-taking. She had remembered the words of the Cree schoolteacher at Budd's Point: *If you don't act like a woman you're going to get into trouble.*

She was in trouble.

7

Woosey had set out for his gold mine that morning. The snow was so soft he wondered if the ice on the lake wouldn't move out in a few days, weeks before its usual time. He wanted to see Stewart, to come to grips with the problem of the ownership of the gold mine. He had no knowledge of the intricacies of business, that was why his intuition had not worked except to give him a general sense of unease, but finally it had clicked even without the knowledge and he was fairly certain of what had happened.

Kate should have been back, and that she wasn't augured some kind of trouble besides the delay due to bad weather. She must have seen the lawyer, used some kind of violence, maybe hurt him; the more he pondered over her absence the more certain he was that Kate had injured him in some way.

She was right in one thing, the lawyer was the key; he had control over the certificates and it was the certificates that gave Stewart the right to carry on as though he owned the mine, and they in turn were bound up with the lawyer's relationship to his boss. He was young, thirtyish; Stewart had picked him out at law school, overwhelmed him with his favours and his easy, good-natured ways. With a fearful clarity his first meeting with the two men returned: his own defenses were down, the sheer exuberance of being the prospector who had discovered a gold mine, and he was taken in by the free camaraderie, the jokes, the easiness, the whole grand abounding assurance of it all. He'd been sized up at once. Stewart was a master of dealing with his kind of fledgling businessman. He was a gentleman, but they were all gentlemen! He'd been duped, and properly.

After he left the office it was smooth sailing for the others. If the lawyer had removed certificates from his envelope and put them into Stewart's, and he was certain he had done so, he could also put them back. He wasn't fundamentally a crook as Kate believed, was probably fairly decent; his problem was weakness and greed, with some laziness, too. The right arguments might convince him to put the certificates back in their proper envelopes and brave Stewart's fury. He was going to give it a try.

Stewart was tramping round the mine site in high boots, thick grey socks, mackinaw carefully fastened, an old grey felt hat pulled well down to his ears when Woosey appeared over the bluffs, carrying his snowshoes. "Hey . . . want to see you," Stewart called.

Woosey chafed at this kind of address, calling back rudely, "You see me."

Stewart's shoes plunged into the soft snow. "Woosey-I-want-to-see-you."

"What have you got to say about my gold mine I haven't heard a hundred times?"

"I'm sick and tired of your arrogance, Woosey."

"You can bloody well be tired and sick too." He marched on and came up close to Stewart.

"Look you—I'm closing the mine."

"You're what?"

"Closing the Kiski."

"Closing my mine—you can't close my mine!"

"Oh can't I?"

"It's not yours to close."

"You idiot. I own 51 percent of the shares—you have 49 percent."

"You've got it turned around!" A sickening assent to his own intuition made his voice weak even to himself.

"Go on back to your traps. You're living in a dream world."

Rage erupted in his veins and his heart was pounding like a sledge hammer against his chest. "You sewer!"

"Certificates were street type anyway." Stewart went plunging away through the snow.

He ran after Stewart: what did the pukka wallah mean by street type, something dirty and tricky? "I'm going to The Pas . . ." his voice lifting to a screech in his own ears, "see that lawyer—he took the certificates from my envelope. I know him . . . you . . .I'll settle this!" It was all he had the wind to say.

"You go to The Pas and you try." He kept plunging away, then wheeled, "By the way, the property's been sold to McKeever's, New York."

He stood, rooted in the snow. His mine gone! Stewart's body wavered, the shaft of the mine blurred. "You swine. I'll see you dead first . . ."

"You'll end up behind bars." Stewart sludged on.

He felt tears come to his eyes.

Never could he remember borrowing dogs from Alborg, crossing back over the lake, leaving the message for Kate and without respite pushing on to The Pas.

8

John Ewing sat in his office stroking the bandage round his broken fingers. His right hand had been strapped to a board, the dickens of a thing to carry about, he complained. "Won't set the bones, bound to a board they ought to heal," the doctor had said.

"Ought to? And what if they don't?"

"Well man, it'll just be too bad. How'd you break *four,* anyway?"

"I told you, I fell downstairs."

The doctor didn't believe him. "But you're young and reasonably spry."

But they hurt, they hurt damnably. The pain gnawed at his fingers, gnawed at his arm, at his shoulder, even his guts. He couldn't sleep, tossed and turned all night.

"Take a couple of aspirin."

That was all the sympathy he got.

It was a funny thing, but he didn't feel any bitterness toward the woman, that so-called partner of the Cockney. He'd tried to glean bits of information, anything the druggist, the shopkeepers could supply. He'd gone about it in a roundabout way. "Say, hear there's a woman prospector comes in every so often," he'd say casual-like. He didn't put it this way to the druggist, since there was no need to be circumspect there. The druggist knew and Ewing hoped to God he was the only one who did know she'd thrown a chair at him. Ewing confessed, "She's a beauty even if she's a wild woman!" What he discovered only intrigued him the more.

No matter what the druggist said, and he'd said, "It's a pure and simple business arrangement between two responsible parties," he didn't believe a word of it. A woman with a face like that didn't form pure and simple business arrangements with a man and live with him under the same roof. And that man was Woosey! What he'd found out by inquiries shook him up. Woosey was an old cavalry man, he'd fought somewhere in Africa or India, his father was a lord or something. Woosey could be a remittance man. No wonder she was so violent on his behalf.

He stroked the bandage, the bones of his fingers shooting pain clear to his shoulder. She almost killed me! He'd asked the doctor how long before he could use his hand. "Maybe two months if you're lucky." "Damned thing to say," he muttered. Damned awkward to carry a board strapped to your arm and hand, hitting every object in sight and the whole damn thing in a sling about your neck!

The daylight was almost gone but there was still light from the sunset filtering through the winter-scarred window pane. The streaks of yellow orange pressed between mountains of blue grey clouds fell with lurid light over the packages on his desk, plunging the rest of the office into gloom. It was a backdrop for an act of violence. Oh God, he hoped not! Once was enough.

On his desk rested two blocks of 8-1/2 x 11 office stationery, a sample letterhead pasted on each block: *Canada Nickel—Burntwood Narrows—N. Manitoba—Canada;The Pas Nickel—The Pas—N. Manitoba—Canada.* What in hell was The Pas Nickel? Never heard of it. Was Stewart forming two companies and employing a whole slew of lawyers? Who knew? That it was a scheme of some kind he was certain.

He hadn't yet received his walking papers from Stewart; the man hadn't taken time out to re-consider him as vice-president of Canada Nickel. He shrugged and pain shot up his hand and arm. He groaned aloud. For a moment he wondered about Stewart's wife down in Winnipeg—did she know or suspect what her husband was up to? He doubted it.

He'd been taken to their home a number of times when he was a law student—she was a scared little woman with pale thin brown hair, the kind that shows the scalp on top, but she was a generous soul and heaped his plate with food; she seemed to know he was always hungry and had little money to spend on food or other necessities. Once, during the meal, the bell had rung; it'd been some kind of church collection, some Bible society or other. Stewart inquired if she had given anything and she'd said, yes, ten dollars.

"Don't you ever do that again, you hear! My money doesn't grow on trees!"

She'd had tears in her eyes. She must have been the kind of complaisant woman he needed, never giving him any back talk or arguments.

He wanted to be free of Stewart, to get out of any association with him and get out as peacefully as he could. He hated rumpuses. He ran the fingers of his left hand over the bandage, so softly the pain eased. Stewart was a manipulator and Ewing longed for order and harmony and the security of the law. He admitted he'd watched and he'd helped Stewart squeeze out prospectors like Woosey but when he got into high finance, when he cheated governments, companies, capitalists in London and New York out of millions, that was scary. Ewing felt guilty about the small guys, guys like Knott where Stewart had simply walked in after the suicide and helped himself to a profitable gold mine. It gave him a queasy feeling to know that it could be done. That was why he must get out. If he didn't, if he stayed on, he'd be lost forever. He'd had it up to the neck, doing the bidding of a swindler. He longed to be associated with an established law firm with a good reputation.

Stewart manipulating the Manitoba Government into building a road into that bloody Burntwood Narrows at a thousand a mile, why it was two hundred miles from here to there, if it was an inch!

Manipulating the Feds to build a railway to his mine, that took gall. But it was nothing to what he'd seen yesterday in the sheet, *The Hudson Bay Herald*. Stewart, being interviewed by an Ottawa reporter, was extolling the beauty of the moon over the vast untrodden wastes of the northern territory, the glorious sunsets and sunrises over the myriad lakes without even a name, and beautiful The Pas, the capital of the greatest mining realm in all Canada, nay in the whole world. What drivel! Ewing closed his eyes. A brutal man making poetry made him physically sick.

He wanted out of Stewart's influence, out of The Pas, out of Selkirk, out of Winnipeg. He wanted to go West, maybe Vancouver, more likely San Francisco. He'd tell his girl over dinner tonight that he was going West. West into law and order, West into a new life, West into a reputation as a man of probity. That was what he wanted; the other kind of life was too scary and nauseating besides.

His girl Lila had been silent and mulish last night after he'd come from the doctor's; her father, the druggist, had never approved of him and since that woman had almost killed him, she'd been cold. No use dreaming of that sleeping bag partner of Woosey's.

Footsteps on the stairs; he recognized them and grimaced. He hadn't expected a visit from him today. More footsteps on the first tread; he didn't recognize them.

The door banged open. Stewart stood in an old felt hat, mackinaw, heavy boots and socks. Stewart larger than life-size—and that was too large—marched in.

"For God's sake, light the lamp—what's wrong with everyone?" He didn't plunk down in his usual place but came on in, aggressive and in foul temper.

The other footsteps on the stairs climbed on, slow, hesitant.

Ewing lit the coal oil steel lamp on his desk, but the glass chimney was carbon smudged and gave out a poor light. Using his left hand (it was clumsy and he had trouble adjusting the chimney) he was too aware of the stormy eyes fired on him. He was nervous too—he had to let this man know he wanted to sever any relationship the two of them had.

"For God's sake, what's happened to you?"

"I fell." His left hand was gently massaging the bandage.

"You're a liar, Ewing! You were in a fight over some business and you got knocked out. It wasn't my business, was it? Was it my business?"

A figure in a bearskin hat with a rifle in his hand stood in the doorway. He breathed heavily and his face was ashen. Ewing stared. The remittance man! The lover of that woman! Odd the two of them had the same interest, a woman.

Stewart wheeled in a fury. "Don't you shoot!" He put his hand to his back pocket.

Woosey was having trouble with his breath but there was an arrogant lift to his head.

Ewing was getting up. The Cockney'd be a crack shot. "No shooting inhere!"

"Put down that gun!" Stewart pointed his revolver at Woosey, coolly transferring his rifle to the other hand.

Ewing rushed between the two men. "For God's sake . . ." He hit the board to which his broken fingers were strapped and cried out in pain.

Stewart's attention was diverted a second. "Ewing, you had your chance—get out of this!"

He had his chance now too, he could defy Stewart, throw off his shackles. *Stand fast, therefore in the right!* Wherever did that old slogan come from?

Woosey ignored Stewart. "I know all about you, Ewing," he was fumbling out his words, "you're not a bad fellow, only weak . . ." His breathing became too difficult.

"You don't know me at all."

"Ah yes, I know you. You took certificates from my envelope, didn't you? Put them into . . ." Unable to finish, he sat down, afraid.

"Ewing, you get to that safe, get my envelope—I'll show him!" Stewart was red-faced with fury.

Between them, Ewing hestitated. How could the Cockney have known?

"Go on!"

Going to the safe, he removed the portfolio. He hated himself.

"Take my envelope out and give the certificates to him. He's had the gall to accuse me!"

Woosey was trying to rise. A terrible pain ripped through his whole body. He closed his eyes.

Ewing threw the portfolio down on his desk. "The man's sick!" He went over to him. "Can you hear me, Woosey?"

"That man's accused me, me! I want this settled!" Stewart put the revolver back in his pocket and reached for the folder. "What's wrong? The corner's missing, looks as if . . ." he was jerking out the envelopes.

Ewing put his good hand on Woosey's shoulder, "Where you putting up?" It occurred to him Woosey hadn't put up anywhere but was camping by the river. He bent over to get the answer.

A whisper. "Bacon's."

That flea joint!

Woosey opened his eyes, pointing a lax finger at the bandaged hand. "You hurt . . ." His eyes were strangely black on Ewing's face.

The peculiar obtuse eyes seared his flesh. "I fell—those stairs."

Woosey's eyes, still unfocused and glazed with black, charged him. "My partner, I ought . . ."

Was he such a bad liar he could convince nobody, not even a dying man? He went for his coat, threw it over his shoulder, and knocking the board strapped to his hand cried out.

"What in God's name you doing, Ewing?"

Helping Woosey to his feet, he half carried him to the stairs.

Stewart waved the envelopes. "Don't move, either of you."

"Get to my left side, that's it."

"I gotta talk to you, Ewing!"

"Easy, easy, lean on my left, we'll make it." They managed the stairs.

Above them at the top, Stewart was beside himself with rage, waving the envelopes above his head, "You come back, bugger—you show that poor stick he owns 49 percent."

9

It was late at night when Ewing returned exhausted, to his office.

He lit the lamp and a swirl of carbon weaved up the chimney, forcing him to turn it low, so low that when he dropped into his chair he was unaware at first of the gaping door of the red safe, the empty pigeon holes, the missing blocks of stationery for Canada Nickel and The Pas Nickel. When he realized what it meant he felt good, he'd been released. But guilt settled quickly and it made him sick; the severance of his relationship with Stewart had been at the expense of Woosey.

The envelopes were gone now and he didn't dare try to get them back: it would be like opening again the can of worms and letting the crawling things spew out. It was too late to do anything.

His left arm fell along the side of the chair, his fingers scraping the floor, the other hand in its sling resting like a weight of stone along his desk. He hadn't an ounce of strength left; it was guilt.

The curious thing was his liking for the cocky little Englishman. He'd got him past the man at the desk of the flophouse by paying twice what had been asked out of his own pocket; they didn't want the sick at that joint. He'd waited after he'd laid him out on the thin straw mattress to see if he was breathing. He couldn't tell by looking and the eyes were closed; he'd had no experience with the sick, especially the mortally sick, and he was sure the man was dying. The only hope was to get help. He'd waited a little longer but there was no change and then he'd run, no, he'd sprinted, (he'd never gone in for athletics), to the druggist.

"You'll have to get him out of there," the druggist told him. "They don't want the sick. The Grey Nuns take a few but they're full up with Indians and Doc Sinclair has gone with his dogs up beyond Flin Flon Lake to Dan Mosher. The old prospector's dying."

"What am I going to do? I can't be responsible . . ."

"Brother, you'll have to stick with him. You'll have to get a guide over in the reservation who has dogs and a toboggan, take the man back to his camp."

"What, me? Can't you?"

"Man, I have the store to mind. I'll take a look at him though."

He'd be forced to go first to the reserve; he knew nothing of the geography of the country behind the boardwalks of The Pas, had no idea where the reserve was, except that it was somewhere vaguely north; everything was always vaguely north of The Pas. He had even less of an idea how he would get there.

"Take the man's team of dogs, cross the Saskatchewan over the new bridge, carry a lantern because when you get across there's only a trail through the snow in a black spruce forest, eventually it will turn left, follow it about three miles to the first shack. Ask there for the guide with dogs."

He'd never mushed with dogs, never travelled lonely trails through a deep forest, let alone at night, never gone anywhere at night except to restaurants or, in Selkirk or Winnipeg, to the occasional silent movie. "I can't! You'll have to!"

"Look, you came to me for help—I didn't come to you."

"I know but . . ."

"Where's the fellow's camp, do you know that?"

"I think it's somewhere near Wekusko Lake."

The druggist's usually mild grey eyes were severe, even accusing him. What'd he done? He was only trying to help a guy. He'd robbed a man, that's what he'd done! Damn his guilty conscience!

"What's his name?"

"It's Woosey." For some unfathomable reason he spoke the name with diffidence.

"Woosey! Dick Woosey? Why in heaven's name didn't you say so in the first place?"

"I didn't know his name meant so much."

"He's about the most well-known man round here, one of the real old-timers like Dan Mosher and Tom Creighton. He's respected, made The Pas what it is today. Why, he helped open up this country in here."

"Well, I didn't make him sick." But he wasn't so sure.

"You johnny-come-latelys, you don't contribute anything, you only take and you take it without the law . . ."

His mind squirmed. How much did the druggist know or guess at?

"Then you clear out with your takings but Dick Woosey and Mosher, they've given everything they had to this country. Dick Woosey sick in a flophouse! I'll go right away and as for you, you'll go for that guide."

And he hadn't finished. Ewing still had to bear the whip of his tongue. "You'll have to tell the guide to take Dick as far as the George Cowan homestead on Cormorant Lake. George will judge if he's fit to go on; if he's not, Cowan will put him up until the guide goes to the camp in Wekusko—it's an island."

So they lived on an island. It sounded romantic.

"The guide will alert Dick's partner—but you know her, don't you?"

The sharpness of the glance burned him as though with a brand of hot iron.

"She knows a lot more than you'll ever know, she'll tackle anything. If he's well enough to go on, the guide will take him to the Diamond Queen's cabin at Mile 82. And she will either keep him or deliver him to his base camp. You think you can remember all this?"

This was too much and Ewing reacted with hauteur. "I'm not a child." He caught himself just in time from saying a babe in the woods. Anyway, he didn't expect Woosey to be alive when they returned to Bacon's.

But he had been alive and Ewing had been forced to beg and borrow everything from boots to mackinaw to lantern.

It had been a ghastly experience. The tiny yellow circle of light, the only live thing in the vast dark world, the noises; the black spruce bush to his right and left was full of noise, wolves or lynx. He was terrified of wolves and once he'd heard the scream of a lynx as it sprung upon its victim and he'd never forgotten it. The matter of a rifle had slipped his mind—he couldn't use one if he did have it. The sudden lack of noise was as unnerving as the crackling sounds. He was certain it was a lynx, stalking him and ready to spring with an awful scream. Returning was a little better. He had the company of another human being, even if that human was a silent Indian, and another team of dogs. He could never deny the power of the black forbidding forest over him.

The druggist was at Bacon's with Woosey when he got back, a rowdy card game going on in the next cubicle. "It's some kind of heart trouble. I've given him digitalis in combination with strychnia."

They carried him down the stairs, rolled in the druggist's fur robes and settled him onto the toboggan; heated bricks were tucked inside. The druggist, dressed in a short fur coat, stroked the unresponsive forehead. "I'll go as far as the Cowan place, may even go on as far as the Diamond Queen's, it's the only decent thing to do." He settled on Ewing a pair of frosty eyes.

Ewing had the feeling of being exposed, his inadequacies, his guilt common knowledge; the act of juggling certificates was about the same as jumping claims and he knew too well what happened to the man found out: strung him up to the nearest tree or shot dead, that's what happened. Supposing it'd been Tom Creighton or that old crust, Dan Mosher who'd found him out? He shivered. If the druggist didn't know then he'd guessed and he'd told his daughter. When he'd gone back to the drug store after seeing the druggist off with Woosey and the Indian she'd run to the back of the store and never reappeared. He'd simply stayed, feeling like an ass. To be guilty was bad, to be found out or suspected, a crime.

It was long after midnight. Extinguishing the lamp, he stumbled down the long, dark stairs, striking the board clamped to his arm and gagged with the pain. He made for his little sterile hot room in The Pas' best hostelry, the Rupert House.

10

She waited for him.

She was outside many times a day with her binoculars, surveying the mouth of the Grass River. She considered starting towards The Pas to meet him on his way back but occasionally during the winter months he'd returned the long way, holing up for a night or two in the old Indian trap cabin east of Cormorant Lake. And at this time of year there was always a question of break-up especially if the abnormal mild days continued. The ice at the mouth of the Grass was pitted and rotting.

She waited four days.

The sound of dogs and human voices brought her to the top of the path leading down to the lake's edge. Two people, a man and a woman and both unknown to her, were lifting a figure wrapped in furs on a toboggan up the steep bank.

"'Ave a care, mate . . ."

The first terrible recognition that the figure on the toboggan was her partner, immobilized her.

"Ere 'e is, your man." The woman was breathing heavily though her mouth. They pushed past her through the open cabin door.

"Don't stand, luv—where do we put 'im?"

In a dream-haze, she followed them.

The first necessary actions brought relief, stripping his brass bed, laying the mattress on the floor in front of the fire. He was lifted from the toboggan onto the mattress. The man brought soft ice from the lake to heat on the stove and the woman chatted cosily, filling in details of Woosey's progress from The Pas as she had learned from the druggist.

"Got to look after your man, matey."

Getting down on her knees beside the mattress, Kate ran her hands over his forehead, pushing away the sweaty tangle of hair. There was no recognition that he was in his own camp, no response in the eyelids, the tight muscles about his mouth. She lifted up one hand which sickness had whitened, refined, but it was still a prospector's hand, horny and tough-skinned, fingers enlarged. It was any prospector's hand and it was his hand; for all the trenching, all the wrestling with roots, rocks, trees, earth, mud, it had a kind of delicacy and she wondered what musical instrument he had played as band-rat. There was so much in his life of which she knew nothing.

She put down the hand, bent her head and touched his in an act of humility. The old alternatives, stay with him or go exploring, were strange and alien now. She belonged here with him. A whole new country opened up in front of her and she was without maps or compass. She'd come to this, this act of submission, she who'd been so heretical in claiming her independence.

"I'm not leaving, I'll never leave you."

There was no response.

The woman, curious, hovered above her but she did not care.

"It's 'is 'art, 'e's to 'ave digitalis and somet'ing else."

"He shouldn't have been moved."

"'Twas the druggist from The Pas that moved 'im—we did wat we was told, miss."

It was all straightening out in Kate's mind. This woman was the Diamond Queen, the former chorus girl from London, England, and the man with the beard was the blacksmith who'd left his wife and children to live with her. She got off her knees.

The little Diamond Queen, who didn't reach Kate's shoulders, surveyed her with critical cyes. Kate, accustomed to stares, ignored her. "Must say, never took to the serious ones, they 'aven't caught on to theyselves."

"What do you mean by that?"

"Never mind, luv—up close you aren't so bad." She stuck a finger into the pail of melted ice on the stove. "Not too 'ot, not too cold. You let your old Auntie take 'is clothes off—you 'ave never seen a nude man."

"How do you know?"

"I know, mate."

The two women bathed Woosey while the man fished through a hole he broke in the soft ice, catching two whitefish and putting them in a pot on the stove.

The Diamond Queen held Woosey's head as Kate poised a teaspoon of fish broth against his mouth. "'E may choke, maybe not good."

Kate pushed gently with the spoon and his mouth opened, an almost automatic gesture, and she deposited the broth on his tongue. Both women held their breaths but there as a swallowing movement. He took three spoonfuls. The fourth time, he choked. "That's it," Kate said. She'd been scared.

The man with the beard stood over them. "Mebbe ice go out tonight, mebbe not—we leave now."

The little Diamond Queen stood at the door. "Used to pity 'im, living with you, but you aren't so bad."

"You speak plainly."

"Yes, luv."

At the path leading down to the lake, "Soon as break-up we take your dogs to Dog Island, let them loose there. Too much nuisance to have around."

"The dogs belong to the Alborgs. They will pick them up later."

"Bye bye sweet pot, 'ope you make it."

"What do you mean by that?"

"Watch your old Auntie, luv."

That evening she lay beside him on the mattress. She took him in her arms, holding him as though she could transfer her own strength to his weak body. "You're going to trench again, going to discover another gold mine, you're going to . . ." She changed it to, "We'll be a strange couple, I think."

A cold wind came roaring out of the north that night, blustering about the cabin walls. The ice would not go out tomorrow, or the next day.

There was no change in his response but she refused to believe he would die. He couldn't die, they had their life to live together; it was as simple as that.

The third day after his return she was holding his head in one arm feeding him the teaspoons of broth, when his eyes opened and fixed on her.

"At nine-thirty p.m. we moved off from Dundee, we had to abandon our field hospitals and our Talana Hill wounded. It was Talana where the whole thing started at five-twenty exactly in the morning of Oct. 12th. The bearing of the Boers was chivalrous, they behaved like gentlemen . . . Kate! You! And here!"

"And where would I be? Not with your Hussars in South Africa, that's for sure."

Then he said something in a completely different tone. "Did you break the fingers on the lawyer's hand?" It wasn't an accusation.

"I threw a chair at him," she admitted and told the whole story.

"Your way might have worked, Mosher or Creighton would have thought so. I brought my rifle and would have used it on Stewart but he had a revolver and we probably would have killed each other. I thought it better to try and persuade Ewing to slip the certificates back into my envelope; I'm quite sure he'd have done it but Stewart was there, and Ewing's a coward, just a scared little pukkah wallah."

"I have no pity for him—he got himself into that bully's clutches with his eyes wide open."

"So did I—have you no . . . pity . . . for me?"

"All my pity is for myself. I've spent too much of my life . . ." Woosey had drifted off into sleep or unconsciousness, she didn't know which but she went on anyway, "energies on auroras, plant life, bird life, every kind of life but my own life, until I've nothing left. I'm a kind of empty shell, full of wind and information that's useless."

But he woke from his sleep or his unconsciousness again soon and asked for food.

It took six weeks of nursing before he was able to stand on his own feet. If the day was sunny she would help him to a chair outside the cabin. All about him the May day burst into new life. The sheltered cliff sides were full of ducks and geese, a woodpecker drummed on a dead flood-scarred pine near the water's edge, Lapland longspurs pressing hard north in a stiff breeze sang their rollicking songs, a loon called from the lake. The Alborgs came bringing a chicken and new bread and various bits of news from the Settlement. The Queen arrived with a duck stew and brandy.

"Cheers luv—I'll dance a jig on the table but first 'and me a tot."

Most of the time he dozed. The nights were chilly so he went to the mattress in front of the fire; Kate moved from her place beside him to her own room. She said nothing about having held him in her arms each night, yet she was certain he knew.

When he was a little better, Kate decided he was well enough to accept the news Ventures had brought to the cabin while he'd been lying so ill: they'd withdrawn their offer of a hundred thousand for her nickel claims, backed off altogether from any further deal. The news had a curious effect.

"You haven't lost them—they're still in your hands." He smiled (never his ingratiating grin) and gazed out over the water in what she'd begun to call one of his long long looks as though he missed something of the old jaunty and doggedly optimistic self and was trying to discover what had happened to it.

It took a long time—five years—before he seemed well again. But it was only seeming. He showed no interest in prospecting or his gold mine. If Kate brought up the subject he would turn away or abruptly change the talk to something else. Once he said, "You have to be a bit of a bounder to be a successful promoter."

"What do you mean by 'bounder'?"

"Simply, a bit of a crook."

Occasionally he would tell his stories, some of them ones she'd heard before, others new. They lived on the fish he caught, winter and summer. He loved to garden, spending hours digging and weeding. The peas, beans, cabbages, potatoes and strawberries became famous round the lake. He sold strawberries to the store at Herb Lake Settlement; he'd take over a tubful of berries in his canoe and sometimes by the time he reached the little town they would be mashed into liquid by the hot sun. Then the storekeeper would refuse to buy.

"It'll make Miss Rice feel badly."

The storekeeper was abrupt. "I can't help that—I'm not buying rotten berries."

He'd return to the island with the tubful of watery strawberries, crestfallen like a small child whose offering has been rebuffed.

The change in him was almost unbearable to her, touching what had been inviolable in her being, something his arrogance, his cheeky gumption never could.

But one night drinking their tea he did mention trapping and prospecting and she believed he must be almost his old self again. "We're a fine pair of camp mates. You're no ordinary woman and I'm just an ordinary bloke—no hero but I've taken part in some heroic battles, witness this scar. I know nothing about business, nothing but a bit of trapping and prospecting and the 18th Hussars."

How he clung to his Hussars. Did she catch another meaning tucked behind the words? They never would be anything more than barrack-room buddies. Perhaps he himself was innocent of the significance of his speech.

With the exception of his gardening and fishing, Kate had assumed most of the burdens about the camp, hauling the water, splitting wood, and doing a little trapping. Rarely did she go to The Pas—the small amounts of sugar, flour, tea and candles she needed, she bought at Herb Lake. Woosey, beginning to notice she'd amost abandoned watching the auroras, insisted she go back to her notes and observations that winter. The weather cooperated with his pleadings, a series of magnificent auroras flashing over Wekusko Lake.

The weather changed from bitter cold to milder days with the resulting foggy atmosphere. The surface of Wekusko Lake became covered with hoar frost. Clusters of little ice fans formed, each fan a full inch across with minutely sharp points of ice. The fans stood upright in thick clusters forming ice brambles. One afternoon Kate observed the astonishing colour of the ice overlaying the body of radioactive ore. After gazing a long time, she came into the cabin. Woosey built up the fire and she finished the last observation on the auroral expression:

> One mid-afternoon, looking from the door of the cabin, I beheld a miracle of colour over the lake. There lay a monster spectrum spread out to a depth of a few feet upon the hoar-frosted surface of the ice—electric blue, green, on through to deep aurora red, extending in all about fifteen hundred feet, its lovely ethereal hues a benediction of beauty against the foil of towering grey cliffs on either hand, with their pine-darkened seams and crests. Looking at it almost horizontally, and at that distance, about the length of a mining claim, and in the daylight, the blue-green end of the coloured acreage had the effect of a highly coloured opal—sometimes it was the green I could distinguish, then it was the blue, or an indistinguishable blending of the two.
>
> But the red end of the spectrum, which was very much greater in extent than the rest, washed up to the very shore on which I stood, so that I could judge of its character without any manner of doubt as to its appearance. It was the deepest colouring possible, short of a spilled vat of carmine paint. Although it was not the hour of sunset, I looked to the west expectantly to see from whence such an unusual reflection could be coming. There was not a hint of these colours in the west, or anywhere in the sky. How to account for it? It was the happening of a lifetime!

She finished the aurora article in the morning (her explanation for the strange phenomena was a discharge of static electricity since radioactive bodies carry a charge of electricity) and posted it at Herb Lake. There, in the Settlement, to her surprise she found herself well-known, a woman who lived openly with a man. The rector of the new St. John's Anglican turned his fine Roman nose away when they passed on the dirt path. The rooming house was filled with young men, engineers on development company orders: they knew of her and gazed, even attempted to speak with her, in their eyes open admiration and, also, curiosity.

In June of the following year she received a formal letter from the Royal Astronomical Society of Canada acclaiming her article; it would be published in its September 1932 *Journal*, a copy of which would be duly sent her. There was no renumeration.

Woosey was happier than Kate at the news. "I told you!" And he whistled all that day about the camp.

A year passed.

On a brilliant day of white sun and numbing air in September Mr. Alborg brought a telegram and a letter for Kate. The telegram read: *Father dead buried letter follows come Mother.*

She took the letter into the small freezing bedroom to read. Her heart could not yet face the telegram and its contents. How the letter had reached her, stained with tears and crumpled with their moisture, she didn't know. She braced herself against the complaints snd self-pity about to face her and ran her fingers under the flap.

Father only gone two days. He was never sick until don't know what What am I to do   rheum   bad   furnace   can't go down cell   you come   mill   owners   bankers   lawyers   your   father   lost belonged to my Family   you own copper mine

Her mother had worked herself into such a lather of selfish grief she'd forgotten to sign her name, state the actual date of his death (it was August 2, 1933) and as for the mine she'd as usual got it wrong: Kate's mine was nickel. She could feel the tentacles her mother was sending out, like strings of steel that once clamped would never let go. She sat at the table in the kitchen and wrote her note of refusal while Alborg waited to take it back to the Settlement. Her mother would never forgive her.

Oh, the profound spaces, the black holes of time! Kate and Woosey became beings with no past, nor did they speak of the long ago, of the east winds that blew, the fair winds and calm waters that brought safe haven, the journeys done, portages taken, waterfalls not taken, lakes crossed, forest fires quenched, animals killed. Their vast knowing of the universe, of rift fissure vein crack crevice cut defile rock rock and more rock they avoided. They lived in a kind of jelled ancient of days, a soft endlessness of moments, hours; each day coming over the horizon, making seasons, the owl-light of winter, the gold and green dream of summer, and they stayed behind their barnacled cliffs.

Rarer and rarer were Kate's trips to the Herb Lake settlement. Her overalls began to show patches, patches over patches until finally her bare knees protruded. Once or twice Woosey protested and then he too sank into the slow slumber that precluded bothering to notice.

It was September 1940 when suddenly he wakened. The breeze was still friendly, but the little birds, all the nuthatches, the warblers and white-throated sparrows had flown to their winter homes. Alborg came with news. War had broken out between Great Britain and Germany.

Woosey had been half asleep by his fire. He came alive. It was as though an electric shock had passed through his body. Smartening his plaid mackinaw, he stood at attention. His eyes glistened. "War! War again! Between those two! This time it'll go hard against old Blighty." He left Alborg and Kate in the kitchen and went outside, for a few minutes gazing with his long long look out over the lake. He came back in. "There won't be any of my old comrades in this, they're dead or old and useless—like me." He smiled at the two who stood watching. It was such a sad smile, it pierced Kate's heart.

"Nothing happen yet," Alborg said.

"Guess my 18th Hussars will be tank now." The moisture in his eyes drying, he lifted his head proud like an old eagle. 'They'll be a crack tank regiment!"

He was fifty-nine years of age. And Kate was fifty-eight.

The next day he said to her, "Look at me, an old cavalry bloke, I'd be cashiered if the Colonel caught me—got to have my hair cut." He laughed. She believed something miraculous had happened; he was his old self. It had happened before.

His hair fell thick and bushy to his shoulders, streaked with grey— Kate had usually cut it, or Alborg, but lately Woosey had objected and let it grow.

"I'll cut it for you."

"Got to find out what the latest war news is."

"I'll take you."

At the surprise of the offer, the eagerness in her voice, he turned and gazed at her as though he hadn't really seen her for a long time. He seemed about to say something but he checked himself. "I have to go by myself. If I don't I'll come to think I'm a creature of your will, and you're strong, Kate, you have a powerful will. You see, don't you, why I must go on my own? You saved my life and I'm deeply grateful, but do you see?" He moved to her, "You've done too much already. Besides I never felt better in my life." Again, he moved to her, again, he seemed about to add something.

She let him go.

He set out. He was certain he had reached some new plateau of well-being, his body was weightless, his mind clear, so clear he knew his thoughts were sharp and true. Kate was a new kind of woman, free and unlimited. He hummed a song sung years before in the camps of the 18th Hussars in northern India on the borders of Afghanistan,

Come into the pawnee, love
For the dark pagodas have flown.
I am here at the dhoby alone

It wasn't right for either Kate or himself. It wasn't right, at all.

He turned off the motor and let the canoe drift. His mind homed to her, as if he had received a new ability, a new kind of prescience; he could think through her, feel as she felt, he understood her now so completely. She was a woman who lacked the vocabulary of love, had no language to express it but it did not matter for he could make no move toward her. At first he had been satisfied to have a partner, someone to share grub, a cup of tea at night, someone to lend an ear to his army tales. His wife May had no importance to him, had never had any importance; it had been a mistake. He'd given up the Hussars for her when his stint was over and for that he didn't know if he could forgive her.

It was Kate herself who had insisted on drawing up a testament, determined on it being signed by them both, thus giving permanence to their partnership. He'd thought of an easy, temporary relationship, a kind of drifting in and out as suited temporary needs and movable camps. But she wanted a durable arrangement, a partnership that was fixed as a marriage with an established base camp; she'd called it, "doing the thing properly," and that to him was whollly female. Kate was a feminine being, though she would go out of her way, marshal all her college arguments, to prove the opposite. There was another part of her that was quite new to him, a willingness to let him be his own person in his own way; this he honoured in her. And now, she was changing once more, was as firm, undeviating in her move toward him as she had formerly been casual and indifferent. Perhaps he did love her but not in the way he had loved his old army life with the Hussars, his only real life and love.

A flock of small birds winged over him, foregathering for their long trip south (it was late for them—it might mean a mild fall and winter) and he lifted his head, the sun turning them into pure gold. It seemed to him a sign; its meaning was just there, just beyond his present searching, if he could extend his own awareness a little, only a little more, he'd know. He sat a long time searching inside himself, just a little greater, just a little higher, the canoe drifting with silken, circuitous movements.

At the dock in front of Lucky Island he tied it up, marched up the incline and along the path to the saloon. The saloonkeeper's mouth gaped, "We'd given you up . . ."

"Don't say it." Woosey fingered his long locks, "Rid me of this, will you?"

"Come along, into the kitchen . . ." he pulled out an armchair. "You're a sight for sore eyes, thought you wouldn't . . ."

Woosey laughed. "You shouldn't say that."

"I won't again."

He sat down. "Good to be back."

"A jiff till I get my scissors." He moved to the dresser.

The Last Call sounding, siren sweet, was it evening? Darn! it must be evening, sounding on the old silver "toey."

"This calls for a snifter of brandy."

There was no answer.

11

She'd been making notes in her little black notebook; suddenly she glanced up and a shiver passed along her body. She was conscious of loneliness, an emotion that had rarely troubled her, of being utterly, terribly alone. A coldness made her push aside the notebook and reach for her mackinaw. She built up the fire in the fireplace, made a fire in the stove, put a pail on for tea. And still she was cold.

She went outside with her binoculars, hugging the mackinaw about her body. It was almost time for him to be returning. Her glasses ranged over the empty lake, sweeping up the light into the lens. She shivered and went inside.

She sat, eyes wide open, gazing at nothing. She sat so long the fire died down, the pail ceased its steaming. Going outside again, she raised her binoculars; it was long past the time he should be returning. The glasses picked up a canoe pointed at the island. It held not his wide-brimmed black felt hat but Mr. Alborg's little knitted cap. Alborg was towing another canoe—Woosey's—and he was not in it. Lowering the glasses, she crossed to the chair he had always used and sat down. The towed canoe was the riderless horse at military and state funerals. Her eyes closed.

Coming up the steep path, Mr. Alborg found her. "Miss Rice, Miss Rice . . . bad news . . . he's dead."

Her eyes flew open and she stood up. "I'll go over. I'll bring him back—he'll be buried on the island."

"No no, Miss Rice—military funeral, The Pas."

She sat down, the burst of energy gone.

"You come, wife come, we bring him The Pas, see praying man, he preach military sermon, flag over coffin, flag over grave, whole town come—proper, Miss Rice."

She went inside, put on her 1906 graduation clothes, packed some tea, flour, sugar, lard, and several cans of beans into her canvas pack sack, threw it onto her back, rolled up her sleeping bag and came out.

"No no, Miss Rice . . . have to carry him three portages on Grass. Change The Pas into funeral clothes—Mrs. Alborg bring proper funeral dress."

She did not change.

She sat with the canvas-wrapped body in Woosey's canoe, pulled by Mr. Alborg's freighter. When they chugged past the island to the mouth of the

Grass River, it was without recognition, without feeling that she gazed upon the rock cliffs, the roof and chimney of their cabin; it was as though it belonged to strangers. At each portage of the river she helped carry the body almost as an act of charity having no connection with her. A whisky jack flying from branch to branch among the pines set up a continuous crying, its uncanny, mythic mourning following their passage. "Oh, stop its wailing—I can't bear it!"

The Alborgs gazed at her in surprise.

Seventy-two hours later they tied up on the bank of the Saskatchewan in front of Christ Church in The Pas. Mr. Alborg took charge: he left to find a coffin to bury Woosey and returned with two men carrying a long box of rough boards. The body was lifted in and the top nailed down. Each blow of the hammer made vicious jabs in Kate's backbone.

The coffin was taken into the Church and set in the chancel. Mrs. Alborg went to the front seat to take her place proudly at her husband's side; she was properly dressed in her black sateen funeral dress bought at a Hudson's Bay post along the Saskatchewan River. Kate, the hem of her long black skirt and coat powdered with dried mud and dirt from the portages, slipped into a pew toward the rear.

The Church was the oldest building in The Pas, excepting the ruins of the French fort, the oldest building still functioning for hundreds of northern bushland miles. Built first as a house in 1840 by Henry Budd, an Indian, it was used as a school and mission for the Indians. Budd had been a clerk in the Hudson's Bay Company, apparently in the Columbia River area, a region of violence in the fur trade. He'd been called to W'passkwayaw, the name of The Pas at the time: in 1853 the church building was raised out of the shell of Budd's house by the Reverend James Hunter with funds collected for the missionary society, pennies from the hot hands of children, from farm and factory labourers, from cramped donations of farmers in dim decent ivy-grown churches throughout England who never in their wildest imaginings would have dreamed of a great river, an artery of water cutting across the solar plexus of a vast land, forming a ganglion of lakes, small rivers, creeks, muskegs and then gathering them all together after its one thousand two hundred miles to unite with Lake Winnipeg only to join with another, the Red River, born close to the Mississippi, and to emerge again into three fast dangerous channels and all these waters through all these fabled fields emerging as one, the Nelson River, ravening north and east into Hudson Bay. Neither could the donors imagine the small trim church on the Saskatchewan's suddenly gentle bank with its slit Gothic windows letting in as little as possible of winter Arctic winds, winter blackness and thus of summer warm breezes and summer long shimmering light, nor could they conceive that this interminable parish, once Opasquai, then W'passkwayaw, then Au Pas, then Le Pas de la Rivière, Le Pas and finally The Pas, built for the spiritual needs of Indians, would ever include trappers, prospectors, traders, promoters, girls, girls with names they would never hear, the Suicide Sallys, the Cut-throat Rosies, Moose Jaw Kids, Giggling Gerties.

On this day it was cold inside the little church and it smelled of old wood—the pews had been built from debris salvaged from Sir John Franklin's Arctic Expedition—old brown varnish, old leather, old paper. It was a chill hand squeezing Kate's heart.

The Rector came, an elderly man with tiny blue veins fretting his thin cheeks; he was a missionary sent out from England, from London, from the green and ordered harmony of its land, and he longed with a secret and terrible hunger for his native country.

Mr. Alborg spoke up. "Dick Woosey, prospector, military man, dead, want military funeral."

Bowing his head, the Rector turned slightly to Mrs. Alborg. "You are the deceased's wife?"

"No no . . ." she said, her eyes floundering about to locate Kate.

In a loud voice, as though attempting to drive certain facts into the Rector's head, Kate said, "My name is Kate Rice. I am Mr. Woosey's business partner."

The Rector had a habit of closing his eyes when confronted with something he could not understand, and he closed them now. He knew prospectors usually had partners, indeed sometimes had several, but a woman claiming with a certain pride—he thought he detected haughtiness in her speech and manner—that she was a business partner of a prospector was a denial of all his ideas on the sanctity of womanhood. He opened his eyes to ask Mr. Alborg a question, "Give me a few details of the gentleman's military career," and closed them again while he was being answered.

Mr. Alborg began bravely but quickly ran into trouble. "Fight India . . ." He could not pronounce Afghanistan and stopped, turning and appealing to Kate.

"He was with the Relief Expedition to Chitral on the border of Afghanistan in 1897. Because of his extreme youth, he began his Army career as a band-rat of the 18th Hussars. It had been a terrible summer of heat . . ." Her voice sounded like Woosey himself, telling once again his story of the storming of Chitral. "Men and horses died to the right and left of enteric fever malaria and exhaustion. Before his regiment was ordered to India he was made a Hussar of the Line! And when he stood before Ladysmith in South Africa he was an NCO. His rallying cry was . . ." In a strange way she'd been taken over by Dick Woosey.

Alborg's eyes blinked with disbelief at the sound of Woosey's voice.

"'Steady, boys!' And he couldn't have been much more than seventeen years of age." It had become her own age.

The old missionary's eyes had been closed when she began the recital but he was so hungry for the glories of England that he opened them now, and they were blurred with his tears. He turned and went into the tiny robing-room, no more than a closet, bringing back a Union Jack and draping it over the rough boards of the coffin.

At once the remains of Dick Woosey, prospector and trapper, were transformed: he'd become Dick Woosey, servant of England, instrument of majesty, soldier of the 18th Hussars, hero of an Empire. The old missionary's hand groped in his sleeve for a handkerchief. Mrs. Alborg wept. Kate, though she could not now and wondered if she ever could accept Woosey's death, was nevertheless moved to tears.

The funeral would take place at seven that evening.

The Alborgs made camp. Walking the dirt road to the boardwalk of the town, Kate found a store which had always bought her partner's raw furs and came away with a small Union Jack for his grave. After paying for the coffin and giving the missionary a gift of money for conducting a military funeral, she would have no money left.

Mrs. Alborg provided a good meal of moose meat, white bread, blueberry jam and tea. Mr. Alborg was the only one to speak.

"Good man, will be good funeral, good military funeral."

Whether he referred to the missionary or Dick, Kate did not know. She would eat nothing, but after pressure from Mrs. Alborg, drank a cup of tea.

The sun was high over the brown Saskatchewan River, the trees making long thin shadows over the side of the old church.

Just before seven they made a small procession, Mr. Alborg leading the way to the front pew, walking very stiff and straight, his little knitted cap in his hand, Mrs. Alborg coming after, stepping with reverence in her black sateen funeral dress. Kate slid into the back pew, along the narrow seat until she was shrouded in the cold shadows of the outer wall. News of an important military funeral, the first of its kind in The Pas, had spread by moccasin telegraph faster than a forest fire, and the church was filled. They had all come, the druggist, his daughter, the editor of *The Hudson Bay Herald*, his notebook open, his pencil poised at the ready to jot down the funeral oration and the list of mourners, two merchants, one from Herb Lake, the saloonkeeper, one or two Indians, perhaps guides, a tall man, one hand fingering his left jaw as though his teeth hurt, two old prospectors, one old lady, properly attired in correct mourning clothes bought at Woolland's in London, England, a black suit of excellent quality and the cut of twenty-five years before, black hat with a black bird on its brim, face swathed in a black veil; she may have been the missionary's English wife.

The missionary appeared sharp on the hour of seven, stood behind the flag-drapped coffin and began his oration without notes: "Ladies and gentlemen, we are gathered here this evening to do homage to Richard L. Woosey" (where he got the middle initial Kate did not know) "and his sorrowing wife . . ." His eyes sought out Mrs. Alborg. "Mr. Wools fought for the glory of England. He offered his life as a very young man, I believe he was but fifteen years of age when he began his career in the service of his country and thereby gave his hand and heart into the making of England into the glory of the world where the sun never sets but it sets on the Union Jack . . ."

The old man had taken off, telling of dim, dusty battles of the Empire, somehow giving the impression that Mr. Wools (sometimes it was Woos) had taken part in them all. He told of Omdurman; "Oh it was a glorious battle, full of the clang of horses, the sounds of musketry, the dust and the interminable sands of Egypt, and the Sudan was won for the eternal glory of the British Empire. We must never forget and must always remember and pay our deepest respects to our old soldiers, to such a one as Richard L. Woos!" He repeated a verse from Lamentations, "And now brethren . . ." mumbled a quick prayer, took the one short step down from the chancel, and shook hands with Mrs. Alborg. And it was over.

But not quite over. The editor of *The Hudson Bay Herald* rushed up to Mrs. Alborg, his notebook open, pencil ready, "I understand your husband also took part in the Boer War?"

Nor yet quite over. Dick Woosey was buried in the churchyard, where half a dozen crosses tilted and slanted towards the weedy earth, the sun hovering only a little lower over the rim of the river, the tree shadows a little more slender, a little longer and more slanting along the side of the old wall. Kate stuck the small Union Jack into the mound made by the coffin; it unfurled and flapped bravely in the breeze. The Vicar to the Indians, the prospectors, the trappers and the girls shook hands again with Mrs. Alborg, his eyes misty with tears. He would go back to the vicarage where his wife of many years would make him a cup of strong tea, laced with a little brandy, content he had preached the military funeral of a lifetime and done his duty for the Empire in this inclement land.

It was over.

The Alborgs rolled in their sleeping bags in their small tent. Kate took hers outside and lay facing into the western sun, red over the river's brown water. As she lay awake, the sun sank lower and lower, more red, more flamboyant over the water until the river ran with red blood, then pink and orange, until finally it became mauvish blue, a living, moving thing, changing in the early dawn to the fairest blue, freckled with yellow and orange, forever changing, forever the same.

The missionary had caught the reason for Dick's often arrogant behaviour; he'd really believed he was a being apart from other prospectors in this land—he was an officer of the Hussars under the British Raj and forever would be. But she could hardly accept that he was dead; he'd be there when she returned to the cabin on the island, waiting for her with a welcoming meal, a cup of tea, a cheery word. He had only failed her once and that was not through a fault of his own, and he wouldn't now. She whispered into the river, "Steady, boys!" and heard his answering voice, "You forgot something." She replied, "What did I forget?" "You forgot 18th Hussars, Queen Mary's Own." His hearty laugh echoed along her veins.

Dick Woosey had entered into the secret byways of her being.

PART IV

1

 he cabin was empty and chilling. The dead flies crunched under her feet. She'd been hungry when she opened the door, eager for his grub, but her appetite dissipated at once in the silent, lonely rooms. She fled outside and sat in his chair, her rifle on the ground beside her.

He had always come when she needed him. Her reason told her he was dead. Dead. Hateful word. Dead. Nothing. No warm cabin, no good grub, no pail bubbling with tea, no stories, no welcome, no rifle even. Nothing. Dead. She could not accept nothing, deadness. He was alive. He had come when she was lost and storm-captive on the Burntwood, when she was half-drowned on the Grass, marooned on Wekusko. She was more lost now than when she crouched on top of a smoking fire, or lay half-dead on a mossed-over portage. It was useless. He was dead. He was nothing.

She ate only a few crumbs of hard tack, slept when her eyes refused to stay open. The days slipped out of sight.

She would find herself standing up, surveying the lake with her binoculars, turning them about the horizon; she couldn't remember what instinct had prompted her to get out of the chair. Once, she found traces of smoke above the black spruce in the west to north sector of the sky where their Chisel Lake cabin was located . . . It was a fire from his camp, he had returned from The Pas by way of Woosey and Cook and Chisel Lakes and he would be here soon. Her heart was missing beats. She relaxed . . . But it wasn't true, was it? It couldn't be, hadn't she listened to a military oration, telling of his heroic deeds; seen the mound made by his coffin, and the Union Jack unfurling and flapping? He was not coming. He couldn't. He was dead. He was nothing.

She jumped up again to check the smoke. It was always the same, never increasing, never smudging out. At the end of an endless day her

187

binoculars picked out the tip of a smoke stack. It was only the new smelter next to their old cabin. She was exhausted.

Mr. Alborg came. He wanted her to plan a new life. "You young Miss Rice, you prospect, you go to Burntwood if you want . . ." When she made no move , nor appeared to listen he watched her covertly, her silence, her preoccupation, her thinness. "Wife bring food, make you fat."

She didn't seem to hear his words. He came over, stood squarely in front of her. "Keep bus', Miss Rice," he said and smiled down at her.

"You smile and it is a false smile."

Every other day the Alborgs brought food, fresh fish, wild strawberries picked round the mine sites by Mrs. Alborg, white bread and tea. They coaxed her inside the cabin to eat but their attempts to beguile her with food, as though food was the answer to her problem, failed. She fled outside to the chair; the cabin was too lonely, too melancholy.

Mr. Alborg followed her out, picking up a handful of seed packages from the ground. "You clean up around camp." He smiled, "Mus' keep bus', Miss Rice."

She rebuked him. "Don't be so false."

She was passive, resigned. She could bring herself to think about his funeral, how the old Rector's sermon had enveloped Dick in an aura of grandeur. She called over to Mr. Alborg, occupied with splitting wood, hauling water. "It was real and it was good, wasn't it?"

Dropping the axe he came over to her with no idea what she meant, but he smiled so hugely the gold work on his teeth gleamed. He opened his arms wide as though to encompass the lake, the island, the cabin on the island, "Yes, Miss Rice, all real, all good."

"You are false, you make false statements."

2

One by one the days vanished, they became shorter, there was a period in the night when it was dark. She sat in his chair, suspicious of all callers, her rifle on the ground beside her. The Queen came with food and cheer. She left her chair, fled to the cabin and barred the door against her. The Alborgs and one or two others she allowed on the island. Around the lake the tales spread: Miss Rice was a hermit.

One day the Alborgs brought her a letter. Opening it for her, they put it on her lap when she didn't take it. She gave the words a brief glance. They began with a Bible quotation: *Weep not for the dead, neither bemoan him (her): for he (she) will return no more, nor see his (her) native country.* Jeremiah 22:10. In conclusion there was one statement: *Your old home has been sold.* It was unsigned. It came from her hometown. Kate let it fall to the ground as the Alborgs watched.

Her mother was dead. She couldn't weep.

On an afternoon when she was alone, the sound of an outboard motor brought her out of the chair. It was not the sound of the Alborg's freighter and it couldn't be Dick, people did not rise from the grave. She raised her glasses to her eyes. A young man was scrambling down the length of a large canoe. She did not know the canoe nor the man.

He lifted his head looking to the top of the path where a tall gaunt woman was standing with rifle raised. "Don't shoot!"

"What do you want?"

"I'm looking for Miss Rice."

"What do you want of Miss Rice?"

"If you're Miss Rice, International Nickel wants to buy . . ."

"If you take one step out of that canoe, I'll shoot!"

"Forty-five thousand for Woosey's nickel claims." Jumping out, he put one foot on the path.

The bullet pinged above his head. "Miss Rice!"

The bullet pinged close to his left ear. "You must be . . ."

The bullet pinged close to his right ear. "Crazy!" He was scrambling back along the canoe to the motor.

She was breathless and sat down in the chair. Dick wouldn't have done that, he'd have spoken to the young man, invited him up to the cabin, given him tea, even if he was an emissary of Stewart. But Dick was slipping farther and farther out of her life and into the past. She was left alone to pick herself up, go on. A shiver passed along her back and across her shoulders. For the first time she was uncertain of herself, for the first time she knew she was not thinking straight. Hadn't Dick said she was the type that could be bushed? She seemed to be coming out of a long and hopeless journey, emerging in bits and pieces as though she'd been almost totally destroyed. Was she bushed and if so, how bad?

Mr. Alborg had left the door of the shed open; she got up to look inside, wondering suddenly about Dick's canoe, wondering if it was inside where he'd left it. It was on the platform he had constructed, the outboard motor stashed in a corner, wrapped in canvas. Why had she wondered now, been in doubt? Everything was there, where Alborg had left it, carefully and neatly in order, waiting. Hanging on a peg in the middle of other pegs from which hung Woosey's traps, his fish net, his coils of rope, was his black felt hat. She reached for it. His hat! As though she'd found some precious object that was uniquely his, she fingered its softness, turning it over; there were letters faded and green, *Christy* still readable—once they'd been gold, once that hat had been fine and expensive and he'd been proud of it because it was of sound British manufacture. She stood gazing out the door into the blinding light of the blue sky, empty and silent, stroking his old wide-brimmed black felt hat.

Presently, the sky was no longer silent. Faint sounds like small waves breaking filtered into the shining air, the sounds of a familiar outboard motor. Stepping out of the shed's cool gloom, she put the hat on her head, turning up the brim in front. And went back to the chair.

Mr. Alborg came. He held out a letter to her.

"What's that?"

"It's a letter, Miss Rice."

"I know it's a letter, but it's addressed to you."

"But look, Miss Rice." His hand slipped inside the envelope, bringing out a clipping. "From paper in Kan-sas. You famous, see." And he thrust it in front of her face.

It was a photo of Kate taken by a newspaper reporter. She was marching along a path in the Herb Lake settlement, her pack sack on her back. Underneath the photo, the caption read: Beautiful Woman Famous Trapper and Prospector in Wilds of North!

"Man come when lotta man come. He come from Kan-sas and he take that picture, as' me about you." His chest puffed out at his knowing so much about the beautiful and famous Miss Rice.

"And you told him everything you knew, didn't you?"

He missed the sarcasm, the anger balled up in her voice.

He was standing squarely in front of her, a habit of his which vexed her. He did not notice her vexation; he had more important information yet to impart.

"Miss Rice, soon two thousan' man here, in winter tractor train go all day, man and tractor train, mebbe here nex' winter. Wife and me leave Settlemen' go far—you come, you too thin. We feed, tak' care . . ." It was the longest, most impassioned speech he'd ever made to her.

She had been certain it would happen some day; now it didn't matter. She'd been emotionally upset finding Dick's hat, and in some strange way it had thrust her back to him. "When I was in trouble he came to me, when I was lost he found me."

It was a queer thing to say. She recognized that as soon as she'd spoken but let it go, didn't even know if she cared.

The words had an instant effect on hm. "Miss Rice, you not well."

She turned away from him.

He stayed close the rest of the day, sometimes on the ground beside her, sometimes doing a little weeding, always with his mouth buttoned down tight.

The next day he came. He was tired and anxious about her and he fell asleep easily in the early afternoon.

The sound of an outboard motor wakened him and he got up. Kate too, got up; he helped her to the top of the path. A young man with a mop of fair curls was getting out of a canoe.

"It's the same canoe, the same motor as yesterday, that International Nickel used, or was it the day before that?" She didn't try to remember.

Mr. Alborg called down. "What you want, man?"

"I want Miss Rice." He kept his eyes on Mr. Alborg.

"Why wan', man?"

"Manitoba Nickel wants to buy Woosey's and Rice's claims."

"How much, man?"

"Forty-five thousand dollars!"

"You sell Miss Rice, you sell, you no money."

"Tell him cash only."

"Miss Rice sell—cash only, man."

"I'll bring forty-five thousand cash in two days," said the young man leaping for the canoe as though he'd opened a Pandora's box of devils.

"Good business, Miss Rice, hear Manitoba Nickel big show."

"It had another name." She was weak and wanted to sit down.

Mr. Alborg left but next day was back again, bringing Mrs. Alborg. He stood squarely in front of Kate.

"Miss Rice, you sick. When money come, we take you, wife and me to The Pas, see Doc. Mebbe you go sou' big hospital. . ."

"What hospital?"

"Big, sou'."

"I know there's a hospital for the insane down south, is that the place you think you'll commit me?"

"No no, Miss Rice, no commit."

"But you think I'm insane, don't you?"

"No no, Miss Rice, no insane."

"What then? You say I'm sick, but what kind of sickness? You don't tell the truth."

"Maybe bushed Miss Rice, maybe bushed bad."

"I wish you'd go, Mr. Alborg, just go."

His eyes had platters of white. Mrs. Alborg came to the cabin door. "Miss Rice, you fine, fine lady."

"Both of you go, just go."

Mr. Alborg was shocked into silence. His wife had brought along a good meal; she left the food on the table and returned with her husband to Herb Lake. They talked over what could be done to help Miss Rice.

She regretted her action. Her thinking took the form of short sentences she could not answer. The Alborgs were her friends and they wanted to help her. She would not have sent them away in the old days. Their offers to help were so clumsy; his manner of standing so squarely in front of her, his foreign accent annoyed her and she lost what equanimity she'd ever had, which was never much, becoming nervous and fidgety until she finally reached the boiling point.

She knew she was enlarging pin pricks into boulders. She was aware that from time to time she made odd statements, but why couldn't he let her remarks go? Why couldn't he leave her alone? Why couldn't his wife? She wanted to be alone.

All night her mind fought with the question: was she as bushed as the Alborgs believed? What about the story Dick brought back from The Pas about Bill Knott who had been seeing faces in the bush and hearing voices? She was not seeing faces or hearing voices but she was not thinking straight. How bushed was she? She was exhausted.

The next morning the sound of an outboard motor sent waves stab-

bing the foggy, fuzzy stillness. She recognized the motor and got out of
her chair; stood at the top of the path leading down to the lake, her rifle
in hand; she was weak and her hand trembled.

The young man with the mop of curls stood up in the canoe,
searching the cliff on top, then stepped over the bow, carrying a canvas
bundle.

"Leave it on the big rock."

He stared up at her. "You must sign this paper first."

"Stewart is great at the signing business, except when it's a
gentlemen's agreement."

The young man came on up, puzzled, not knowing who she was
talking about. Handing her the paper, some kind of legal document, he
held it while she signed her name.

"He's great on the legality business, your boss."

"Ma'am?"

The name on top of the document read: International Nickel.

"I thought it was Manitoba Nickel." She had already signed,
questioning was useless. "But it's all the same, isn't it?"

"Ma'am?"

After the young man's canoe had chugged away from the island she
climbed down, picked up the canvas bundle, pulled out a handful of
crisp new hundred dollar bills and tried to count—she'd never seen so
much money before—but could not make her mind work. Stuffing the
loose bills into the top of her sweater, and bloated with money, she
climbed back up the path.

She went into the cabin, into Woosey's bedroom. Her footsteps echoed
in the emptiness, too loud, too desolate, and she stood, listening. There
was nothing, no sound at all, and she reached for his old canvas pack
sack hanging empty from a peg. She loaded it with the money and stood
gazing about the room, senses strangely alerted as though his sleeping
quarters held something peculiarly for her. In a corner sat his rifle, the
little Queen and her man having brought it with him that day; the stock
was on the floor, barrel upright. She dropped the sack of bills to clasp
his rife. It was like no rifle she'd ever held, heavy, nine or ten pounds
in weight, long nd lean, clean-shaped and plain without the smallest
decoration. It made her own look like an over-fanciful toy. The barrel was
well oiled, the butt constructed of some very solid wood, probably teak
to resist tropical insects, and smooth as satin. He could have used it in
Afghanistan, might have had it in his hand when he sailed away from
Portsmouth with bands playing and flags snapping, when he saw his
mother for the last time.

Putting it against her shoulder, she lifted the barrel to the ceiling,
squinted through the two sights and pulled the trigger. The bullet made
a clean hole in the ceiling where the sky like a small blue eye stared down
at her. She searched for shells, knowing he must have a store of them
and found a box of 303's in another corner.

When she came out into the kitchen, the table was set with the food Mrs. Alborg had left. A sudden ferocious hunger seized her and she sat down, the Lee Enfield on her lap, the sack of money by her side. She ate the cold fish, the chicken—Mrs. Alborg must have killed one of her hens—the blueberries, the thick white bread, ate it all, and drank the cold tea in the tea pail. Her strength began to come back and she was fired with decision and purpose. Had she forgotten she was a woman of action?

She had a lot to do. First thing was to find the shovel. Dick always kept it in the shed after digging, wiped and clean. Behind the cabin, to the north and east, near the clump of bush willows she started to dig; rain had not fallen recently and the ground was hard, her muscles weak. The shovel struck thin roots, tough as wires of steel, clinked against rocks and stones. When the hole was deep enough, she got down on her knees, cleared the hollow of stones and rocks, tore at the tenacious roots. Picking up the canvas pack sack that had seen hundreds of journeys and now, instead of supplies, was stuffed with hundred dollar bills, she lowered the sack into the hollowed resting place. Shovelling earth back over, smoothing, tamping, throwing leaves and willow branches as a covering blanket, she stood still, breathing fast. Only the sharpest eye would know anything was buried beneath that spot of earth. She wiped the shovel with leaves, put it back in the shed and closed the door.

She leaned against the door, suddenly aghast. Why had she done it? Why had she buried the money? She gazed up at the vacuous and unresponsive sky for an answer. There was none.

She packed only the foundation of a load, about seventy-five pounds, all necessities. Once before she had packed such a load, long ago at Beaver Lake, to take on the Sturgeon-weir and its rapids and hairpin twists. With Woosey's Lee Enfield in one hand she closed the door of the cabin behind her.

The pack sack rested on her back, the seventy-five pounds weighing so heavily it bowed her over; she'd have to accustom herself to carrying weight, to fighting fatigue, to overcoming loneliness, to being always on the alert for any queer, quirky actions which could bring disaster down on herself. In truth she was a little frightened of herself.

The sleeping bag was rolled on top of the pack sack, tea pail hanging from the roll, and her belt hung with a pick and an axe. She remembered Dick's shovel, and went for it in the shed. Leaning slightly to grasp it, she almost toppled with the weight on her back; she would need to re-learn the whole art of camping. On her way out a small green notebook was tucked into one of the wooden supports; it was a diary of some kind. She placed the Lee Enfield against her body, picked up the book and thrust it into her pocket. Then she clasped the rifle and shut the door with care.

She made her way down the cliff side to the lake. A light wind whistled against her ears under the wide brim of Woosey's hat; the lake was smooth but the wind foretold a change.

The Duckling rested on the water where Mr. Alborg had left it. She stowed the pack sack in between the thwarts; the tea pail, and other equipment was handily placed in the bow. Stepping in, she pushed the hat back, brim turned up in front, and gazed at the island. Only the chimney of the cabin was visible. But now it was a stranger's base camp. She began to paddle. The canoe settled in the water, accepting her; passage in the beginning was slow, her arms ached, but gradually the Duckling was gliding through the water towards Snow Creek and Squall Lake. When it crossed the Burntwood, found some feeding creek or river, she would have reached the new frontier.

It was the journey she had started on years before, but how different it was from her dreams. She could only recall a snatch of her father's words: *Kit Carson was true to the seed planted in him . . . to push back the frontier . . . and still there is more land*—or was that what he had said? But it was all she could remember and there'd been much more, so much more, of bravery and excitement and glory.

The lake was sullen now, waiting for the wild wind and the rain; the storm.

GLOSSARY

ASSAY   Analyze chemically samples of an ORE, alloy, etc. to find out the amount of metal in it.

AURORA BOREALIS   A brilliant nocturnal radiance suffusing the sky of high northern latitudes; also known as northern lights.

BANNOCK   A kind of pancake or bread eaten by prospectors and trappers in the north. Made from flour, salt, water and sometimes lard or fat from fried meat, as often as not it was stirred with a finger rather than a spoon by the prospectors, each of whom had his own version of this basic recipe.

BLACK JACK   A purely local name for a formation in the bedrock usually indicating a showing of SILVER ZINC. It is dark-coloured with a resinous lustre over a light-coloured streak.

BUSHED   A malady of the bush. Prospectors—particularly those who lived alone and far from civilization—after long periods of time in the bush might develop strange symptoms: hearing voices and seeing shapes or bodies in the woods when there were none.

CHALCOPYRITE   A rich copper ore consisting of a SULPHIDE of COPPER and IRON; copper pyrites.

CLAIM   A tract of public land staked out by a prospector for mineral exploitation.

COPPER   A tough but malleable reddish-brown metallic chemical element. Like other metaliferous metals lying at or near the surface, copper is altered by the effects of surface water and produces malachite which leaves green-blue stains on rocks when present. *See also* GOLD.

DOLOMITE   A light-coloured magnesia-rich sedimentary rock, resembling limestone but harder and more resistent. Much so-called white marble is actually dolomite. Dolomite forms the cap of Niagara Falls.

DRIFT   Rocks, gravel, stones and other material deposited by a glacier, river, etc. on top of a mineral VEIN.

FISSURE   A cleft in the rock. *See also* FRACTURING, RIFT.

FOUR-IN-HAND   A necktie tied in a slip knot with the ends left hanging.

FRACTURING   Cavities or breaks in the rock. Of special interest to prospectors because secondary minerals or gold may be preserved as filings in these fractures.

FREE GOLD   Fine particles of gold lying in an exposed VEIN and visible to the naked eye.

GABBRO   A coarse-grained igneous rock. Because it is magnetic, a compass should not be used near this formation.

GALLUSES   Suspenders for trousers.

GAUNTLET   A stout, heavy glove with a wide, flaring cuff.

GOLD   A primary mineral as opposed to secondary ones such as COPPER, NICKEL and IRON. Primary deposits are still in their original form while secondary deposits are those which have been derived from the deterioration of primary ones.

GOLD PANNING   The process of attempting to isolate gold from the effluent deposits in the beds of rivers, streams, etc. by gradually allowing the other materials to escape from the gold pan until only the gold remains. *See also* PROSPECTOR'S PAN.

GOLD STRINGER   *See* VEIN.

GOSSAN   A deposit containing secondary minerals having a characteristic rusty look. All gossans merit investigation using a pick or blasting down to the primary minerals or the heavy sulphides such as COPPER or NICKEL.

GRANITE   A common light-coloured rock. Eighty percent of all granite rocks were formed in Precambrian times and thus are over 570 million years old.

GRUBSTAKE   Supplies or funds advanced to a prospector in return for a promised share of the profits. The term grubstaker may also refer to a prospector who traps in the winter to raise the stake money for the summer's prospecting.

HARD TACK   A dry biscuit commonly used by trappers and prospectors.

HEMATITE   A form of IRON ORE. A useful mineral in itself, it is often found in gossans and its presence may lead to GOLD and valuable SULPHIDES.

HIGH GRADE   A commercially valuable metal of superior quality which may be easily extracted in large quantities.

HUSSARS   One of the oldest and most famous of England's cavalry regiments. They carried the glory of England to India, Egypt, Balaclava, Waterloo, Mons, Ypres, etc. The names of its officers read like a page from Debrett's. Winston Churchill was the most famous Hussar of them all. Queen Mary was the Colonel-in-Chief, hence the name, Queen Mary's Own. Part of the romance of the Hussars rested on its colourful uniforms, discarded for khaki during the Boer War.

IRON   The commonest and most useful metal; a secondary mineral. *See also* GOLD.

LOBSTICK   A tall, prominently situated spruce or pine trimmed of all but its topmost branches, originally used by the Indians as a talisman and marker. Also used by trappers and prospectors in the north as a memorial to an honoured comrade.

LODE   A VEIN of metal ORE. *See also* MOTHER LODE.

MINERALIZATION   The transformation of metal into a mineral by oxidation.

MINING CERTIFICATE   A stock certificate issued when a mine is formed. *See also* STREET TYPE CERTIFICATE.

MOTHER LODE   The main VEIN of ORE in an area or mine.

NICKEL   A secondary mineral. *See also* GOLD.

NICKEL ARSENIDE   A compound of NICKEL and arsenic. It is a secondary mineral producing an apple-green stain on rocks where it is present.

OPTION   The right to purchase a claim at a later date, usually following testing to determine the value of the claim.

ORE   A mineral or aggregate of minerals from which a metal can be mined or extracted.

ORE SHOOT   A large and usually rich aggregation in a VEIN.

OUTCROP   A part of the bedrock which has come to the surface. Prospectors will pierce the outcrop to search for minerals.

OVERBURDEN   Any unconsolidated material such as gravel and rocks overlying and hiding a deposit of useful minerals.

PEGMATITE   Igneous rocks of coarse grain, largely granite, sometimes rich in rare elements such as uranium.

PIT   Dig or SCRAPE.

PROSPECTOR'S PAN   A sophisticated pie pan about sixteen inches in diameter with sloping sides and a depth of two inches or more. It is usually constructed of sheet iron because if it is too highly polished or greased it won't retain the fine grains of gold. The pan is filled with soil and gravel and immersed in a slow-running stream or in a lake or pond. When it is stirred gently the soil is washed away, then the large pebbles are taken out by hand. Next, the pan is alternately shaken or rotated under water then raised to the surface at an angle so that the upper material is washed away. The process is repeated until only the heavy gold grains, if any, remain. *See also* GOLD PANNING.

PROSPECTOR'S PICK   The essential prospector's pick or rock hammer is usually short-handled for use with one hand with a hammer head on one end and a pick at the other. The hammer end is used for knocking off pieces of rock; the pointed end is used for picking into overburden or decomposed rock, prying rocks loose, removing moss and picking out small specimens.

PYRRHOTITE   A bronze-coloured, slightly magnetic IRON SULPHIDE, sometimes containing NICKEL.

QUARTZ   A silicon rock worthless in itself and thus known by prospectors as gangue but which may contain valuable minerals.

REMITTANCE MAN   Someone who lives abroad on money sent from relatives back home. Many were men whose families for one reason or another (moral turpitude?) wanted to get rid of them. They came from the upper class or nobility of Victorian England and were usually sent to Canada, Florida or Australia. Hugh Vickers, the first man to prospect north of The Pas was such a man. On weekdays he dressed in his old prospector's clothes, but on Sundays, true to his upper class roots, he wore magnificent tweeds.

RIFT   A narrow cleft or FISSURE in a rock. *See also* FISSURE, FRACTURING.

SAMPLING   The random sampling of bedrock taken with a view to determining the average mineral content.

SCHIST   A medium- or coarse-grained metamorphic rock. Its composition is dominated by micaceous minerals, a mineral group with sheet-like structures.

SCHISTOSE   *See* SCHIST.

SCRAPE   Remove moss or other overburden from the outcrop of rock in order to investigate the appearance of a deposit or more importantly, to reach the deposit.

SEDGE GRASS   Found everywhere, it is especially common in the Arctic where it is a native of wet soil. Sedge grass grows in what is known as a beaver meadow, where the beavers have worked, flooding the land slightly. The sedge stems are triangular and solid in contrast to other grasses with their round hollow stems.

SHEARING   Similar to FRACTURING. Both shearing and fracturing can indicate the presence of valuable minerals.

SILVER   A primary mineral like GOLD.

SLUDGE   Broken stone, rocks and heavy gravel.

STREET TYPE CERTIFICATES   A stock certificate on which the owner's name is not specified and thus owned by whoever possesses them.

STRINGER   *See* VEIN.

STRIPPING   Removing OVERBURDEN.

SULPHIDE   A combination of a mineral and sulphur.

TRACING FRAGMENTS   The sign by which the presence of GOLD or other minerals may be located. Because these signs are often barely discernible, it is frequently necessary to use a special lens. Once the tracing fragments have been located a prospector will follow them to their source.

TRAP SHACK   A crude cabin put up by trappers as temporary shelters near the traplines. A trap shack sometimes lacked windows, or had only a piece of burlap for the door, but always there was a fireplace for cooking and for heat. Indians, who always travelled to their winter traplines with their families, built the largest and finest trap shacks.

TRAPLINES   The route along which traps to snare fur-bearing mammals are systematically spaced.

TRENCH   A narrow ditch or excavation from which all OVERBURDEN has been removed to expose the bedrock in promising places. A shovel and a pick are required; if the excavation is through solid rock a steel drill, power drill or dynamite is used. Because most trenches were made in low marshy ground they filled with water and some were wide enough for a canoe to pass through.

TRENCHING   *See* TRENCH.

TREWS   Tight-fitting trousers or breeches, usually tartan.

VEIN   The most common and important of mineral deposits. A typical vein is a regularly-shaped occurrence composed of one or more minerals occupying a FRACTURE or fault. A STRINGER has the same properties but is too small to be classed as a true vein. Generally, any vein measuring less than an inch or two is known as a stringer.

VOLCANIC ROCK   Any rock extruded or ejected from a volcano.

ZINC   A secondary mineral occurring in other minerals such as SILVER.

BIBLIOGRAPHY

PRIMARY SOURCES

Interviews with the following: the late George Bartlett, Snow Lake, Manitoba; Carl Beck, Toronto, Ontario; Emily Crosby, Snow Lake; Joe Kerr, Snow Lake; the late Mrs. Lincoln Rice, St. Marys, Ontario; Hall and George Thompson, and the Misses Edith and Rose Thompson, Cranberry Portage, Manitoba; Vernon Wang, The Pas, Manitoba; Mrs. Whitaker, The Pas.

Letters (fifty) to the author, 1977-1981, relating to Kathleen Rice and Dick Woosey, in the possession of the author.

Tapes (eight) from Charles Vance of Chilliwack, British Columbia, in reply to questions from the author, 1977-1979.

Diary (unpublished) of an unknown trapper, ca. 1921 in the collection of the Little Northern Museum, The Pas, Manitoba.

Manuscript (unpublished?) entitled *Reminiscences,* n.d., by Les Charles, in the possession of his daughter, Mrs. Babs Friesen, Winnipeg, Manitoba.

Clippings, papers and speeches of John A. Campbell, M.P. for constituency of Nelson, 1917-1921, in the collection of the Manitoba Archives.

SECONDARY SOURCES

Books and Articles:

Blaxland, Gregory. *The Buffs.* London: Leo Cooper, 1972
Bocking, D.H. *Saskatchewan, A Pictorial History.* Saskatoon: Western
    Producer Prairie Books, 1958
Crozier, John. "This Woman Lives Dangerously!" *World Digest:* vol. 1,
    no. 2 London, 1938
Dana, James D. *System of Mineralogy.* New York: J. Wiley & Sons, 1883

Edwardes, Michael. *Bound to Exile; the Victorians in India.* London: Sidgwick & Jackson, 1969

Guest, Captain Freddie. *Indian Cavalryman.* London: Jarrolds, 1959

Hough, Emerson. *The Way to the West.* New York: Grosset & Dunlap, 1903

Johnson, Joseph C.F. *Getting Gold.* London: Charles Griffin & Co., 1917

Kincaid, Dennis. *British Social Life in India, 1608-1937.* New York: G. Routledge & Sons, 1939

Maitland, Francis Hereward. *Hussar of the Line.* London: Hurst & Blackett, 1951

Malet, Colonel Harold. *Historical Records of the Eighteenth Hussars.* London: W. Clowes & Sons, 1869

Rice, Kathleen. "Aurora Borealis." *Journal of the Canadian Astronomical Society,* September 1932

Rice, Kathleen. Article in *Toronto Star,* September 5, 1939

Turner, Frederick J. *Significance of the Frontier in American History.* Ann Arbor, Mich.: University Microfilms, 1966

Wilkes, F.A. *They Rose From The Dust.* Saskatoon: Modern Press, 1958

Wilton, Sidney. *The Pas: A History; Adventure and Romance.* The Pas: The Pas Chamber of Commerce, 1970

Wright, James Frederick Church. *Saskatchewan, The History of a Province.* Toronto, McClelland & Stewart, 1955

Periodicals and Other Publications:

Annual Report, vol. XIII, 1900 and vol. XIV, 1901. Geological Survey. Canada

Bulletin, September 1918. Canadian Mining Institute

Canadian Mining Journal, vol. XXXV, 1914

Dictionary of American Biography. (Entry for Daniel Boone)

Dictionary of Canadian Biography. (Entry for Dr. Samuel Dwight Rice)

Guide for Prospectors in Manitoba. Winnipeg: Manitoba Department of Mines and Natural Resources, 1936

Memoirs, vol. 30, 1913; vol. 109, 1918; and vol. 208, 1937. Geological Survey. Canada

Mining and Mineral Prospects in Northern Manitoba. Northern Manitoba Bulletin, Manitoba. 1919

New Manitoba District Canada; Its Resources and Development. Department of the Interior, Department of Natural Resources, Intelligence Branch. Canada. 1918

The Pas: Golden Jubilee. Pamphlet. The Pas, 1962

Prospecting in Canada. Department of Energy, Mines and Resources. Canada. 1906

Saga of Snow Lake. Pamphlet. Snow Lake, n.d.

Snow Lake Salute to the Trail Blazers. Pamphlet. Snow Lake, 1967.

Summary Report, 1901, 1905, 1906, 1910, 1914, 1915, 1916, 1917, 1918, 1922, 1930. Geological Survey. Canada